ANDY WARHOL
FILM FACTORY

Edited by
Michael O'Pray

BFI PUBLISHING

First Published in 1989 by the
British Film Institute
21 Stephen Street
London W1P 1PL

Copyright © British Film Institute 1989
Individual essays copyright
© the original authors

Designed by Andrew Barron
Typeset by Fakenham Photosetting Ltd,
Fakenham, Norfolk
Printed and bound in Great Britain
by W. S. Cowell PLC, Ipswich

British Library Cataloguing
in Publication Data
Andy Warhol: film factory
   1. American cinema films. Directing. Warhol, Andy
   I. O'Pray, Michael, 1945–
791.43'0233'0924

ISBN 0–85170–250–3
         0–85170–243–0 pbk

Cover: Frame stills from *The Thirteen
Most Beautiful Women* (Andy Warhol, 1964)

Warhol film stills by courtesy of the Warhol Estate

Photographs on pp. 11–13 by Peter Gidal, 1967

For

Joanna, Stephen, Frances and Thomas

CONTENTS

ACKNOWLEDGMENTS

I would like to thank Ed Buscombe and Geoffrey Nowell-Smith for their enthusiastic support for this book, Roma Gibson for her editorial help; and John Smoker for handling production. For the generous use of their private Warhol archives and research and their personal support, I'd like to thank David Curtis, Simon Field, Peter Gidal and Keith Griffiths, and in particular Peter Gidal for the use of his photographs of Warhol and the Factory.

Thanks to Jonas Mekas and particularly Nadia Shtendera at Anthology Film Archives, New York for their help and advice. My gratitude also to Jon Gartenberg and Charles Silver at the Museum of Modern Art, New York for their assistance in arranging screenings, and to the British Film Institute Stills Collection.

Warm thanks to Marjorie Keller and P. Adams Sitney for their friendship and hospitality and to P. Adams for sharing his memories and ideas on Warhol. And not least, thanks to the following for their help: Joanna O'Pray, Stephen Koch, Kathleen Maitland-Carter, Judith Preece at the Polytechnic of East London, Jayne Pilling, Hilton Als, London Film-makers' Co-op, and John Hanhardt at the Whitney Museum of American Art, New York.

Thanks to Kate Leys for helping it all to happen.

Finally, thanks to A. L. Rees for his friendship and continual debate and to Jill McGreal for everything.

NOTES ON CONTRIBUTORS

Kathy Acker is a novelist living in London. Her most recently published fiction is *Young Lust*.

Paul Arthur is a film-maker and writer and lives in New York. His book on film noir, *Shadows on the Mirror*, is to be published this year.

Gregory Battcock was a leading American art critic. He edited many books, including *Minimal Art*, *New Artists' Video* and *The New American Cinema*.

Gretchen Berg is a photographer living in New York.

Vivienne Dick is a film-maker renowned for her Super-8 films made in New York in the late 1970s. She now works and lives in London.

Mark Finch works in the Distribution Division of the British Film Institute and is also co-programmer of the London Lesbian and Gay Film Festival.

Peter Gidal is a film-maker and author of *Andy Warhol: Films and Paintings*, *Understanding Beckett* and *Materialist Film*.

Gary Indiana is a writer and poet living in New York.

David James teaches at Occidental College in Los Angeles.

Stephen Koch is a writer and teaches at both Columbia Graduate School and Princeton University.

Margia Kramer is an artist and writer on civil rights. She has also published books on the FBI surveillance of the actress Jean Seberg.

Jonas Mekas is a film-maker, writer and poet. He is director of Anthology Film Archive, New York.

Michael O'Pray is co-director of the Film and Video Umbrella and co-editor of the film magazine *Afterimage*.

Tony Rayns is a freelance writer.

A. L. Rees is a lecturer in Film at the Kent Institute of Art and Design at Maidstone and co-editor of *The New Art History*.

Ronald Tavel is a leading American writer and playwright. He was Warhol's script-writer (1964–6) and founder of the New York Theatre of the Ridiculous.

Parker Tyler was an influential and prolific American film and art critic and author of *Underground Film*, *Magic and Myth of the Movies*, among other titles.

Peter Wollen is a film-maker, teacher and writer.

INTRODUCTION

Warhol died suddenly in 1987, while in hospital recovering from a relatively straightforward gall-bladder operation. He was fifty-eight years old and had not made a film for over a decade. Between 1963 and 1968, an amazingly short period of time, he had produced his major film work, most of which was hardly shown at the time and remained largely unseen throughout his lifetime. Paradoxically, his public reputation or infamy rested as much on these rarely-seen films as it did on his paintings, yet they have attracted scant serious critical attention. For example, the catalogue accompanying the first major retrospective after his death barely mentions them. In stark contrast to his painting, the legacy of his films is a chaotic and obscure one, riddled with myths, half-truths and sheer ignorance. To make matters worse, Stephen Koch has recently stated (in conversation) that as far as he is concerned his filmography of 1973 based on Mekas's brilliant attempt in 1970 has hardly any scholarly status. In his book *Stargazer*, Koch describes finding the Factory's cupboards filled with unmarked reels and its archives 'the perfection of carelessness and chaos'. As for Warhol and Morrissey, there was not 'a single statement either one of them made to me . . . that, upon examination, turned out to be true'.

Consequently, an extensive period of archival retrieval, restoration and cataloguing of the films has begun under the direction of John Hanhardt of the Whitney Museum of American Art. Not surprisingly, the present touring exhibition has provided only a dozen or so films including extracts from two films *Sleep* (1963) and *Empire* (1964) which should be shown in their entirety given that their central aesthetic concern is the nature of cinematic duration. Hardly any of Warhol's early films have been in proper legal distribution. In Britain, for instance, *The Chelsea Girls* (1966), *Lonesome Cowboys* (1967) and the later Morrissey films (*Flesh* (1968), *Trash* (1970) and *Heat* (1972)) have for years been the only ones legally available. Some of the infamous classics – *Empire*, *Sleep*, *Blow Job*, *Vinyl* – have rarely been seen even by afficionados of Warhol's cinema. Ironically and fittingly, for the artist who both attacked the aura of art and made it the commodity par excellence, many of the films have been illicit since their withdrawal from distribution by the Factory in the 70s and have led an 'underground' existence as pirated dupes. According to Warhol's biographer, Victor Bockris, as early as 1970, the project to rent Warhol's films to colleges run by his close friend and associate Gerard Malanga was discontinued as Morrissey attempted to withdraw the early films from distribution. Warhol's own move towards mainstream narrative cinema in the late 60s and early 70s may have had its effect on the circulation and reputation of the earlier films. Paul Morrissey described people who acclaimed *Empire* as

Andy Warhol in The Factory

'snobs'. Whether Warhol shared such a view seems unlikely, nevertheless he did produce the Morrissey films and geared his film ambitions towards commercial success and a mass audience.

The present volume of essays has been put together against this background. Very few of the contributors are fully familiar with all of Warhol's films, which means that, in many cases, the most basic prerequisite for research is unfulfilled. However, as a conceptual artist Warhol's work is perhaps more accessible through its 'idea' than a narrative film-maker's might have been. For

Andy Warhol in The Factory

instance, we know about the fixed camera, the use of unedited 100 feet rolls of films, the silence and mundane subject-matter. But this attitude is dangerous, for many viewers, upon seeing them for the first time, have been shocked by the sheer *visual* quality of Warhol's films, thus generating the paradox that the best of conceptual art still has to be experienced as well as understood. Too much can be made of the Duchampian quality of Warhol's

films, as if they existed simply to make a philosophical point. Many of the early films are not reducible to such an understanding.

There have been only two books in English about Warhol's films – Peter Gidals' *Andy Warhol* and Stephen Koch's *Stargazer*, each taking different stances on the work and Gidal's being long out of print. This present volume was conceived as a remedy for this situation by making available some of the classic writings on Warhol from the 1960s and early 70s. Consequently, many critical, literary and theoretical dialectics, so to speak, jostle against each other, as they should when dealing with Warhol's diverse and enormous range of interests and artistic projects. I have included Mekas's characteristically polemic contribution to the Coplans' catalogue; Parker Tyler's witty and sceptical critique 'Dragtime and Drugtime'; the late Gregory Battcock's on-the-spot analysis of four Warhol classics; the dramatist and Warhol script-writer Ronald Tavel's account of the making of *Harlot* and his script for the latter, plus Gretchen Berg's much quoted and hilarious interview for *Cahiers du Cinéma In English*.

The essays which have been specially written for this volume range widely and establish different approaches and starting points, from the theoretical to the anecdotal, from the fine-art to the cinematic to the literary-based. I accept them, as I'm sure many of their writers must do, as the beginnings of a serious study of Warhol's films. I felt that it was crucial to preserve and present the broad fascination and influence of Warhol's film work, for it was unique. It represented a watershed not only for avant-garde or underground film practice and theory but also for art cinema and Hollywood. Its influence was pervasive and often difficult to pinpoint. It seemed to include, among other innovations, how the camera was used, how actors acted, how sex was treated and how reality was depicted. It was as if a transformation of the way films could be made had been subtly achieved and new possibilities of style and subject-matter had been presented to audiences and film-makers alike. Only Godard's work of the same era was as radical and as apposite for the times.

Broadly speaking, five major interpretive areas can be discerned in these essays although many writers incorporate more than one area: a modernist aesthetic related to the minimalist-inclined work of avant-gardists like musician John Cage, dancer Merce Cunningham, painters Jasper Johns and Frank Stella; this is expressed in Battcock's essays. Secondly, an avant-garde theatricality related to performance, high camp and popular culture found in the work of Jack Smith, Ronald Tavel's Theatre of the Ridiculous and the Fluxus events and happenings of the early 60s. These issues are discussed in Peter Wollen's 'Raiding the Icebox'. Thirdly, there are the pieces by Peter Gidal, David James and Paul Arthur, which are rooted in contemporary film theory, and fourthly, the viewpoint from the avant-garde film tradition itself, articulated in very different ways by Jonas Mekas, Parker Tyler, Vivienne Dick and A. L. Rees. Last, but not least, the later 'Morrissey' films are discussed by Tony Rayns and Mark Finch, the latter also examining the virtually unexplored relationship between Warhol's gay films and the gay movement itself.

Two strands of Warhol's work do not receive attention. Firstly, the collection lacks a critique or, for that matter, celebration of Warhol from a feminist perspective. The cold stare by the 80s on the 'sexual revolution' of the 60s with which Warhol was closely associated, has perhaps made his work unattractive, to say the least, to latter-day feminists. In fact, writing by and about the female superstars has been prolific compared to that emanating from the male contingency of the Factory – Viva and Ultra Violet have both written books and Edie's role was discussed in Jean Stein's study. I strongly believe that there is still much to say about such matters. Equally Warhol's involvement with television and

The Factory

pop videos has been ignored and awaits its critical moment. Warhol became involved in this area in the last decade and his impact is still being felt.

Inevitably, we suffer from being too close to the period. Warhol's films have experienced (with the notable exception of the forever popular *The Chelsea Girls*) the present decade's reaction against the hard-line formalist and sexually 'naive' concerns of much work of the 60s. For many of us involved in British film culture, Warhol was someone we encountered in our formative years in that

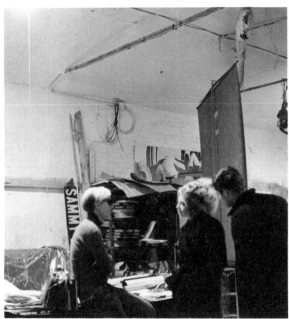

decade and like other major cultural figures, objects, events and movements of that period (Godard, Marx, pop music, Vietnam, drugs, Maoism . . .) he shaped and altered forever in some way, like phantasies, our very perceptions and conceptions ■

Michael O'Pray
London
May 1989

RAIDING THE ICEBOX
PETER WOLLEN

Fordist mass production inevitably demanded mass marketing and mass consumption as its corollary.[1] Thus the long post-war American boom saw the development of a massive merchandising machine, in the advertising, packaging and media industries. This Great Leap Forward of marketing and publicity was predicated, of course, on a Great Leap Forward in the production of images: in the streets, in the press, on television. The seismic change in the form of mass culture, as it both proliferated and was subordinated to the drive of mass production and consumption, was finally reflected in the narrower and traditionally 'purer' spheres of the arts and high culture, unable to delay or resist confrontation with the new visual (and, indeed, verbal) environment or the economic weight and pressure of the new communications industries. In this sense, the arrival of Pop Art in the early 60s was just one element in a much more general cultural shift – Warhol and Lichtenstein should be seen alongside cultural critics such as McLuhan (or Eco or Barthes), writers like Burroughs, obsessed by advertising, the image bank, the word virus and the 'Reality Studios', and, of course, film-makers like Godard. Artists had to come to terms with the new images, whether through irony, celebration, aesthetic enhancement, or détournement. But if Warhol stands out among them as anything more than a harbinger of this new parasitism of art on the media, it is because his work has a more complex meaning. Like his great contemporary, Joseph Beuys, Warhol (another master of disguise) was able to shift the optical and semiotic field of art towards a new, and potentially troubling, theatricality. This in turn left an important political, as well as aesthetic, legacy – in the case of Beuys, to be found in the Green Party, and in the case of Warhol, in the Gay Liberation Movement.[2] Warhol's key achievement, within the field of Pop, was to bring together the apparent contraries of 'minimalism' and 'camp' in a paradoxical and perverse new combination.

The minimalist current into which Warhol tapped began (or re-began) with John Cage (after Gertrude Stein, after Satie).[3] Cage, in revolt against the authoritarian systematicity of his teacher, Schoenberg, invented a form of music which rejected the traditional ideology of composition, with its pillars of harmony, structure, order and control. This, in turn, led him to abandon the whole idea of the artist as organisational source and master of the work. Instead Cage developed a philosophy (inspired by Buddhism and a certain pantheism) which equalised all the parts of a work and stressed duration, repetition and random elements. Art, according to Cage, should be brought back into relationship with everyday life. It should use found objects (or found sounds) and respect the uneven rhythms of day by day existence, even its banality, 'dead' periods and

Allen Ginsberg in Fifty
Fantastics and Fifty
Personalities, *1965*

ordinariness. At the limit, Cage was fascinated by silence, which posited duration with a special intensity, while negating the traditional appeal of music as melody and even the unthought-through concept of audibility – because, in a certain sense, silence was the most 'audible' register of all. Silence, too, foregrounded the incidental and the not meant-to-be-listened-to, re-focusing our perception of the acoustic environment, removing the aural 'frame' which marked 'music' off from 'everyday life'. Like the artists of Cobra, in Europe, Cage also placed 'everyday life' in relationship to 'play', to non-purposive, free activity.[4] Thus everyday life would be aestheticised as art was re-contextualised as part of, rather than separated from or exterior to, daily life. But for Cage, unlike the Cobra artists, with their surrealist background, this was primarily a spiritual rather than a political project.

Cage's ideas and practices gradually spread out of the music world into the related dance world (especially through his collaboration with Merce Cunningham) and eventually into the art work, through Black Mountain College (to Rauschenberg and thence to Johns) and through the Fluxus group (to De Maria, Morris and others). It was through this 'radiation' of Cage's aesthetic that minimalism came to Warhol, although Cage himself notes analogies between his own love for Satie's 'furniture music' and Warhol's manufacture of Brillo and other boxes which could be (and actually were) used as furniture, being treated as coffee-tables.[5] Rauschenberg and Johns were initially, of course, Warhol's role-models in the art-world. Like him, they designed window displays for Bonwit Teller, but, unlike him, they were recognized in the gallery world for their fine art.[6] Like him, too, they were gay artists who came from art-starved provincial backgrounds who had fled to New York to nurture their will-to-art. They offered an alternative avenue to those who, like Warhol, could hardly identify with the straight, macho posturing of the Cedar Tavern

and the claims of abstract expressionism to seriousness and mastery. Rauschenberg knew Cage from 1951 (when he collaborated with him on an 'automation' piece in which Cage drove his Model A Ford along an inked section of roadway and then across twenty pasted-together sheets of paper) and grew close to him in 1952 when they both spent the summer at Black Mountain.[7] Rauschenberg meanwhile had been working on all-white and all-black paintings, analogous to Cage's work in their early minimalism, but the important collaboration which took place there was at the now-legendary 'Event', a precursor of the multi-media performances and events of the 60s. Rauschenberg operated the gramophone for Cage and films and slides were projected on to his white paintings, beneath which Cunningham danced, poems were read and Cage's music played.

The Black Mountain 'Event' was the first of a series of artistic collaborations between Merce Cunningham and Rauschenberg which persisted till the mid-60s. Rauschenberg worked on other dance performances too, designing sets and/or costumes, and after 1960 he became deeply involved in the work of the Judson Dance Theater, founded by dancers from Cunningham's company, deeply influenced by Cage. They were joined by other dancers who performed at the Judson Church,[8] a space and refuge made available to artists in many fields and from different backgrounds, a catalyst for the arts, avant-garde, bohemian and 'underground', whose activities had a deep and lasting impact on Warhol. In fact, it was because of Rauschenberg's involvement, Warhol said, that he first went to the Judson Church. It was there that he encountered the theatricalisation of minimalism, and it was there too that he saw that theatricalisation reach into the realm of glitter, extravaganza and camp.[9]

'Camp' of course, emerged as an art-historical category with Susan Sontag's brilliant 'Notes on "Camp"', first published in *Partisan Review*[10] in 1964. This was the year in which Warhol had his

'Flowers' show and made his first sound film in the Factory which Billy Linich had decorated all over with silver foil a few months previously. Reading that essay today is like reading through a litany of Warhol's tastes, allusions and affinities. It is all there: the Tiffany lamps, the *Enquirer* headlines, the Bellini operas, the Firbank novels, the old comics, the bad movies, the idolisation of Garbo, post rock'n'roll pop music, 'corny flamboyant femaleness', dresses made of millions of feathers. . . And, on a more theoretical level, the redemption of banality, the transcendence of 'the nausea of the replica', the volatile intermixing of sheer frivolity with passionate commitment, the taste for excess and extravagance, 'dandyism in the age of mass culture'. Camp, of course, involves a rejection of the whole late-modernist aesthetic, that citadel of high seriousness and good taste as elaborated by Greenberg, who saw himself as defending the gates against the barbarians of kitsch massed without.[11] In this sense, camp taste, with its hyperbolic aestheticisation, its playful connoisseurship of kitsch, was fated to play a decisive part in the demise of modernism. At the same time, it was pushing insistently towards performance, towards the theatricalisation of everyday life.

Warhol's own version of camp is visible everywhere in his commercial art work, where, however, the inclination to excess is prudently held in check.[12] There are limits – limits which often seem calculated in their containment. Gold leaf remains decorative, foot fetishism remains whimsical, boys and cherubs remain charmingly precious. It was not till the Factory days that camp was let off the leash of good taste, no longer limited by a self-conscious censorship (to be evaded in 'private' books, like the 'Foot Book' and the 'Cock Book') but channelled within a rigorous and austere aesthetic. It was minimalism that enabled Warhol to release an orgy of camp. And it was at the Judson Church that this encounter of minimalism and camp crystallised for Warhol, to be transposed later into a new register. There the discipline of minimalist dance met the flagrant masquerade of femininity. Warhol was, of course, already aware of the minimalist direction in which the art world was moving. He had acquired a set of small paintings by Frank Stella (through De Antonio, who was Stella's agent, as well as Rauschenberg's and Johns', and who played a crucial role in encouraging Warhol himself to paint and exhibit) and must have also known the Stella black painting that De Antonio owned.[13] He was also a dedicated gallery-goer. Moreover, he prided himself, when he was a commercial artist, on his facility, his ability to draw fast with only one line, and he had also always been interested in print media, in techniques of replication, such as the blotting technique he made his own and the stamps he carved out of erasers. His longstanding interest (encouraged by commercial considerations) of doing as much work as possible as fast as possible was bound to push him towards a minimalist reduction. But he was also interested in content and in performance. Here the example of dance was crucial.

The exemplary minimalist dancer and choreographer at the Judson Church was Yvonne Rainer.[14] Her first work, 'Three Satie Spoons', at the Cunningham Studio in 1961, had a repetitive structure, based on Cage's work and performed to music by Satie. The next year, Warhol was at Judson to watch her 'Ordinary Dance' and in 1963, 'Terrain' (lit by Rauschenberg). This included a series of partly rule-governed activities (walking, jostling, passing, standing still), of choreographed walks, runs, falls, somersaults, ballet and cheesecake postures, games (with a ball, wrestling), and a love duet in which 'she delivered hackneyed expressions ("I love you", "I don't love you", "I've never loved you") in a flat monotone which one critic likened to the recitation of a grocery order'. In 1966 Yvonne Rainer wrote a retrospective manifesto for the dance work of the period, drawing parallels between sculptural and dance minimalism ('A Quasi Survey of Some "Minimalist" Tendencies . . .'), in which she likened the 'energy equality and "found" movement' of dance to the 'factory fabrication' of sculpture (or 'objects'); 'equality of parts, repetition' to 'modules'; 'repetition or discrete events' to 'uninterrupted surface'; 'neutral performance' and 'tasklike activity' to 'nonreferential forms' and 'literalness', etc.[15] Though she was presumably thinking of other artists than Warhol, the parallelism would still hold good, both for Warhol's gallery work (including the 'sculptural' Brillo boxes), except for 'non-referential

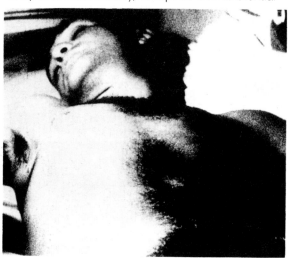

John Giorno in Sleep, *1963*

forms', and for his film work, except that Warhol's predilection for exhibitionistic 'routines' replaced 'neutral performance', at least in the later films. (Early work like *Sleep*, *Eat*, or indeed *Empire*, was often neutral). There is a sense, perhaps, in which we can think of Warhol's relationship to Rauschenberg as analogous to Rainer's relationship to Cunningham.

Before she became involved with the founding and programme of the Judson Dance Theater, Rainer had worked with the James Waring company of dancers. Later she recollected that 'Jimmy had an amazing gift which because I was put off by the

mixture of camp and balleticism in his work – I didn't appreciate until much later. His company was always full of misfits – they were too short or too fat or too unco-ordinated or too mannered or too inexperienced by any other standards. He had this gift of choosing people who "couldn't do too much" in conventional technical terms but who under his subtle directorial manipulations revealed spectacular stage personalities.'[16] Here a completely different parallel with Warhol and his Factory 'company' is plain, one which also relates Waring and Warhol to the other camp and gay performance groups of the 60s, such as the Playhouse of the Ridiculous or Jack Smith's 'mouldy' extravaganzas.[17] Indeed, Warhol was particularly enthralled by one of Waring's star performers, Freddy Herko, who also danced in a number of pieces and programmes with Yvonne Rainer. Herko shared an apartment with Billy Linich (Billy Name), who moved into the Factory and became Warhol's longest-lasting and most enigmatic associate of the 60s. Warhol made three films with Herko, and was fascinated by his beauty, his 'star quality', his use of glitzy window-display materials, paste jewels, feathers, glass flowers, the whole tawdry fairyland of fake glamour transcended by a spectacular stage presence. For Warhol, looking back on Herko's career after he became a speed freak and, in 1964, 'choreographed his own death and danced out of a window' in a sensational camp suicide, the roots of the tragedy were in Herko's lack of confidence, concentration and discipline.[18] It was a career of unchannelled excess.

Warhol transposed his own interior discipline into the exterior form of the machine and the factory as site of automation and of productivity. But this factory was a minimalist factory that simply recorded rather than transformed its raw materials. The techniques of standardisation, repetition and assembly line through-put were used, not to assemble complex finished products but literal replicas of what was already there, more or less unaltered. (Though art critics and connoisseurs, of course, have often chosen to stress the tiny percentage of 'personal touch' they are able to trace.)[19] Warhol's Factory was a travesty of a real factory. Warhol had farmed out work to assistants and friends when he was a commercial artist, holding 'colouring parties' when he produced hand-made books, and experimenting with hand-made printing devices.[20] His assistant, Nathan Gluck, did original drawings for Warhol which he then corrected, as well as doing the blotting which was part of Warhol's technique. Warhol's mother was entrusted with doing lettering. His practice at the Factory was simply to update these habits and procedures as new, relatively inexpensive technology became available to him: the silk-screen, the polaroid, the tape recorder, the film camera. All these devices simplified and speeded up the work and removed Warhol himself from arduous involvement. It was much easier that way (as, indeed, it was for Ford).

But Warhol's rationalisation of the work process was half-serious, half-theatrical. In an article on Fordism published recently, Robin Murray describes the impact of Ford's methods and ideas in the Soviet Union: 'Soviet-type planning is the apogee of Fordism. Soviet industrialisation was centred on giant plants, the majority of them based on Western mass-production technology. So deep is the idea of scale burnt into Soviet economics that there is a hairdresser's in Moscow with 120 barber's chairs. The focus of Soviet production is on volume, and because of its lack of consumer discipline it has caricatured certain features of Western mass production, notably a hoarding of stocks, and inadequate quality control.'[21] These 'caricature' elements of Soviet mass production are precisely the ones Warhol prized: volume ('Thirty Mona Lisas are better than one'), hoarding and (deliberately) inadequate quality control, leaving errors of alignment uncorrected, etc.[22] It is easy to imagine

Baby Jane Holzer, Jack Smith, Beverly Grant and Ivy Nicholson in Batman Dracula, *1964*

the delight Warhol would surely have felt at seeing the 120 barber's chairs! Warhol often reiterated the ideology of Fordism (Americanism, or 'commonism' as he once called it) in the form which Robin Murray describes: 'In the welfare state, the idea of the standard product was given a democratic interpretation as the universal service to meet basic needs.'[23] Warhol frequently commented on the way in which post-war Fordism produced a form of basic social levelling (without, of course, redistributing wealth), through standardising consumption (Campbell's Soup, Coke, and so on).[24] But, of

course, Warhol's own standardisation production was precisely on the 'barber-shop' scale.

Warhol's attitude to the mass-consumption commodities whose packaging he replicated is often described as 'ironic'. But I think it might be better understood in terms of theatre, of performance or masquerade. Rather than producing images of commodities, he was re-packaging packaging as a commodity in itself. In this process it was the element of display that fascinated Warhol, the transfer to a new space (the art gallery) of images whose display was already familiar in different spaces (the supermarket, the daily

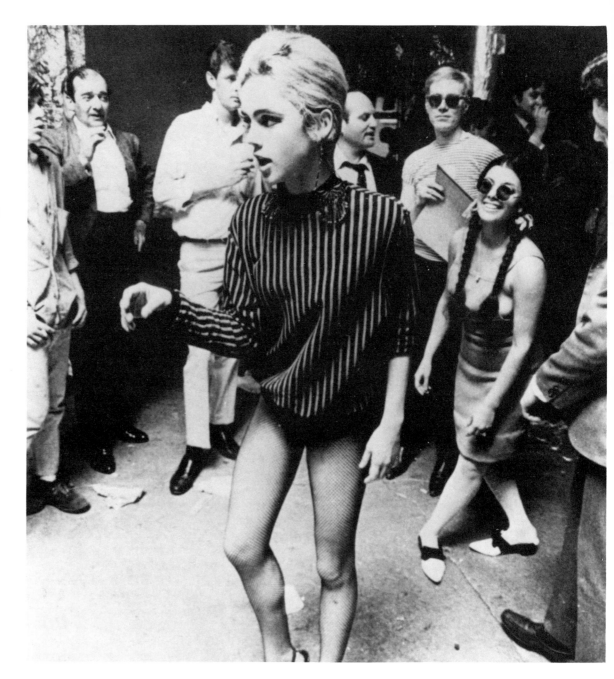

Edie Sedgwick in Cíao! Manhattan, *1972*

newspaper, the fan magazine). It was precisely the proliferation of 'spectacle', of the 'to-be-looked-at', the saturation of everyday life by a new scopic regime, that Warhol chose to replicate in a further gesture of theatricality. Warhol was not particularly concerned by the problem potentially posed in terms of loss of originality or authenticity. He was already used to working on assignment in the commercial art world, where he was told what kind of image to produce and then produced it as fast as possible in a given format. He was already used to copying and tracing from photographs (in fact, his first recorded drawing was a childhood copy of Hedy Lamarr in a Maybellene ad)[25] and was a frequent visitor to the Picture Collection of the New York Public Library where 'he would often come and check out *hundreds* of pictures'.[26] To produce work for gallery spaces he acquired an 'iconographic programmer' (Henry Geldzahler) and re-structured his system of production. The innovation of Warhol's gesture was that of displaying display.

In this circuit of display, Warhol's particular position was to be with, to be alongside the recording apparatus. Indeed, he seemed both to identify with the apparatus and to perceive it as an extension of himself, a prosthesis or, as he came to call his tape-recorder, a 'wife'.[27] At the same time the apparatus 'machinised' its controller, turning Warhol himself into a phantasmatic machine, in line with his desire: 'The reason I'm painting this way is because I want to be a machine. Whatever I do, and do machine-like, is because it is what I want to do.'[28] Only if the apparatus was too complex or tiresome to operate would Warhol let go of it – the 35mm still camera he gave to Billy Name because there were too many controls to work (and which Billy Name used to document the scene at the Factory). Similarly, Warhol hired Gerard Malanga to do the silk screens because it was too much effort to do it all himself. To Geldzahler these pieces of apparatus were 'baffles' which Warhol needed to function in the interpersonal world. He could only have a conversation over the telephone, and, only then if it was being recorded. He took his tape-recorder to dinner parties and took Polaroids of the other guests. He wanted everybody who came to the Factory to be filmed in one of an endless series of 'screen tests'. It is as if by submerging himself into machine-like-ness, Warhol could enter, in phantasy, a world of pure seriality and standardisation, in which, at one and the same time, the 'otherness' of the image of the 'other' was effaced and the identity of the self obliterated through the agency of an impersonal machine-like 'Other'. Thus imaginary difference was erased and the identity of the subject reduced to the purely symbolic dimension of the name, functioning like a logo: 'Andy Warhol', like 'Coca-Cola' or 'Walt Disney'.[29]

This idyllic vision of the Andymat stands in obvious tension with the camp world of caricature and masquerade. Yet the 'baffle' was itself a form of mask, a shield or screen which promised immunity from the exchange of intersubjective looks, while permitting a whole economy of voyeurism and exhibitionism in the form of recorded spectacle. Here the excess and extravagance of masquerade and displays was neutralised by the apparatus, framed, registered and re-projected on the exterior blank of screen or wall, under the supervision of the passive yet sovereign master of ceremonies.

At the same time, recording was also a form of storage. Warhol recorded everything. He ended up becoming a compulsive hoarder of every detail of his daily life. Not only did he have fourteen hundred hours of taped telephone conversation with Brigid Berlin alone, but he saved records and samples of everything that passed through his hands, packing it all up in boxes each month and sending it to storage as 'time capsules'.[30] This mania extended far beyond the bounds of an artistic strategy. It became constitutive of Warhol's being-within-the-world, so to speak. Once again this accumulative drive was channelled into a serial form, that of the regular scheduled 'time capsules': 'what you should do is get a box for a month, and drop everything in it and at the end of the month lock it up. Then date it and send it over to Jersey.' This indeed is what Warhol did – accumulate 'clutter' and then empty it out of his immediate space into his 'closet' in Jersey in an orderly fashion, accumulating an endless series of identical sealed and labelled boxes.

In 1970 Andy Warhol[31] was invited to curate an exhibition selected personally from the storage vaults of the Museum of Art at the Rhode Island School of Design in Providence. In his preface to the catalogue ('Raid the Icebox') the museum director remarked that 'there were exasperating moments when we felt that Andy Warhol was exhibiting "storage" rather than works of art, that a series of labels could mean as much to him as the paintings to which they refer. And perhaps they do, for in his vision all things become part of the whole and we know that what is being exhibited is Andy Warhol.' It is as if the label 'Andy Warhol' would signify, not a person, in the sense of a human subject, but storage: boxes, reels, spools, polaroids, all labelled 'Andy Warhol'. It would be an immense museum of junk (or rather, since it could all be metamorphosed into commodity form, a department store or gigantic thrift shop).[32] At the root of this attitude we find once again many affinities with Cage's aesthetic – the refusal of hierarchy or consequence or narrative (hierarchy and consequence of events over time). Everything is equally worth recording and storing and hence all that is needed to record and store it is an automatic process, the simplest possible algorithm. The recording/storing apparatus should not make evaluative distinctions and to avoid 'clutter' (the single aesthetic imperative) it should adopt a serial procedure of segmentation and ordering, based on arbitrary data (the length of a reel of film) or decisions. (For his second exhibition in Los Angeles, in 1964, Warhol sent a roll of silkscreened Elvises, with a request to 'cut them any way you think it should be cut. I leave it to you. The only thing

I really want is that they should be hung edge to edge densely around the gallery. So long as you can manage that, do the best you can.')[33]

'Raid The Icebox' records another poignant moment. 'Back in his office, Robbins [the museum director] informed the curator of the costume collection that Warhol wanted to borrow the entire shoe collection. "Well, you don't want it all," she told Warhol in a somewhat disciplinarian tone, "because there's some duplication." Warhol raised his eyebrows and blinked." In fact he wanted all the shoes, all the hatboxes (without taking the hats out), all the American Indian baskets and ceramics, all the parasols and umbrellas, all the Windsor chairs, and so on. 'All of them – just like that.' This is the same attitude that inspired Warhol's approach to film-making. He would shoot a single reel of film for each episode or each movie. He would shoot only one take. Then he would show the movie (the take) either as a work in itself or, like *Kiss*, as a serial – a different *Kiss* opened every screening at the Film-Makers Co-op for a period of time. Or, as with the longer works, such as *The Chelsea Girls*, a series of ten-minute takes would be joined up and shown end to end. There was no editing. Nothing was selected within each take and, since there were no second takes, there was no selection between takes.[34] Here Warhol's approach is completely the opposite to that of William Burroughs, who also tape-recorded and photographed everything incessantly, but precisely in order to edit it, to cut the word lines and re-organise the images in complex photo-collages. Burrough's paranoid fear of being taken over by alien words and images is the exact converse of Warhol's 'reverse-paranoid' desire to be taken over. Both recorded compulsively, in order to sabotage (Burroughs) and to facilitate (Warhol) the workings of the semiotic machine.

Warhol's reluctance to edit was a constant in all his activities. Unedited tape transcripts became the basis for his novel *a* and, later, for his magazine *Interview*. With Cage this refusal of selectivity had both an aesthetic and a spiritual, quasi-religious foundation, but with Warhol we can sense another dimension, a more social and psychological fear of rejection, which could express itself in the attempt to re-integrate the rejected. Talking about Freddy Herko and the Factory 'company', the San Remo crowd of faggots and amphetamine freaks, Warhol recollected that 'the people I loved were the ones like Freddy, the leftovers of show business, turned down at auditions all over town. . . . You had to love these people more because they loved themselves less.'[35] Warhol surrounded himself with 'leftovers' and set about turning them into 'stars' – not just ordinary people, as in the Hollywood myth, but rejects, people 'turned down at auditions all over town'.

In 'Raid The Icebox', Daniel Robbins remarks that Warhol 'picked an entire row of Windsor chairs, but from an antique connoisseur's point-of-view the chairs he chose were of secondary interest. In fact, they had been kept, according to a venerable entry, for use in spare parts!' Robbins continues, commenting, 'What violence the idea of spare parts does to our fanatical notion of uniqueness and the state of an object's preservation. Our present curator will not allow a piece to be exhibited at Pendleton House if it is "married" – that is, if all parts are not original to it.' Of course, Robbins is right – Warhol's aesthetic does challenge ideas of uniqueness and authenticity. But it is also important to note that the chairs in question 'were of secondary interest'. In fact, they were the leftovers – the understudies, the rejects. Elsewhere Warhol says, 'I always like to work on leftovers, doing the leftover things. Things that were discarded, that everybody knew were no good. . . . When I see an old Esther Williams movie and a hundred girls are jumping off their swings, I think of what the auditions must have been like and about all the takes where maybe one girl didn't have the nerve to jump when she was supposed to, and I think about her left over on the swing. So that the scene was a leftover on the editing-room floor – an out-take – and the girl was probably a leftover at that point – she was probably fired, so the whole scene is much funnier than the real scene where everything went right, and the girl who didn't jump is the star of the out-take.'[36]

I don't think there is much doubt that the girl on the swing in the fantasy scenario is Andy – the childhood reject and misfit, beaten up at school, kept in bed with nervous disorders, 'the girl who didn't have the nerve'.[37] The fear is mingled with the anxiety of not being like everybody else, like the ninety-nine other girls on their swings. So, on the one hand, we have the deep desire to be exactly like everybody else. 'I don't want it to be essentially the same. I want it to be *exactly* the same.'[38] And, on the other hand, there is the identification with the rejected. It was 'the stars of the out-take' that Warhol loved, who were meaningful to him. The others, the ninety-nine, had no emotional charge for him. 'I want it to be *exactly* the same. Because the more you look at the same exact thing, the more thhe meaning goes away, and the better and emptier you feel.' Warhol's fascination with images was bound up with his dissatisfaction with his own image, his unattractiveness. He had hair that fell out, blotchy, odd-looking skin, a bulbous nose that reminded people of W. C. Fields (his family called him 'Andy, the Red-Nosed-Warhola'). He had a nose-job and kept out of the sun and acquired a wig. 'I really look awful, and I never bother to primp up or try to be appealing because I just don't want anyone to get involved with me.'[39]

Tina Fredericks, his first picture editor (at *Glamour*) comments, 'Like the harem guards at ancient courts, he had the power that comes from being totally unthreatening and endearing.'[40] The power, that is, which emanates from an imaginary castration. In his novel *a*,[41] Warhol is called 'Drella', that is, a mixture of Cinderella and Dracula. The magical transformation from out-take to stardom was achieved for Warhol through voyeurism, as a kind of ocular vampirism. The look recorded, appropriated and re-projected as spectacle the magical transformation of other leftovers into stars. At the same time, it conferred a magical aura on Warhol himself. He acquired not beauty or attractiveness but glamour and fame. For Warhol, the kind of love that counted was that of the fan for the star – a love that linked private fantasy with public image, a love at a distance, mediated through merchandising, maintained by the obsessive hoarding of fetishes: the process described so well in Edgar Morin's book *The Stars*, that Warhol acquired, I assume, when it was published by Grove Press in New York in 1960.[42] And as Warhol acquired confidence and assurance, as he began to savour his own success and fame, he turned more and more to 'the stars of the out-take', a process only ended when he was shot by one of the out-taken in 1968.

Viva in Lonesome Cowboys, *1967*

In 1965, in Paris, Warhol announced his intention of giving up painting. He had started making films two years earlier and, on his return to New York, he would soon become involved with the Velvet Underground and the world of music. The Soviet artists who moved out of painting in the 1920s did so in order to enter the field of commercial and industrial art: advertising, design and even their own functionalist version of fashion. This, of course, was the world Warhol was coming from. His trajectory was towards performance. In retrospect, it is possible to see tell-tale signs of the impending move in the art works themselves. There is a move from the generic products as subject-matter (Campbell's Soup, Coca-Cola) to the stars (Marilyn, Liz, Jackie) and then the increasingly 'frivolous' flowers and cows (subjects from Dutch genre painting helpfully suggested by Geldzahler and Karp). At the same time, the gallery space was being theatricalised: the wrap-around Elvis paintings, the Brillo boxes littered all over the gallery floor, the cow wallpaper with the inflatable silver balloons (perhaps the turning-point was 1963,

when Warhol first wore a silver-sprayed wig). Warhol was deeply impressed by the scene at his opening in Philadelphia in 1965, when a crowd of fans screamed at Warhol, Edie Sedgwick and his entourage. 'It was incredible to think of it happening at an *art* opening. . . . But then, we weren't just *at* the art exhibit – we *were* the art exhibit, we were the art incarnate and the 60s were really about people, not about what they did; "the singer/not the song", etc. Nobody had even cared that the paintings were all off the walls [removed because they were in danger of getting crushed by the crowd]. I was really glad I

was making movies instead.'[43]

In one sense, of course, films were just another form of wallpaper – wallpaper that slowly began to move out of stasis and silence into movement and sound, even eventually into colour. But in another sense they ratified Warhol's need for theatricality; they made possible his plunge into the world of camp, the underground, the bohemian avant-garde.[44] Warhol traces his interest in film back to the days when he would go to 'bad' movies on 42nd Street with De Antonio, and this camp inflection of his taste was strongly reinforced by the films he saw at the Co-op screenings organised by Jonas Mekas, especially films from the gay scene, like those by Jack Smith. This led him on to even 'worse' films like Arthur Lubin's cut-price stagey desert melodramas. But Warhol's key decision was to combine the minimalist aesthetic he brought with him, and which was naively present in many 'bad' cheaply made films, with an equally minimalist refusal to direct. His instructions to his 'script writer' Ronald Tavel (who Warhol approached when he acquired the Auricon sound camera) were that he wanted 'situation' and 'incident' rather than 'plot' or 'narrative'. At first, he wanted Tavel to invent situations and provoke responses from off-screen. In fact, much of the sound track came from off-screen comments. Later, he realised that with a cast of confessional exhibitionists, he could dispense with the idea of a writer entirely. Given a forum, they would talk.

Moreover, Warhol made it clear that his non-interventionism meant that there would be no censorship. Warhol benefited from the freedoms which had been won by others, who had to face legal actions: Allen Ginsberg, William Burroughs, Jack Smith (and Jonas Mekas), Kenneth Anger. The liberties Warhol enjoyed meant that not editing meant not censoring. This was an outcome of the minimalist aesthetic which accommodated Warhol's own voyeurism and love of sexual gossip, and made it possible to combine minimalism with a scabrous sense of the histrionic and the breaking of tabu. Warhol believed so strongly in a certain kind of literalism, that he was worried when filming *Sleep* that he was missing moments because of having to change the reel in the camera. (Later when he was recording interviews for his book *Pop-ism*, he would come with two tape-recorders and start them at different times, so nothing could escape). To make up for the missing moments, Warhol slowed down the projection speed of the film, so that it would be the length he felt it should have been, without the gaps, It is exactly this literalism, this insistence on missing nothing, on suppressing nothing, that made

the connection between minimalism and outrageous camp performance.[45]

Finally, Warhol moved into the music world, with the Exploding Plastic Inevitable, a mixed-media performance environment, with movies, light show, 'expressive dancing' and the Velvet Underground.[46] Warhol recognised in the Velvets a group which already shared the same aesthetic, minimalist and outrageous. John Cale had been a student of Cornelius Cardew in England, where he had already absorbed Cage's ideas. In New York, he was close to another minimalist composer, LaMonte Young, and played in John Cage's 1963 eighteen-hour performance of Satie's 'Vexations', a series of 840 repetitions. (This was a performance which Warhol attended.)[47] At the same time, Lou Reed brought a star presence, as bard of drug-taking and paranoia. Warhol both expanded the theatricality of the Velvets by turning every performance into a mixed-media Event (shades of Black Mountain) and also sought to minimalise the performance.[48] 'One of the ideas he came up with, which was very beautiful, was that we should rehearse on stage, because the best music always took place in rehearsals.'[49] Similarly he had irritated Tavel by preventing any rehearsal for films, so that the take was, in effect, of the rehearsal.

Warhol was many things. He was the revenge of graphics on fine art. He was the revenge of the 'swish' on the 'macho'.[50] He was the revenge of camp on high seriousness and the underground on the overground. Perhaps, one might even say, the revenge of the Ballet Russe on the Great Masculine Renunciation.[51] His legacy has passed to different hands in a number of different directions. The most obvious has been assimilated into mainstream post-modernism and simulationism. But the potential of the other dimension: the underground, the camp, the Velvets, is still available. It left its trace on punk and on the emergence of militantly gay art. In the last analysis, it may be, to borrow Walter Benjamin's categories, that he will be remembered not as the artist of the 'copy', but, more subversively, the artist of 'distraction', whose Chelsea Girls rampage through the aesthetic gangland of the underground imagination[52] ∎

Notes

1 I have discussed the historic impact of Fordism on culture more generally in my 'Cinema/Americanism/The Robot', *New Formations*, no. 8, Summer 1989.

2 For Josef Beuys, see Josef Beuys, *Ideas and Actions* (New York: Hirsch & Adler, 1988) and *Skulpturen und Objecte* (Berlin: Martin-Gropius-Bau, 1988).

3 For John Cage and his influence on Rauschenberg and others, see Calvin Tomkins, *The Bride and the Bachelors* (New York: Schirmer, 1981). See also Michael Nyman, *Experimental Music: Cage and Beyond* (Harmondsworth: Penguin, 1976).

4 For Cobra, see my 'The Situationist International', *New Left Review*, no. 174, March–April 1989.

5 See John Cage's comments in the 'Madame Duchamp' section of *Andy Warhol*, transcript of David Bailey's ATV documentary (London: Bailey Litchfield/Mathews Miller Dunbar, 1972).

6 For Rauschenberg in general, and the work he did with Johns for Bonwit Teller in particular, see Calvin Tomkins, *Off the Wall* (Garden City: Doubleday, 1980).

7 For Black Mountain, see Martin Duberman, *Black Mountain: An Experiment in Community* (New York: Dutton, 1972).

8 For Warhol and Rauschenberg see Emile De Antonio's comments in Patrick S. Smith, *Warhol: Conversations About The Artist* (Ann Arbor: UMI Research, 1988).

9 For Judson Church and New York bohemia in general, see Ronald Sukenick, *Down and In: Life in the Underground* (New York: Macmillan, 1988); Barbara Haskell, *Blam! The Explosion of Pop, Minimalism and Performance 1958–1964* (New York: Whitney Museum, 1984); and Sally Banes, *Terpsichore In Sneakers* (Middletown: Wesleyan, 1976).

10 'Notes on "Camp"', in Susan Sontag, *Against Interpretation* (New York: Farrar, Strauss and Giroux, 1966), first published in 1964. For a modernist response, see Matei Calinescu, *Faces of Modernity: Avant-Garde, Decadence, Kitsch* (Bloomington: Indiana University Press, 1977).

11 See Walter Hopps' comment in Jean Stein with George Plimpton (eds.), *Edie* (New York: Knopf, 1982): 'No chic, no chi-chi, no frills, no nothin'!' For Warhol's own comments, see Andy Warhol and Pat Hackett, *POPism: The Warhol 1960s* (New York: Harcourt Brace Jovanovich, 1980): 'It was exactly the kind of atmosphere I'd pay to get out of . . . I tried to imagine myself in a bar striding over to, say, Roy Lichtenstein

and asking him to "step outside" because I'd heard he'd insulted my soup cans. I mean, how corny.'

12 For Warhol's commercial art, see Smith, *op. cit.*; Jesse Kornbluth, *Pre-Pop Warhol* (New York: Random House, 1988); and Donna M. DeSalvo (ed.), '*Success Is A Job In New York*' (New York: Grey Art Gallery, 1989).

13 For De Antonio's impact on Warhol, see Emilio De Antonio, *Painters Painting* (New York: Abbeville, 1984), and Warhol and Hackett; Stein and Plimpton; and Smith, *op. cit.* These three works remain the basic source material for Warhol's life.

14 See Yvonne Rainer, *Work 1961–1973* (Halifax: Nova Scotia College of Art and Design, 1974).

15 'A Quasi Survey . . .', Rainer, *op. cit.* and reprinted in Gregory Battcock (ed.), *Minimal Art: A Critical Anthology* (New York: Dutton, 1968).

16 Rainer, *op. cit.*

17 See Stefan Brecht, *Queer Theatre* (Frankfurt am Main: Suhrkamp, 1979), and 1960s numbers of *Film Culture passim.*

18 Warhol and Hackett, *op. cit.*

19 See Richard Morphet's essay in Morphet (ed.), *Warhol* (London: Tate Gallery, 1971). In contrast, see Malanga's comments in Smith, op. cit.: 'This one he may have purposely decided to leave that corner blank. But, as far as this part here is concerned, we didn't know what was going to happen.'

20 According to Malanga, *ibid.*: 'Andy even had his mother's penmanship – the script – made into Letrasets so that he would have instant lettering.'

21 Robin Murray, 'Life after Henry Ford', *Marxism Today*, October 1988.

22 Nathan Gluck remembers an early example of lack of quality control, in Kynaston McShine (ed.), *Andy Warhol: A Retrospective* (New York: Museum of Modern Art, 1989): 'If the drawing needed a caption, Mrs Warhola would painstakingly copy it out letter-by-letter, but sometimes she mistook one letter for another and would write *Marlyn Monore* for *Marilyn Monroe*, for example. Andy loved these errors.' See Benjamin Buchloh's essay in the same volume for other examples.

23 Murray, *op. cit.*

24 Nathan Gluck remembers, in Smith, *op. cit.*: 'You know, at one time, when the movement first got started, he wanted to call his stuff "Commonist Painting".'

25 Isabel Eberstadt, in Stein and Plimpton, *op. cit.*

26 See Alfred Carlton Walters, in Smith, *op. cit.* For his fine art, Warhol used an old file of UPI photos he had acquired.

27 See Andy Warhol, *The Philosophy of Andy Warhol* (New York: Harcourt Brace Jovanovich, 1977).

28 G. R. Swanson, 'What Is Pop Art?', *Artnews* 62, November 1963.

29 Or more still of a *beance*: 'I always thought I'd like my own tombstone to be blank. No epitaph, no name. Well, actually,

I'd like to say "figment".' In Andy Warhol, *America* (New York: Harper & Row, 1985). Compare Billy Linich: 'People would ask me what my name was and semifacetiously I would say my name is Name.'

30 Brigid Berlin, 'Factory Days', *Interview*, February 1989. See also *The Andy Warhol Diaries*, (ed.) Pat Hackett (London: Simon and Schuster, 1989).

31 Andy Warhol, *Raid the Icebox* (Providence: Rhode Island School of Design, 1969).

32 For Warhol as a collector, see the five volumes of Sotheby's catalogue, *The Andy Warhol Collection* (New York, 1988). In his preface (printed in each volume) Fred Hughes observes that: 'Andy was an omnivorous observer and recorder of everything, and his collecting habits were, in some way, an extension of this.' He goes on to describe the difficulty he had in persuading Warhol to 'deaccession' some of his collection in order 'to upgrade it'. 'I have no doubt, however, that the disposal of even the smallest items would have been a long, hard struggle as Andy considered himself to be a natural bargain hunter, feeling that everything he bought should have increased in value thousands of times. He had strange anxieties that made him extravagant at times and really quite stingy [i.e. minimalist] at others.'

33 Cited by Irving Blum in Smith, *op. cit.*

34 This minimalist approach would be serialist when it was easier to put together pre-fabricated or pre-measured units, such as photo-booth portraits or reels of film, or when the production process could be mechanized, as with the silk-screens. See John Coplans, *Serial Imagery* (Pasadena: Pasadena Art Museum, 1968) for an early (and pretentious) attempt to deal with Warhol's serialism. Coplans' work has been superseded by Rosalind Krauss, *Grids: Format and Image in Twentieth Century Art* (New York: Pace Gallery, 1978).

35 Warhol and Hackett, *op. cit.*

36 Warhol, *Philosophy* . . .

37 In Smith, *op. cit.*, Fritzie Wood remembers Warhol asking, 'Do you think I dare go up to such-and-such theatre where he or she is playing, and ask if I could sketch. Would I dare? Would I dare?'

38 Warhol and Hackett, *op. cit.*

39 Warhol, *Philosophy* . . .

40 In Kornbluth, *op. cit.*

41 Andy Warhol, *a* (New York: Grove, 1968).

42 Edgar Morin, *The Stars* (New York: Grove, 1960). The Frontispiece of this book consists of a repeated serial image of an advertising poster featuring Marlon Brando. Warhol collected both fan magazines and books about stars. His own involvement with star-making may have been modelled, I suspect, on David Bailey's success in creating stars. One of these, Jane Holzer, enthused: 'Bailey is fantastic . . . Bailey created four girls that summer [1963]. He created Jean Shrimpton, he created me, he created Angela Howard and Susan Murray. There's no photographer in America like that. Avedon hasn't done that for a girl, Penn hasn't, and Bailey created four girls in one summer.' (See 'The Girl of the Year' in Tom Wolfe, *The Kandy-Kolored Tangerine Flake Streamline Baby* (London: Cape, 1966). Warhol met Bailey at a dinner party given by Jane Holzer, who became his own first 'superstar' the next year, 1964, after her success modelling for Bailey. The word 'superstar', incidentally, occurs in Morin's *The Stars*, referring to Marilyn Monroe.

43 Warhol and Hackett, *op. cit.*

44 Stephen Koch's *Stargazer* (New York: Praeger, 1973), remains the best book on Warhol's films. See also Jonas Mekas, *Movie Journal* (New York: Macmillan, 1973) for both comment and context. For Warhol's 'pre-film' interest in film, see also Charles Lisanby's account in Smith, *op. cit.* He remembers how Warhol 'thought that the "Kodak" and all the dots and everything at the beginning or at the end of the leader . . . was as important as anything else [in his home movies].'

45 There is a sense in which Warhol's fine-art phase was bracketed by the much more obviously gay affiliation of both his earlier work (personal and commercial) and by his subsequent film work. (Although there is a trace of 'camp' and 'belle' in Campbells!) On the 'gay sensibility' in the earlier work see Trevor Fairbrother's essay, 'Tomorrow's Man', in De Salvo, *op. cit.*

46 See Victor Bockris and Gerard Malanga, *Up-Tight: The Velvet Underground Story* (London: Omnibus, 1983) for information on Warhol and the music scene. See also, for the Exploding Plastic Inevitable, Marshall McLuhan and Quentin Fiore, *The Medium Is The Massage* (New York: Bantam, 1967).

47 See the accounts by George Plimpton and John Cage in *Edie*.

48 There is an obvious line of descent from the Velvets both to glam rock (one of Bowie's early songs is called 'Andy Warhol') and to punk.

49 Bockris and Malanga, *op. cit.*

50 In Warhol and Hackett, *op. cit.* Warhol remembers asking De Antonio about why he was not accepted by artists of the previous generation. De replied: 'Okay, Andy, if you really want to hear it straight, I'll lay it out for you. You're too swish and that upsets them.'

51 See my 'Fashion/Orientalism/The Body' in *New Formations* 1, 1988. In this interpretation Warhol plays the part of a street Diaghilev.

52 Where, perhaps, they might just encounter William Burroughs' Wild Boys.

NOTES AFTER RESEEING
THE MOVIES OF ANDY WARHOL

JONAS MEKAS

**From *Andy Warhol*
ed. John Coplans,
New York: New York
Graphic Society, 1970**

On reseeing the movies of Andy Warhol, in bulk, old and new – a task which involves a good number of working days – the first thing that strikes one is the uniqueness of the world presented in them, and the monumental thoroughness with which it is presented; a uniqueness in the sense that there is no other artist in cinema similar either in subject, form, or technical procedures. Warhol went into his work with such an intensity, concentration and obsession that one whole area of experience – the people, the visual ideas, the ways of doing it – was so totally covered that there is practically nothing left for anybody else to do in that area.

We have other similar instances in contemporary cinema: Stan Brakhage, Gregory Markopoulos and Jean-Luc Godard went about their work the same thorough way: there is nothing much left for any other film artist to do in the areas they passed through. Huge areas of form and content have been covered in all four mentioned cases, with all the formal questions, technical procedures, solutions explored. In Brakhage we have one area of content, form and technical procedure explored; in Markopoulos another; in Godard still another; in Warhol again another. Neither the content, nor form, nor style, nor technology is the same in any of the four cases. Each artist came and revealed a different vision of the world.

Sometime in 1965, Stan Brakhage came to New York. On his mountain, in Colorado, nine thousand feet high, he had heard about Warhol and *Sleep*. He sat down at the Film-Makers' Cooperative and he said: 'Enough is enough. I want to see the Warhols and find out what's the noise all about.' So he sat and looked through reel after reel of *Sleep*. I think he even said he looked through all of it. I was working by the table, and Stan stood there, suddenly, in the middle of the room, and he started raging, in his booming mountain voice. He told us that we were taken in, that we were fools for sure. Plus, he said, he was leaving New York. Something to that effect. Sitney was there too, I think, and perhaps Kelman. I walked ten times across the room, listening to Stan's rage. Something shot through my mind: 'How did you project the film, 16 frames per second or 24 frames per second?' I asked. 'Twenty-four,' said Stan. 'Please, Stan,' I said, 'do us a favor. I know it's hard for you, but please sit down again and look at *Eat* and *Sleep* at 16 frames per second, because that's how they were intended to be.' Which Stan bravely did, honoring us, and for which I honor him. We went across the street, to Belmore, for some coffee and for some wound-licking, and we left Stan alone to watch the films. When we came back, much later, we found Stan walking back and forth, all shook up, and he hardly had any words. Suddenly, he said, when viewed at 16 frames per second, suddenly an entirely new vision of the world stood clear before his eyes. Here was an artist, he said,

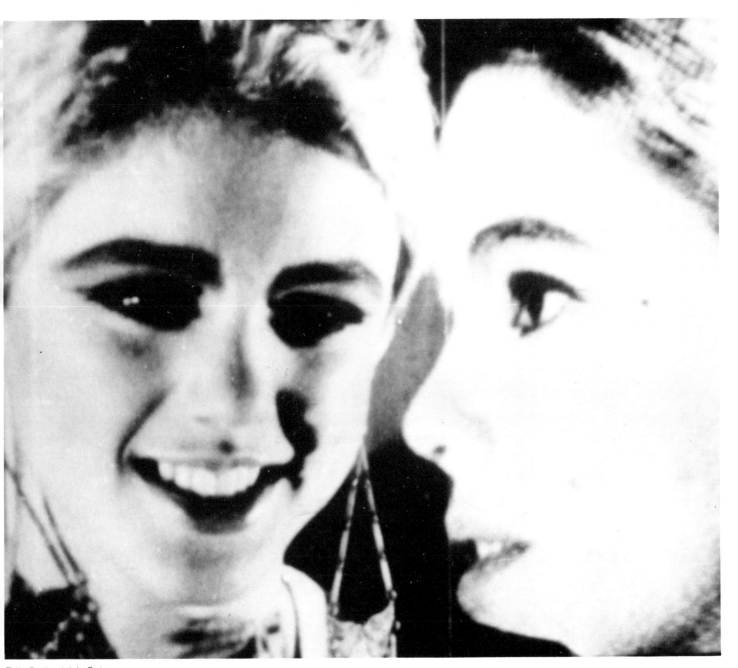

Edie Sedgwick in Outer
and Inner Space, *1965*

who was taking a completely opposite aesthetic direction from his, and was achieving as great and as clear a transformation of reality, as drastic and total a new way of seeing reality, as he, Stan, did in his own work. Stan left the room, without any more words, and had a long walk. I have never seen him before, nor ever since, as shaken up by another aesthetic world as he was that day after watching the movies of Andy Warhol.

A very simple, a very simple displacement indeed. From 24 frames to 16 frames per second. But that's the story of all of Warhol's art: it's always

Tom Baker in I, a Man, *1967*

so unbelievably simple a thing that makes it work. One little thing rightly chosen shifts the whole to a totally new angle, becomes the key to the essence of the work. To see that one simple but unique angle, that one unique formal idea (or concept), has been the Warhol talent alone, a talent that runs out over the boundaries of his art and spills into the areas of life in general. It's commonplace knowledge by now, from *Vogue* to *The New York Times*: it is the unique eye of Warhol to discover, to single out the right faces. A face that Andy Warhol singles out will eventually reach the covers of *Look*, of *Life* or *Vogue*. The same goes for shapes, objects and ideas. If one could call the cinema of Brakhage a cinema of retinal impacts, or simply a cinema of

impacts – then one could call a great part of Warhol's cinema a cinema of presences. One of the special gifts and marks of Warhol's cinema has been this ability of distinguishing, of finding, of seeing the cinematically and conceptually photogenic.

'But it's so easy to make movies, you can just shoot and every picture comes out right.' – Andy Warhol.[1]

Only the next decade will begin to gain some perspective on the cinema of Andy Warhol. As I sat, now, reseeing all his movies again, I was again getting involved in them from the beginning and in a new way. One of the problems of preparing a Warhol filmography, for instance, is that the original presentations of his films have been so much like the films themselves. For example, at the original show, the different reels of the film entitled **** were projected in double superimpositions (one reel on top of the other). Today, on the shelf, what's left of it is a pile of individual 30-minute reels with no information of any kind as to how to look at them. One can look at them any way one wants. I viewed them as separate 30-minute films; one reel – one film. *More Milk, Evette*, during the premiere screening was projected as a double-screen movie – there was another movie, I don't remember which (and no use asking Andy, his mind is blank on such matters), projected beside *Evette* on the same screen. A number of other Warhol movies were shown sometimes in single projections, sometimes in double projections, sometimes in superimpositions; sometimes two 30-minute reels were projected one after the other, running for 60 minutes; at other times the same two reels were projected side by side at the same time, running for 30 minutes. At the end of 1964 and throughout the year 1965, immediately after the Expanded Cinema Festival (at the Cinemathèque), Warhol went through a period of projection experiments, experiments which culminated in the Velvet Underground series at the Dom, and *The Chelsea*

Girls. During such experimental projections the projectionist could do practically anything he wanted – with Andy standing behind him, of course. The projections at The Factory were always very casual, that is, with people milling around, walking in front of the screen, the music going on at the back. The chance aspects of *The Chelsea Girls*, the overlappings of reels in sound and image, drove some reviewers to desperation: they never knew if they were seeing the same film as their colleagues. In short: the aesthetics that went into the making of these films spilled out into the presentations of the films, into the theater. This uncompromisingness and thoroughness of the cinema of Andy Warhol is carried thus to its ultimate purity (or call it extreme) in every area, whichever area of his cinema we happen to touch.

This thoroughness of the cinema of Andy Warhol sometimes provokes curious paradoxes. For instance: as huge and monumental as the achievement and body of the cinema of Andy Warhol is, one could also entertain an argument – and it's a quite popular argument in certain circles – that Andy Warhol doesn't exist at all in practicality. Andy Warhol is a concept, an idea, a myth, a Madison Avenue concoction, a product of the advertising agents.

'The problem is that he had almost nothing to say, and therefore substituted camp and, at best, put-on. He was and is, however, a cunning self-publicist, and there are always some unweary critics around ready to find significance in amateurish improvisation.' – Hollis Alpert.[2]

Warhol is like America: America is only an idea, after all, they say. They say, even New York is not America. The early Warhol is all LaMonte Young, or Jackson McLow, or Paik. The later Warhol (I'm speaking about Warhol's cinema) is either Ronald Tavel or Chuck Wein; still later it's maybe Viva, or maybe Paul Morrissey, who knows. And the mystery of it all remains how it all holds together! Again, it's like the United States: the idea, the concept, they

say. That is, the essentials ('the Revolution') come from Warhol, and the particulars, the materials, the people come from everywhere and they are molded and held together by the central spirit, Andy Warhol – Andy Warhol who has become almost the symbol of the noncommittal, of *laissez-faire*, of coolness, of passivity, of *tabula rasa* – almost the Nothingness Himself.

'In many ways inaction is preferable to unintelligent action, for it has at least the merit of not creating further sanskaras and complications. The movement from unintelligent action to intelligent action (i.e. from binding karma to unbinding karma) is often through inaction. This is characteristic of the stage where unintelligent action has stopped because of critical doubt, but intelligent action has not yet begun because no adequate momentum has arisen. This special type of inaction which plays its part in progress on the Path should in no way be confused with ordinary inaction which springs from inertia or fear of life.' – Meher Baba, *Discourse.*[3]

I have watched Andy Warhol at work, and I have seen certain ideas grow and come into existence; and I have seen some ideas grow and change and never reach realization because something somewhere didn't click: the approach, the angle, the shape, the set-up didn't exactly work out. So I know well that nothing or little that Warhol does during those 'passive,' 'careless' and 'casual' shooting or painting sessions is really that careless or that passive. His aesthetic senses are behind it all, always awake, letting it all happen. But when everything is 'just happening' and when everybody thinks that 'things are happening by themselves' – there he stands, like he isn't even there, and with an unnoticeable, single, simple switch from 24 to 16 mental or formal 'frames' – with one single conceptual switch he transposes the 'uncontrolled' realism into an aesthetic reality that is Warhol's and nobody else's. Those '16 from 24' switches are very unnoticeable – it may be a shrug, it may be a word, it may be a deadpan, it may be a touch or a swing of the camera – they may be very slight but they are always there, and nobody sees them – neither their meaning nor even their very existence – but the Artist himself; and that's exactly where the origin of the myth of the Permissive Andy comes from, from the fact that he is the Total Artist and sees what no one else really sees.

'Why is *The Chelsea Girls* art? Well, first of all, it was made by an artist, and, second, that would come out as art.' – Andy Warhol.[4]

'Marcel Duchamp reduced the creative act to choice and we may consider this its irreducible personal requirement. Choice sets the limits of the system, regardless of how much or how little manual evidence is carried by the painting.' – Lawrence Alloway.[5]

This controlled, and I stress, totally controlled cinema – I insist on this view of Warhol as an artist, I insist that instead of total permissiveness he has been exerting a total control – because of this inversion, the ying and yang of permissiveness-control, the film division of The Factory attracted to itself all the sad, disappointed, frustrated, unfulfilled, perverted, outcast, unreleased, eccentric, egocentric, etc., etc., talents and personalities. A whole generation of the Underground Stars produced by Jack Smith, Ron Rice and Ken Jacobs were there, on the brink of Waiting to Be Used. And there he was, Saint Andy, letting them all into his orbit, into his quarters. Effortlessly and painlessly he moved them and coordinated them and used the energies and forces that were pouring in, balancing them, clashing them – a most subtle maneuvering of the most extreme temperaments and personalities in town, a maneuvering that culminated, on one hand, in *The Chelsea Girls*, and on the other in the Velvet Underground light projections. The Dom series of the Velvet Underground, with projections, were the most energy-charged performances I have ever seen anywhere. The film-maker here became a conductor, having at his fingertips not only all the different creative components – like sound controls, a rock band, slide projectors, movie projectors, lighting – but also all the extreme personalities of each of the operators of each piece of the equipment. He was structuring with temperaments, egos and personalities! Warhol maneuvered it all into sound, image and light symphonies of tremendous emotional and mental pitch (Exploding Inevitables was the other name) which reached to the very heart of the New Generation. And he, the conductor, always stood there, in the balcony, at the left corner, next to the projector, somewhere in the shadow, totally unnoticeable, but following every second and every detail of it, structure-wise, that is.

'The Plastic Inevitables (Velvet Underground; Warhol and Company) performances at the Dom during the month of April provided the most violent, loudest, most dynamic exploration platform for the intermedia art. The strength of Plastic Inevitables, and where they differ from all the other intermedia shows and groups, is that they are dominated by the Ego. Warhol, this equivocal, passive magnet, has attracted to himself the most egocentric personalities and artists. The auditorium, every aspect of it – singers, light throwers, strobe operators, dancers – at all times are screaming with an almost screeching, piercing personality pain. I say pain; it could also be called desperation. In any case, it is the last stand of the Ego, before it either breaks down or goes to the other side. Plastic Inevitables: theirs remains the most dramatic expression of the contemporary generation – the place where its needs and desperations are most dramatically split open. At the Plastic Inevitables it is all Here and Now and the Future.'[6]

The exhausted and tired academic art squeezes all and any content into worked-out, accepted, likeable forms. They are no longer aesthetic forms: they are molds. They give the illusion of strength, security and harmony. There is this aspect of new art: a feeling of things placed on the verge of out-of-balance. It's like Taylor Mead. I saw him the other day at The Factory. He was complaining about a film he was doing with somebody, how he was cut and edited to pieces. 'Wynn said he'll keep in *only the essential parts* of my scenes, where *the thing happens.* Nothing will be left,' he said, 'only the controlled.' Because what his scene was really about – and Andy understands this and permits it – can be revealed only by means of *duration.* Yes, the duration, that's the word. There are certain ideas, feelings, certain contents which are structured in time. The literal meanings you can spell out through climaxes, through the scenes 'where the thing

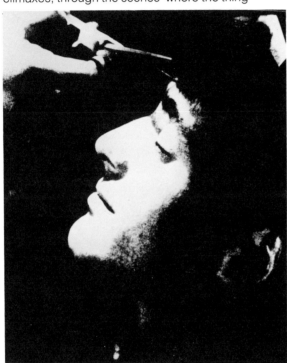

Billy Linich in Haircut, *1963*

happens.' That's why Godard's films are so literal. But the real meaning, the one that is beyond the literal meaning, can be caught only through structuring in time. That applies equally to feelings and thoughts. One of the essential misunderstandings about art and thought has been the belief that thought is opposed to aesthetic activity, to art. And particularly that thought has no place in cinema, which is images, man, images! But the modern scientists tell us that the thoughts are governed by the same structural processes as art, that is, by pace, rhythm, duration; the durations and repetitions of thoughts and feelings and actions. Much of philosophical and mystical writing attracts us not because of the ideas but because of the rhythms and pacings, the structures of thoughts, the meditative and contemplative structures of those writings. The literal meanings are of secondary importance. Most of the criticism of Andy Warhol films (apart from the 'poor technique') rests on the fact that his movies seem to be lacking any literal meanings, any ideas, any scenes in which 'things happen'.

'With us, people can be whatever they are, and we record it on film. If a scene is just a scene, with a lot of ideas that have nothing to do with the people, you don't need to make a movie, you could just type it.' – Paul Morrissey.[7]

When you go beyond the literal ideas, beyond the sensory shocks, when you begin to deal with more essential movements of thought and spirit, when you try to register more subtle human qualities – and the cinema of Andy Warhol has always been concerned with man – you begin to structure in time.

'These other Yankees don't know that I'm from the South, so they don't bother me, but the South has a feeling toward the human being that the North doesn't have.' – Andy Warhol.[8]

'I still care about people but it would be so much easier not to care. It's too hard to care . . . I don't want to get too involved in other people's lives – I don't want to get too close . . . I don't like to touch things . . . that's why my work is so distant from myself . . .' – Andy Warhol.[9]

'With film you just turn on the camera and photograph something. I leave the camera running until it runs out of film because that way I can catch people being themselves. It's better to act naturally than to set up a scene and act like someone else. You get a better picture of people being themselves instead of trying to act like they're themselves.' – Andy Warhol.[10]

We have one more of those curious paradoxes with which Warhol's work abounds. There is this popular notion that Warhol is *the* commercial artist of the Underground. That notion is promoted by both the wider public and by the aestheticians of the avant-garde. The paradox is that the cinema of Andy Warhol, more than any other cinema, is undermining the accepted notions of the American entertainment and commercial film. The cinema of Brakhage or the cinema of Markopoulos or the cinema of Michael Snow has nothing to do with the entertainment film. They are clearly working in another, non-narrative, non-entertainment area, as in a classical way and meaning we say all poetry is in a different area. But the cinema of Warhol, *The Chelsea Girls*, *The Nude Restaurant*, *The Imitation of Christ*, is part of the narrative cinema, is within the field of cinema that is called 'movies,' it deals with 'people,' is part of it. Is part of it, but is of a totally different ilk. That's why the movies of Andy Warhol cannot be ignored by the commercial exhibitors. At the same time, once they are in, and they are In, they are undermining, or rather transforming, or still more precisely, *transporting* the entertainment, the narrative film to an entirely different plane of experience. From the plane of purely sensational, emotional and kinesthetic entertainment, the film is transported to a plane that is outside the suspense, outside the plot, outside the climaxes – to a plane where we find *Tom Jones*, and *Moby Dick*, and Joyce, and also Dreyer, Dovzhenko, and Bresson. That is, it becomes an entertainment of a more subtle, more eternal kind, where we are not hypnotized into something but where we sort of study, watch, contemplate, listen – not so much for the 'big actions' but for the small words, intonations, colors of voices, colors of words, projections of the

International Velvet in The Chelsea Girls, 1966

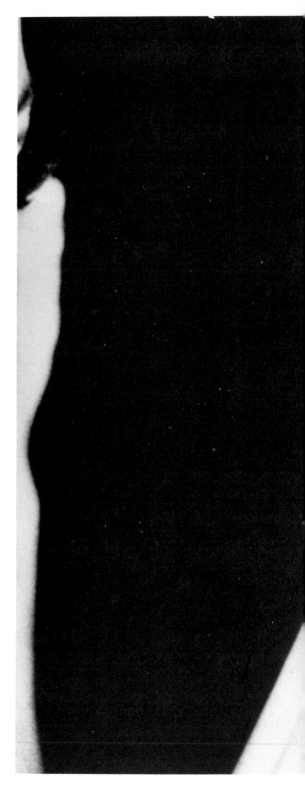

voices; the content that is in the quality and movements of the voices and expressions (in the Hitchcock or Nichols movies the voices are purposeful, theatrical monotones) – a content of a much more complex, finer and rarer kind is revealed through them. And these faces and these words and these movements are not *bridges* for something else, for some other actions, no: they are themselves the *actions*. So that when you watch *The Imitation of Christ*, when you watch this protagonist who does practically nothing, who says very little – when you watch him from this new, transported plane of the New Art (all minimal art exists on this transported plane) – you discover gradually that the occupation of watching him and listening to him is more intellectually fruitful, more engaging, and more entertaining than watching most of the contemporary 'action' and 'entertainment' or serious 'art' movies. A protagonist emerges with a unique richness of character. All the mystical and romantic seekers of Truth and God have left their marks in this character. Patrick is the hero of the end of the 20th century. Every little word, sound, hesitation, silence, movement reflects it totally and completely. Not that Warhol *made* him act that way, to be that way: he chose him perfectly and flawlessly and allowed him to be himself within the context, and chose him for those qualities and in that place.

'"I'm so mad at Andy," she said. "He just *puts* you out there and makes you do everything."' – Ingrid Superstar.[11]

'I have Andy now to think ahead and make the decisions. I just do what he tells me to do.' – Viva.[12]

And this is one of the achievements of Warhol's work, as one discovers when one reviews it again today: this total exploration of these unseen, imperceptible aspects of changing reality, of using his art and the technology of cinema to register them; to structure with those subtle human qualities and changing, emerging, new realities which escape even the wizards of the Cinéma Vérité.

'What Warhol does not permit is that his machine

and technique become the stars of the film. In most so-called ''documentary camera style'' features being screened these days, the supremely slick results and absolutely astonishing feats of technical wizardry defeat whatever hope of evoking reality the film's creators may have had in mind. Their standards, in which all things are perfect, may be said to establish a visual fantasy. Warhol's technique establishes visual reality, in which nothing is perfect. But it is real, and his films are all the better for it.' – Dennis J. Cipnic.[13]

– And do not think for a moment, dear reader, that

the actions, the choices of the artist, *why* he chooses this or that procedure at that particular moment in history, are meaningless, or do not express man fully! Do not ask him to explain it all to you, why he did it that way, and please do not say, when you find that he can't answer, that his silence means that he *didn't* know what he was doing. No, every moment of his life, his whole past grew and grew and grew and mounted and led to this moment of unconscious choice. What I'm saying is that the protagonist and the feeling and the content of *The Imitation of Christ* is pure Warhol.

'Warhol himself, I suspect after talking with him, doesn't know where he's really at, what he's really stumbled into.' – Richard Whitehall.[14]

Gerard Malanga and Edie Sedgwick in Vinyl, *1965*

What amazes one, when one resees Warhol movies, the entire bulk of his film work, is the amount, the vastness of the gallery of the people, of different dreams, faces and temperaments that his films are filled with. Andy Warhol is the Victor Hugo of cinema. Or maybe Dostoyevski, a little bit sicker, that is. And then, again and again this preoccupation, or should I say obsession, with the phenomenal reality, with the concrete reality around him, as he's trying to grasp it and record it again and again, and each time it escapes him. As if the deeper you dig into the human aspects, the more you swing into the material aspects – one deepens the other.

'All my films are artificial, but then everything is sort of artificial. I don't know where the artificial stops and the real begins.' – Andy Warhol.[15]

'"I've been thinking about it," conceded Warhol. "I'm trying to decide whether I should pretend to be real or fake it. I had always thought everyone was kidding. But now I know they're not." He looked worried. "I'm not sure if I should pretend that things are real or that they're fake. You see," said Warhol, craning his head absently, "to pretend something real, I'd have to fake it. Then people would think I'm doing it real."'.[16]

'"Well, I guess people thought we were silly and we weren't. Now maybe we'll have to fake a little and be serious. But then," Warhol said, going on like a litany, "that would be faking seriousness which is sort of faking. But we were serious before so now we might have to fake a little just to make ourselves look serious."'.[17]

The reality seems to be constantly slipping away from under the feet, so he turns to another way of doing it, coming to it from another angle – again and again – with such untiring persistence and obsession that it borders on both the titanic and the insane. Yes, only in a factory, it could be done only by a factory, and not by a human effort. No, the face, held for no matter how long on the screen, no, it doesn't reveal it *all*; nor do the endless

conversations reveal or register it *all*, they do not reveal the existence totally. So he zooms in and out and swings the camera and runs it wild, at the Dom, and in the studio, trying to catch it through the medium itself, through the materials and chances of his medium, indirectly, sneakily, from the sides – putting blind snares to catch the truth, the reality, the existence – and that doesn't do it either. So he goes to two screens, to three screens, to superimpositions, and strobes, and music – or he just leaves the camera by itself – maybe it will do it when nobody sees it, looking at *IT* by itself, as the eye of a newborn baby – maybe it's there, *IT*, but we don't know how to see it again – yes, how to see it or look at the world as if you have never seen it? So he places the camera there and it watches life – it stares at life, like a baby, and it's difficult to stand it, that naked look, so you become conscious of it, you begin to reveal yourself to the child, you show to the child what you'd never reveal to even the closest of your friends, those certain secret emotions, certain secret subtle fragile curious motions of the soul.

'. . . Experiencing things and objects as things and objects is the outcome of holding certain attitudes, and to hold and apply these requires a constant effort.' – Sinclair.[18]

The other day, I was looking through some old English texts. Then I dug out *La Chanson de Roland*, and *Vogelweide*. Oh, the beauty of the Old French, and the High German, and the Old English! Why is it so that languages seem to become slicker with time? They seem to lose those raw edges, that earth quality. Or is it only an illusion, all those mysterious spaces, those unknowns and those inbetweens? Anyway, I thought, whatever the case, the language of the Warhol sound movies (I am talking about the language of cinema) and the language of much of the Underground in general, beginning with 1960 or thereabouts, when compared with the Hollywood film or the European art film, has all the qualities of the Old English, of the Old French, of the High German. It has those raw edges, those mysterious areas where the imagination can roam, where we can erect our own under-textures and under-structures – those mysterious blanks, spaces, muddled noises which can be interpreted two, three, four, ten different ways – that crackling sound – that unpolishedness, which at some point becomes pregnant with personal meanings. Like LaMonte Young's music into which, while listening, you can project one million of your own melodies. That's about the most significant difference between the language of the New Cinema (the Underground) and the film language of the Old Cinema. The only thing is that usually *Old* refers to the origins, to the sources – but in cinema, until now, *Old* meant everything that had become so polished, had reached such a degree of functionality, specialization and practicality that it had lost all mystery and all origins. The only parallel between the Old English and a similar notion of cinema would be to speak about Lumière. And that's where the early cinema of Andy Warhol went: to the cinema of Lumière. He did it very instinctively, but with that act he rehabilitated the meaning of *Old* in cinema, he pushed it all the way back to the true origins. At the same time, he became the first modern film artist who went back to the origins for a readjustment of his art, for the refocusing of the medium.

'Andy Warhol is taking cinema back to its origins, to the days of Lumière, for a rejuvenation and a cleansing. In his work, he has abandoned all the 'cinematic' form and subject adornments that cinema had gathered around itself until now. He has focused his lens on the plainest images possible in the plainest manner possible. With his artist's intuition as his only guide, he records, almost obsessively, man's daily activities, the things he sees around him.

'A strange thing occurs. The world becomes transposed, intensified, electrified. We see it sharper than before. Not in dramatic, rearranged contexts and meanings, not in the service of something else (even Cinéma Vérité did not escape this subjugation of the objective reality to ideas) but as pure as it is in itself: eating as eating, sleeping as sleeping, haircut as haircut.

'We watch a Warhol movie with no hurry. The first thing he does is he stops us from running. His camera rarely moves. It stays fixed on the subject like there was nothing more beautiful and no thing more important than that subject. It stays there longer than we are used to. Long enough for us to begin to free ourselves from all that we thought about haircutting or eating or the Empire State

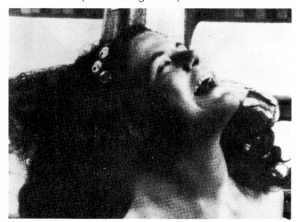

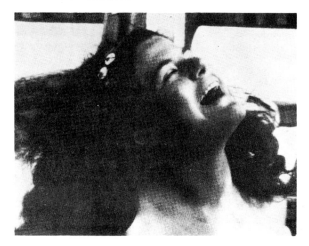

Naomi Levine in Tarzan and Jane Regained, Sort of . . ., *1963*

Building; or, for that matter, about cinema. We begin to realize that we have never, really, seen haircutting, or eating. We have cut our hair, we have eaten but we have never really seen those actions. The whole reality around us becomes differently interesting, and we feel like we have to begin filming everything anew. A new way of looking at things and the screen is given through the personal vision of Andy Warhol; a new angle, a new insight – a shift necessitated, no doubt, by the inner changes that are taking place in man.'[19]

'In effect, then, Warhol insists on *our* personal

Joe Spencer and Ingrid Superstar in Bikeboy, *1967*

commitment, to ourselves, rather than his (the observer can no longer be as passive toward art as he has been for the last four hundred years or so), by giving so little and demanding so much. (How do you fill the time in which you are supposed to be looking at the picture?) . . . Like it or not, it appears that we are being expected to alter our accustomed patterns of perceptual rate, our attention span, and our notions of fitness.' – Alan Solomon.[20]

The viewer is, thus, confronted with his own blank mind. Here is cinema that doesn't manipulate him, doesn't use *force* on him: he himself, the viewer, has to search, to ask questions, sometimes unconsciously, other times consciously, and still other times by throwing objects at the screen. The *serious* art and the *good* entertainment are supposed to shake *you* up. Here, however, is an art which asks that *it* be shaken up; by *you*, filled up with ideas, by you! An art that is a *tabula rasa.* A cinema that leaves the viewer standing alone, in front of it, like looking into the mirror. Didn't we always say that art mirrors reality? So here it really is! Before, it was always true that man mirrored art. Now we straighten things out. We liberate man from art's slavery . . . Isn't the mirror empty and silvery too, like Warhol's face, like the silver of his hair, like the silver of Warhol's Silver Flotations, the silver of The Factory walls, the silver of his paintings?

'To do this once is forgivable. It is a kind of dadaesque joke mocking art – and hell I'm all for it. People and artists do tend to take themselves too seriously at times. If one has enough money for selling Brillo boxes at $200 apiece to waste on six hours of raw stock and developing (such as in the movie *Sleep*) to create a mammoth joke – well man go ahead. But to do it again and again and then ask people to sit through it is pushing things a bit too far. A joke's a joke, but I for one would be embarrassed to play the same boring joke on people more than once.' – Peter Goldman.[21]

During the early years of the decade, the early period of Warhol's film work, whenever I went to a university, lecturing, I used to take one of Andy's films, usually *Eat*. And always the same thing used to happen. The film starts rolling, the audience sits quietly, for a minute or two. The catcalls and crack remarks begin. In the fourth or fifth minute, however, they begin to realize that I have no intention of stopping the film, and the reports from the back lines reach the front lines, that the reel is *big* (45 minutes). The most unsettling, however, is the fact that no amount of noise or cracks seems to do any harm to the film! Its nonchalant, obstinate and don't-give-a-damn imperturbability on the screen seems to reject or absorb anything you can throw at it. It almost grows stronger with every whistle. So the students begin to leave the auditorium. After ten minutes or so the impatient ones leave or give up, others resign, and the rest of the show proceeds quietly. Later, from the discussions, it becomes clear that there is always a period – to some five minutes, to others fifteen, to some still longer – a period of *jumping the reality gap*, or what we would also call the period of aesthetic weightlessness; a period of adjusting to the aesthetic weightlessness, to the different gravitational pull. From there on you are floating through your mind, from there on the movie – *Sleep, Eat, Haircut*, and exactly the same applies to the later sound movies, say *The Imitation of Christ* – from there on everything becomes very rich. You are watching now from a new angle, every detail reveals a new meaning, the proportions and perspectives change – you begin to notice not only the hundred-mile movements but also one-inch movements; not only a crashing blow on the head is an action, a touch of a butterfly wing is also an action. A whole new world opens because of this shifted angle of vision, of seeing, a world in which there is as much action, suspense, tension, adventure, and entertainment as on the former plane – and more!

'When we speak of fashions in thought, we are treating philosophy lightly. There is disparagement in the phrases, "a fashionable problem," "a fashionable term". Yet it is the most natural and appropriate thing in the world for a new problem or a new terminology to have a vogue that crowds out everything else for a little while. A word that everyone snaps up, or a question that has everybody excited, probably carries a generative idea – the germ of a complete reorientation in metaphysics, or at least the "Open Sesame" of some new positive science. The sudden vogue of such a key-idea is due to the fact that all sensitive and active minds turn at once to exploiting it; we try it in every connection, for every purpose, experiment with possible stretches of its strict meaning, with generalizations and derivations. When we become familiar with the new idea our expectations do not outrun its actual uses quite so far, and then its unbalanced popularity is over. We settle down to the problems that it has really generated, and these become the characteristic issues of our time.' – Susanne Langer.[22]

One could say that the cinema of Jean-Luc Godard is the cinema of applied propaganda. His is an ingenuous and total usage of all the means of cinema, the vocabulary, the syntax, for the purpose of putting across certain literal ideas. As a result, the medium is misused, and the ideas themselves distorted, as all propaganda is.

The cinema of Brakhage is the cinema of the truth of the eye, of seeing. The preoccupation with the processes of seeing in its own turn revolutionized the means of registering the seeing, it expanded the medium through which man expresses or retains his visual memories and ideas.

The cinema of the Cinéma Vérité authors is the use of the film medium for the purpose of 'catching life as it is', 'catching truth as it is.' By putting a special stress on life and truth 'as is', they made it feel self-conscious; the truth became singled out, undressed, stripteased, and thus out of the proper truth context. The truth became a fiction, a fantasy.

The cinema of Andy Warhol is also about the truth and life as is, or, rather, men as they are. It is a cinema or a passion to record the people and their feelings as they are – but without any stress on it, without any illusions, without any sales talk about truth and life as is – in other words, doing it but remaining silent, letting the thing itself speak for itself. Everybody, all the Cinéma Vérité film-makers are trying to catch the truth in order to show it to *others*; Warhol is doing it as a private passion. The truth caught in Warhol movies remains in the shadow, under the palm trees, no light is being thrown into its face, and it's visible only to those who themselves put in effort to see it, who light their own lamps, so to speak. The very humble and transitory look of his films seems to pay respect to the truth's privacy.

Again, it was Stan Brakhage who, on his last visit to New York – as he has done on every other of his previous visits – was lamenting the transitory aspects of his art. He slumped into the chair with his long legs on the floor, helpless, almost defeated, talking about the cathedrals and frescoes, and wondering which of his films, if any, will remain in the year 2200, when some of the originals already are fading and crumbling today. There was Jerry Joffen, we remembered, six years ago, who worked, had influence, including influence on Warhol at some early stage – and where is his work today? It all went with the wind, only the memories left. The ephemerality of Warhol's screenings, all the chance elements of them, and the changing states and shapes and lengths and even the titles of his films – Warhol seems to have incorporated all the transitoriness of things into his very aesthetics, looking at his own work nonchalantly, and cool, very cool, no dramatics, no lifted voice about it. And that's why it seems to me that his cinema is really about the transitoriness of the medium and the transitory state of all things. About the transitoriness of all existence and all art.

I bumped into Andy the other day. We spoke about this and that, and about my own film diaries. He spoke about how much he wanted to do the same: to record everything that he saw, everything that happened around him. 'But it's impossible,' he said, 'it's impossible! I tried, but it's impossible. It's impossible to carry with you a movie camera, a tape recorder, and a still camera at the same time. I wish I could do it.'

So he is still at it! Still trying to catch it all – by all possible means. It's an obsession unto death!

'We're going to start making serious movies,' said Andy ■

Notes

1 Andy Warhol, quoted by Gretchen Berg in an interview, *L.A. Free Press*, 17 March 1967.
2 Hollis Alpert in *Saturday Review*, quoted in the advertisements of the film, *Coming Apart*.
3 Meher Baba, *Discourses*, p. 113.
4 Andy Warhol in an interview with Gerard Malanga, *Arts Magazine*, vol. 41, no. 4, 1967.
5 Lawrence Alloway, *Systemic Painting*, The Solomon R. Guggenheim Museum catalogue, 1966.
6 Jonas Mekas, *Village Voice*, 26 May 1966.
7 Paul Morrissey, quoted in an article by Neal Weaver, *After Dark*, January 1969.
8 Andy Warhol in an interview with Gerard Malanga, *Arts Magazine*, vol. 41, no. 4, 1967.
9 Andy Warhol, quoted by Gretchen Berg in an interview, *L.A. Free Press*, 17 March 1967.
10 Andy Warhol, quoted by Gene Youngblood, *L.A. Free Press*, 16 February 1968.
11 Ingrid Superstar, quoted in *The Realist*, August 1966.
12 Viva, quoted by Barbara L. Goldsmith, *New York* magazine.
13 Dennis J. Cipnic, *Infinity*, September 1969.
14 Richard Whitehall, *L.A. Free Press*, 28 April 1967.
15 Andy Warhol, quoted by Gene Youngblood, *Los Angeles Herald-Examiner*.
16 Andy Warhol, quoted by Leticia Kent, *Village Voice*, 12 September 1968.
17 Ibid.
18 Sinclair, *Conditions of Knowing*, quoted in the Stable Gallery program note (Warhol show).
19 Jonas Mekas, excerpt from text of sixth independent Film Award, in *Film Culture*, no. 33, 1964.
20 Alan Solomon, Boston Institute of Contemporary Art catalogue (Warhol show, 1967).
21 Peter Goldman, *Village Voice*, 27 August 1964.
22 Susanne Langer, *Philosophy in a New Key* (Harvard University Press, 1942).

FOUR FILMS BY ANDY WARHOL
GREGORY BATTCOCK

FOUR FILMS BY ANDY WARHOL
GREGORY BATTCOCK

FOUR FILMS BY ANDY WARHOL
GREGORY BATTCOCK

FOUR FILMS BY ANDY WARHOL
GREGORY BATTCOCK

FOUR FILMS BY ANDY WARHOL
GREGORY BATTCOCK

From *The New American Cinema: A Critical Anthology*, New York, Dutton, 1967

Potentially the most influential of the New York film-makers is Andy Warhol, a comparative newcomer to cinema, to which he turned only after having acquired a considerable reputation in the plastic arts. The early films of this artist were deceptively simple: they had a minimum of content and were made with a minimal technique. Warhol first became well known as a film-maker for his use of the still image – the device whereby the action on the screen is reduced to small variations in the posture of a single image. Action is even further reduced, in most of Warhol's films made prior to 1965, by the film-maker's refusal to move the camera. And it may not be farfetched to draw an analogy between this film approach, on the one hand, and the approach toward painting followed by the minimal painter, on the other, in which attitudes toward the surface, the shape of the canvas, and scale and proportion are criticized.

Early Warhol movies emphasized the cinema as a medium for experiencing time, rather than movement or event. They included *Empire*, made by focusing a camera on the Empire State Building for several hours, and *Sleep*, which applied the same technique to the subject of a sleeping man. In this period, Warhol made scarcely more effort to direct the action (or inaction) when making films with waking human actors than when working with a building or an 'actor' who was fast asleep. Thus *Henry Geldzahler, The Thirteen Most Beautiful Boys, Eat,* and *Haircut,* the titles of which precisely delineate their contents, are essentially similar to *Empire* and *Sleep.* The following observations on *Empire* can be applied, with only slight modifications, to all the other films in this group.

Since it may be assumed that the first purpose of *Empire* is to present the essential character of film as a medium, it may then be asked why wasn't a blank or exposed film simply run through the projector? Simply because, while doing so might suffice as a provocative statement, the use of plain film, which is uniform in color, would make impossible the exhibition of contrast and gradations between black and white; and the black-and-white dialectic is probably the second most important restriction and distinction of the film medium. The decision to film *an object* thus made possible the presentation of the full range of tones from black to white. It might be argued here that filming a block of wood could certainly present the full range (black, white, grey) of tones. Why, then, was the Empire State Building used?

If a block of wood were filmed, the audience would be forced to consider that block of wood as *art,* as sculpture – junk or 'found,' Abstract Expressionist or Dada; a concern that would be irrelevant to the purpose, or subject, of the movie. The choice of the Empire State Building seems logical. It's not some faceless building in Queens that demands identification or clarification, nor is it

Marie Menken in The
Chelsea Girls, *1966*

a building from which any aesthetic pleasure or stimulation can be gained (at least not at this time). It is, simply, a big nothing – perhaps the biggest nothing, except for the Pan Am Building, around. It's better known, more familiar, seemingly more permanent than the newer colossus uptown. It's New York, America – yet not a moment like the Statue of Liberty with which one can identify emotionally, either in glorification or vilification.

As if to emphasize that the selection of the Empire State Building is primarily a device by which to present the full range of tones from black to white, the first reel of this long (eight-hour) movie shows the dramatic change of all the original darks or blacks to lights, and the original lights gradually moving through the entire spectrum to blacks. During the first fifteen minutes the image of the building is obscured almost entirely by fog. This provides a dramatic beginning, and one that acknowledges traditional methods of film art. It recalls the first appearance of Garbo in *Anna Karenina*, when the face of the actress is almost totally obscured by steam from a train. Dramatic evolution is confined to the first reel, leaving the rest of the film free to concentrate on a more important limitation of the medium.

In this work Warhol has clearly dismissed the idea that 'movement' is an essential characteristic of movies. Movement can, after all, be presented and experienced in other media – the dance, theatre, now even sculpture – so Warhol has chosen not to deal with it in this film essay on the reidentification of the essential message of cinema. Sound is dispensed with also, and its absence is consistent with the object photographed, since the Empire State Building does not, *qua* building, make noise.

Silence has been dramatically employed in films almost since sound became available. Generally, sound has been erased from portions of films to heighten the dramatic impact of certain scenes, such as the mirror scene in the Marx Brothers film

Duck Soup (1933). The documentary, or non-fiction character of *Empire* is not altered by the absence of sound, and its message is appropriate to the electronic age. Black and white and everything in between is one subject of this film. Another, even more important, is time.

Warhol's decision to film the slow passing of dusk and night emphasizes the importance that he as artist gives to the element of time. In commercial films events are rarely presented in their full time span. Time is distorted in such films – usually by compression. The time in *Empire* is distorted in a different way. It is distorted, perhaps, simply by its *not* being distorted when one would reasonably expect it to be. In addition, the action in the first reel is clearly speeded up, possibly so that the change from day to night, the major 'event' in the film, could be summarily disposed of in order to clear the way for the timeless 'real' time of the unchanging image of the building. Time is perhaps the most important single element that distinguishes film from the other visual art forms. In looking at still objects, the viewer chooses his own time. In dance and the theatre, time is, to some extent, controlled by the director and performers. Warhol then, may not force the viewer to look at his films – in which case there is only one thing left to do, and that is, to sit through them.

The intellectual content of *Empire* clearly overshadows the visual, and the exaggerated time element is in opposition to the 'telescoping' of incidents typical of the commercial cinema. In *Empire* and his other early films, Warhol re-examines communicative procedures in art. In so doing, he has focused upon the very *presence* of the art object itself in a way that recalls modern handling of some commercial products. Indeed, the presence of an object, and its intrusion upon the audience, or consumer, is receiving renewed attention in several areas. Recent advertisements for a new television set read: 'New Westinghouse Jet Set. Doesn't stare back at you. It's considerate television.' In film, of course, the time is decided by the film – that is, by the film-maker. The projector runs at a predetermined speed; the projectionist is not yet an artist.

The subject of *Empire* is, then, an investigation of the presence and character of film – a legitimate if not a requisite concern for the artist. And the terms established for this investigation are the black and white of film technology and the obvious, yet frequently denied, limitation of time.

Empire is now a classic of the avant-garde. In a short period it has received extraordinary

Empire, *1964*

acceptance, which suggests it appeared at the right moment. Whatever influence it may have had, film will not be quite the same again. Neither, perhaps, will the Empire State Building.

From the deadpan 'new realism' just described, with its mind-destroying concentration on insignificant incidents and situations, Warhol has recently moved on to more explicit ironies.

In *Horse* Warhol produced an apparently straightforward parody of the traditional Western – complete with oppressed Mexican (played by Tosh Carrillo), sheriff, boy outlaw, and cowboy – that yet succeeds in revealing the disguised eroticism of the genre. Ron Tavel, who wrote and directed *Horse* and *Vinyl*, also wrote *Screen Test* (with Mario

Montez) – a transitional work in both form and content. It is one of the first of Warhol's sound films, yet the still camera is retained.

In *Screen Test*, as in other still-image pictures, slight variations of image become all the more important because of their scarcity. Presence of the Abstract Expressionist sensitivity heightens their impact and therefore makes the films much more interesting. The strong black-and-white contrasts in *Screen Test* demand a consideration of the flat negative-positive values of the surface, and as in a painting by Franz Kline, it is uncertain whether it is a line or a plane, a white picture on a black ground or a black on white – and it doesn't really matter. The usual half-tone pictorial characteristics seem somehow absent from the picture and bring the picture more toward painting; at the same time the film limitations, which give the work its identity, are not denied.

A single actor, 'in drag,' is shown on the screen for the entire duration of *Screen Test*. Mario Montez is certainly at his best here, for he seems to expose himself utterly in this new revelation of the duality of acting and experience. In effect, the experience cannot be separated from the acting, and the question of determining whether or not Montez is actually acting is thrust upon the audience. His totally convincing performance is heightened by the rather sloppily applied make-up and wig, which speak of Genet and Greenwich Avenue in a startlingly real and cruel manner. And if the wig, make-up, and sex are distortions, so also is the length of the screen test – seventy minutes.

The sound of *Screen Test* consists of two voices: the off-stage voice of Ron Tavel commands the actor to repeat over and over certain words and phrases self-consciously chosen and frequently vulgar and juvenile; Montez does so with embarrassed distaste.

The burden of appreciating the film rests squarely on the audience. The audience, never catered to, is abused, exposed, and ridiculed. It is, at the same time, very much considered. The use of film as a device to torment its audience may be understood as an intellectual challenge; certainly it forces an alert viewer to come to new terms with art. The popular value structure is shattered and not in the terms of the value structure. When engaged in the protest and destruction that is art, Warhol does not subscribe to the notion that calls for the toppling of the old order within the terms of the older order. By demonstrating consistent respect for his medium, he will challenge the existing order on all levels, using his own terms, even though they will be unacceptable to most people and delay acceptance of his art. Quick acceptance of a statement which attempts to subvert within the conditions and restrictions of the status quo and according to its lexicon is to be expected, even though that statement must ultimately be false. If *Sleep* or *Empire* were films to turn on to, *Screen Test* is actively interesting because the viewer is forced into an immediate and not altogether unfamiliar involvement.

As has already been intimated, the actual subject of all Warhol's early movies is film itself and its attendant hypocrisies. *Screen Test* is no exception, though its apparent subject may be transvestism. Here too the intellectual content dominates the visual; the film apes Hollywood and movies in general. In presenting these disturbing challenges to the nature of the medium, Warhol hinders understanding and sympathy by his choice of vehicle. However, sexual dualism as represented on the screen can be taken as further proof of Warhol's intent to unmask the sexual fraud of the contemporary cinema. The usual presentation of sex is a product of the art of packaging technology and it is illusion, facade, and gesture that we buy and that Montez's posturing lays bare.

Representative of the next stage in Warhol's development as a cinematic artist is *Kitchen*, a film noteworthy for the changes it introduces in the concept of the 'superstar', a concept that Warhol is credited with contributing to the iconography of the underground cinema. In the introduction of this latest device, Warhol consciously refers, yet again, to the basic structure of the professional Hollywood cinema. This time the star system itself becomes the subject of scrutiny. In the early still-image movies, the so-called superstar was the sole figurative element recognizable on the screen. More recently, as critical attention has been directed to attempts to identify and license the superstar, Warhol has been engaged in changing the use and presentation of the whole idea. The changes can be seen moving in several directions. Peculiarities of the set, props, script, and audio elements are exploited in a leveling-off process that, in *Kitchen*, acts as a bridge between the earlier films and such new works as *The Chelsea Girls*. Paradoxically, the real superstar in *Kitchen* is the least obtrusive, and the one who behaves mostly like a prop. His participation in the film is less than marginal, and many of the props are assigned a more aggressive role. Though he is always on the set, only at the end of the film is the non-super superstar (played by René Ricard) allowed genuine human identity as he socializes on an equal level with the other people in the film. Here Warhol is obviously trying to equalize in prominence all figurative elements – both figures and objects. Thus the resultant redistribution of emphasis is of a type associated with painting. If the characteristic feature of the superstar in *Kitchen* is seen as a confusion of identity on one hand, coupled with a questioning of traditional patterns of communication on the other, then the real superstar is the most silent and inanimate one.

I should like to discuss the film with several considerations in mind – namely, the role of the set and props, the sound direction, and the superstar.

The title, the director, and the scenarist (Warhol and Tavel, respectively) are audibly introduced along with the actors and their parts, the set and its furnishings, and the procedure followed in making the film. The audience is reminded that the script is planned and that the actors deliver prepared lines, copies of which are distributed around the set in case they forget. Thus, the artist draws the audience into his confidence. No sentimentality is involved in the device, as it does not alleviate the responsibility demanded of the audience, which, as always in any meaningful art offering the promise of intellectual reward, is considerable. In the introduction, as in criticism of a painting, the various items, including format and figures, are given equal billing. Thus, early in the film, a special approach to the various figurative items is indicated. A sort of equalization is begun. The superstars, the ice box, and the kitchen table all have an equal start. All their identities are reshaped.

The spatial organization of the set in *Kitchen* is fixed and defined in a way that recalls the early Renaissance manner of Bouts, Campin, or Van Eyck. Walls, floor, and ceiling act as extension and reinforcement of the frame. Warhol does not move the camera in this film, and, once again, there is little reason for him to do so. The side and rear walls of the kitchen where the movie takes place determine the edges of the picture and the movements of people and things are confined within them. Warhol has telescoped, in a sense, the development of Renaissance space (of this type) from early to later stages, for his subsequent films do away with the rigid spatial delineation and the space is limitless – the entire studio in *Camp*, the great outdoors (filmed on location) for *My Hustler*, and the indefinite 'unseen' limitation in *The Chelsea Girls*. These films are without fixed spatial limits, and both actors and, in a new departure for Warhol, camera wander. In them, the limitations of the surface are decided by the frame of the camera, rather than physical restriction by the set.

The clean white kitchen and its introduction as a 'clean white kitchen' have special significance. It may not be a coincidence that the ubiquitous white walls of modern interiors are contemporary with the practical realization of the existential predicament.

In any room with white walls the occupants are forced into a deeper awareness of and attitude toward the objects that the walls enclose. The antiseptic, unnatural, unfinished whiteness (bare like canvas waiting to be painted – then often not painted) rejects both objects and occupants equally and places them in an intimate relationship with each other. Moreover, white walls give a sense of limitless space, without actually providing the challenge of such a space in reality; decorated walls, on the other hand, decidedly confine space. As the urban environment has been extended beyond the walls of the city to include the entire globe (the 'wild' spaces enclosed, protecting them from us), so the existential presence of white walls reflects a change of our position as regards the immediate landscape.

Quite naturally, the objects within the white non-limitation, in this case the kitchen, gain new importance; at the same time they are no longer 'permanent' in the way that art could once be said to be. Permanence implies a type of decision alien and impractical to the modern philosophic process. Thankfully, the new unlimited environment contains only disposable items (appliances, mates, art objects, emotions); the environment itself becomes temporal and disposable – clipped, treated, planned, and renewed. The intellect, obviously, transcends the object; even the film doesn't have to be seen, and understanding may be experience. Description of the film can suffice; the experience the film offers is understanding, not seeing, it. Bookcases have movable shelves and paper books along with 33 r.p.m. records are seen by the garbage. New books, better recordings, and new art (ideas) will and must replace them and accommodation for the replacements is built in ahead of time. Preparation is made for accommodation of the future rather than preservation of the past.

If Warhol forces a new appreciation of objects in *Kitchen*, he simultaneously urges a reconsideration of their relationship with people. The objects introduced at the beginning of the movie, and which play important roles include mixer, ice box, stove, kitchen sink, kitchen table, etc. Throughout, the kitchen table assumes considerable responsibility. It is placed in the center of the frame, and is used, abused, cluttered, sat on, exercised on, and when it is finally cleared, a murder takes place on it. In the end it is as it was in the beginning, ready to go through it all again. It alone among the objects and people in the movie seems to have followed a formal narrative and to have gone through a conventional pattern of communication with information and events radiating from centers to margins (if that is the conventional pattern), from beginning to end, as they perhaps no longer do. With its own clearly defined space, the table exists as something of a mirror-image; a play within a play. The disordered, compulsive cluttering on the table surface may represent the old order, and is accordingly ridiculed and abused.

The audio introduction of the parts and mechanics of the film is interrupted by the actors' sneezing. Throughout the entire film the male and female stars sneeze at one another, at intervals. The sneezes seem to acknowledge each other as they communicate some sort of information which, in this film, words or sexual behaviour do not. Information and experience are not necessarily transmitted through the printed or spoken word, or by sexual contact or suggestion, or anything else. But sex and words are used to transmit information to the audience even though the actors do not communicate with each other by these means.[1]

The new position of the dialogue is made clear late in the first reel of the movie. An electric malted-milk machine is turned on and the incessant noise from it all but obscures the remaining speech. Sometime in the second reel the machine is turned off, much to the relief of everyone, both actors and audience ('I can't stand that damn noise'). The direct and functional relationship between the dialogue and other sounds, and the fact that the film is on two reels, is demonstrated by the way the malted machine is used. As the second reel of the film begins, the actors are seen sitting around waiting, and the machine is turned off. After a spoken introduction to reel two, the actors arrange themselves and the machine is turned on again, symbolically representing the connection between the two reels. Warhol seizes on the physical fact of the separation between the two reels for particular attention, just as he has pointed up so many other hitherto ignored or obscured realities of film-making. Orderly, literary connection between the two reels of the movie exists solely in terms of the machine, not through dialogue or human behavior, both of which are deliberately interrupted in order to heighten further the separation.

At intervals, a photographer enters the set from the foreground and takes snapshots. Frequently the actors pause momentarily for the picture. The effect is to heighten certain moments in the film, and the device may be intended as yet another reminder of the unimportance of the plot, lest we get sufficiently carried away, even for a moment to become involved with the events portrayed.[2] Whatever the reason, one cannot help but feel the gesture is a little obvious. In addition, it tends to distract from other more appropriate aspects of the film. But *Kitchen* is, on the whole, a dignified and honest attempt at realization of the sociological and aesthetic problems attendant on the new art.

Among Warhol's more recent films, *The Chelsea Girls*[3] is in some ways different from any of its predecessors, for it has the full complement of sound, movement, multiple images, and story line that the artist had laboriously discarded in his earlier cinematic work. The introduction of enriched content can be taken as yet another attempt by the artist to criticize formal cinematic procedure. For in this film, it is most particularly the way a movie is looked at and the way the information is assimilated by the audience that comes under scrutiny. As in

Screen Test, the apparent and the real subject are two different things.[4] In *The Chelsea Girls* two different films are shown simultaneously side by side on a wide screen. Occasionally they may overlap. The pictures are said to suggest a series of rooms at the Chelsea Hotel (on West 23rd Street in Manhattan) and to depict what goes on in them. Each program is more or less the same, with the films (some black and white and some in color) shown in the same order. The films last about half an hour apiece and follow each other without interruption. The series plays for about four hours.

René Ricard and International Velvet in The Chelsea Girls, 1966

At each showing of *The Chelsea Girls* that has so far taken place, the two movies have always been two different pictures; not two prints of the same picture.[5] It might indeed be interesting to see two *identical* prints shown in this manner. In that event, however, critical attention would be directed elsewhere since the artist's concern would be with questions of comparison and time in the cinema image; questions that are not of the moment and not now of much interest. Moreover, the purpose of the experiment would immediately be clear, and, as Nicholas Calas writes in *Artforum*: 'Not clarity but ambiguity rules art. . . .'

On some occasions one of the films on the screen has been black and white, the other in color. In some of the new color films, Warhol has used exceptionally vivid and travelogue-y color combinations. They have all been seen before and parts of them are abstract, in a way similar to figurative Abstract Expressionist painting of the fifties. These films appear equally dated and their emphasis seems to be misplaced. (That is, unless they were specifically made to be shown on a two-picture screen in the present manner.) Most of these movies are somehow a little bland. Did Warhol decide to show all these films two-at-a-time because he realized that they were unable to stand on their own? Or did he make them for this type of presentation? Whatever the answer, it is clear that *The Chelsea Girls* represents a new direction (predicted some time ago in *The Village Voice* by Mekas) in the films of Warhol.

Numerous problems that do not exist in the showing of ordinary films crop up in this special event. The whole point is that *The Chelsea Girls* is not an ordinary cinematic experience. Two films being shown at the same time can be considered a type of media-mixing, and simultaneously raise problems of display and presentation. The reader may ask just how *The Chelsea Girls* differs from other Warhol experiments in media-mixing – such as *The Velvet Underground*, a combination of noises, dancing, props, tactile effects, and films. Although *The Chelsea Girls* employs only film, the most important feature differentiating it from other inter-media operations (including those of Whitman, Rainer, Cage, Paxton, and Rauschenberg) is probably that *The Chelsea Girls* takes place in a movie theater and the screen is where it belongs — up on the stage in front. Thus everything about the movie-going experience remains traditional except the movies themselves. Attention is focused upon a re-evaluation of the movie as movie and not as movie combined with the various other effects — which in the long run may be less outrageous and less offensive.[6] After all, the mixed-media events of the artists noted above can be taken as positive efforts to create a new art form; whereas Warhol's efforts, true-to-form (and true to art), appear to subvert cinema as an art medium.

And, of course, they do.

If this conclusion is accepted, it is possible to see that Warhol is then consistent with his earlier cinema projects. He still questions the very nature of the medium and its relationship with the cultural matrix and the contemporary value structure — for which he clearly holds no brief. He is determined to prove that only vital institutions can provide vital art statements; his challenges to the medium serve ultimately to assure its legitimacy. If in his earlier movies he attempted to redefine the nature of film and to clarify its limitations, the new works may be

Marie Menken and Gerard Malanga in The Chelsea Girls, *1966*

said to check out the remaining restrictions of the art form. These include such physical aspects as the two distinct types of images (the retinal-visual and cerebro-visual), as well as the nature of the auditorium, projection, and screen. Future Warhol films will probably explore farther in the same direction.

One of the principal characteristics of many contemporary Happenings, theater pieces, movies, and inter-media events is the role played by chance and accident; a role that is, as it were, built into the event. The concern with chance is a result of the direct and continuing influence of the Abstract Expressionist school of art. Typically and humanistically, the artist in this case is attempting to acknowledge the role of the audience, the unpredictability of existence, and the integrity of individual identities, by planning a spot in his work for the unplanned. He is, in effect, stepping back and at least pretending to give up control, to proscribe his Romantic position as god and seer; by so doing he may prove the role of the artist unnatural, obsolete, and unnecessary. The inevitable abrogation of Romantic responsibility in

Ingrid Superstar and Ondine in The Chelsea Girls, *1966*

art has led toward the tendency to abstraction, the various 'outrageous' forms, and the variety of 'dehumanized' results. Thus, when the term 'dehumanization' is appended to the new art, it is, to the modern artist an encomium. Such is his very goal.

One result of the intentional use of 'accident' or 'chance' in art events is that no two presentations of any given event will be exactly the same. Sometimes the differences may be slight, sometimes considerable. In any case, they will be noticeable even to the obtuse. Differences in

Brigid Polk in The Chelsea Girls, *1966*

performance of an elaborate theater-event can be observed in so many ways. There is no point in delineating the numerous possibilities for variation – the opportunities for error. Actual image differences in the various evenings in *The Chelsea Girls* are not very great. The major difference or changes apparent in the presentation from performance to performance are in timing by the projectionist and some of these changes are in reality beyond his control. Although he attempts to follow the same order in showing the various parts of the schedule it is impossible always to have the same two images complementing each other on the screen on every occasion. (Such precision could only be obtained by some sort of automated

programming of projection.) Thus exact and dependable repetition, an expected feature within the film medium, is very simply and immediately challenged. At the same time, it's not at all obvious and my interpretation of the event could very well be entirely wrong.

The Chelsea Girls is, up to the present, the only one of Warhol's movies to have achieved a successful commercial presentation, and it has received fairly wide coverage by the popular press. It is dismaying to see how critics attuned to the productions of Hollywood, to conventional narrative in cinema, and to the European commercial cinema, have thoroughly managed to miss the point. An exception was Richard Goldstein in the *World Journal Tribune*, who handled the sociological aspects of the film with considerable perception, though giving relatively little attention to its artistic merits. Nearly all the other critics writing in the popular press dwelt with lugubrious insistence on the squalidness, sordidness, perversion, etc., of the lives depicted in the film.

In stripping the cinematic medium of its pretensions and decorations, Warhol has produced an art statement that is likely to be acceptable only to the very few. If they are to be seriously considered as art, Warhol's films demand a new aesthetic; their admirers would say the artist has already gone some way toward constructing one. Whatever one's opinion of the merits of the films, it must surely be admitted that Warhol has finally forced a realignment of the purpose, place, and function of the artist, who is no longer solely a technician, or a decorator, but is now strictly an idea man and director. Much of his subject matter is, in one way or another, the subject matter of the commercial artist; in this manner big business and the immediate past, probably the two most difficult things for the contemporary artist to come to terms with, become for Warhol both the content and the product of his art.

In this procession of films, there is no pause for

reflection and little self-indulgent repetition. If, by now, the earlier works are classics of the avant-garde, the newer ones continue to present the challenge, uncertainty, and polemic that is art ∎

Notes

1 The dialogue between the actors is interesting and occasionally very amusing, though it is important only because it is there, and not for what it is about. It is based on obvious caricatures of Freudian psychology (e.g. 'I've failed you. Both as a mother and lover I've failed you.' and 'Isn't a mother a boy's best friend?'). So, too, sexual roles are at once confused and paradoxical. The two main characters are both sexy – Edie Sedgwick displaying lovely legs all over the place and Roger Trudeau in levis without a shirt. The male lead reveals he has just come from the shower where he had sex with Joe ('Which Joe, dear?'). And later in the picture, someone else finds he has sexually 'attacked' the wrong person, because of a confusion in names. (Question: 'Why does everyone in this movie have the same name?' Answer: 'You don't have sex with a name, do you?')

2 The use of the 'photographer' reminds me of a peculiarity attendant to Warhol movies. Note that the 'photographer' occasionally walks directly in front of the *camera* and obscures, momentarily, the picture. On several occasions during a recent screening of *Kitchen*, people in the front rows of the auditorium turned around to see who had walked in front of the projector. During the screening of Warhol's films (often on portable apparatus) people interject themselves between the projector and the screen with surprising frequency. Interestingly, the 'less' there is on the screen, the more likely this is to happen. The action may be a demonstration of hostility toward the film which has apparently 'nothing happening' on it. Similarly, 'black' paintings by Ad Reinhardt are said to attract tactile attention at a high rate; they are protected by ropes at the Museum of Modern Art and by little platforms at the Betty Parsons Gallery. Equally, many people will not think twice about interrupting others' views of paintings by Barnett Newman or Kelly or Noland, although the same people will excuse themselves if they happen to obstruct the view of a Van Gogh (or a De Kooning, probably). Is Warhol perhaps protecting his work from this sort of thing by creating his own obstruction to preclude the necessity of further interruption?

3 In this film, the familiar Warhol superstars appear without using fictional names. Of course, this is not an entirely new idea. The characters in the W. C. Fields movie *International House* (1933) also retained their own names.

4 Critics writing in the popular journals have pointed out the 'dirty' subject matter of this film. Other writers have made an analogy between the subject matter of *The Chelsea Girls*, on one hand, and the napalm and torture of the Vietnam war, on the other. In this sense, the popular critics may therefore be accurate – however, it is the absence of sentimentality coupled with a total and unfeeling dedication to *vérité* within this movie that makes the comparison with the ghastly war in Vietnam an appropriate one. A somewhat different view has been taken by Nicolas Calas, writing in *Arts*, who feels that Warhol's selections are frequently sentimental and that the film suffers because of this sentimentality. Calas says:'Warhol is full of self-pity. One after another his hermaphrodites dissolve into a Mimi and Mignon sentimentality with canned soup in the tradition of Praxiteles and Cocteau.' (*Arts*, vol. 41, #4, February 1967.) A different observation is noted by David Ehrenstein (*Film Culture*, no. 42, Fall 1966), who writes: 'Warhol has no ax to grind, he's just an innocent bystander at the scene of the accident. No moralizing, no message you can wrap up and take home with you, just the facts.' The movie must have had some kind of moralizing effect on Ehrenstein, however, for he ends his article: 'Can our lives be filled with such intense pain, our minds diseased, our souls ravaged?'

5 Only one of the films, *Pope Ondine*, does not fit into the scheme. It is about a Papal pretender and his response to an accusation from an inept young coed who is making a confession. The film is placed in an important spot in the sequence – at the end. Sound for the accompanying film is always turned off, rather conspicuously, when *Pope Ondine* begins. It's obviously a major event in a situation which does not want a major event. *Pope Ondine* speaks entirely for itself. Distraction is irrelevant. It's an extraordinary film with exceptional presence. It's entirely engrossing with sharp wit and brilliant camera usage, and the message is something other than only the medium. In addition, the formal narrative is important, and it must be followed completely. Naturally, when one's attention is directed equally to two different events, it is impossible to follow the narrative of both at the same time. Warhol is only one of several artists who have contributed, in the past, to the ultimate destruction of formal narrative in film. The removal of this type of narrative or literary content from film form was an essential development and a prerequisite to the radical departure represented in *The Chelsea Girls*.

6 Other critics have pointed out an innovation of a different sort – that in this film the camera is very close to the subject (figures). The surrounding 'background' material is cut away by the frame, and the figures generally occupy the entire surface. It has been suggested that this manner of Warhol recalls Caravaggio. It also recalls a popular device employed by many makers of filmed television commercials.

NOTHING TO LOSE
AN INTERVIEW WITH ANDY WARHOL

GRETCHEN BERG

Gretchen Berg *Cahiers du Cinéma in English* no. 10, 1967

Andy Warhol – I'd prefer to remain a mystery, I never like to give my background and, anyway, I make it all up different every time I'm asked. It's not just that it's part of my image not to tell everything, it's just that I forget what I said the day before and I have to make it all up over again. I don't think I have an image, anyway, favorable or unfavorable. I'm influenced by other painters, everyone is in art: all the American artists have influenced me; two of my favorites are Andrew Wyeth and John Sloan; oh, I love them, I think they're great. Life and living influence me more than particular people. People in general influence me; I hate just objects, they have no interest for me at all, so when I paint I just make more and more of these objects, without any feeling for them. All the publicity I've gotten . . . it's so funny, really . . . it's not that they don't understand me, I think everyone understands everyone, non-communication is not a problem, it's just that I feel I'm understood and am not bothered by any of the things that're written on me: I don't read much about myself, anyway, I just look at the pictures in the articles, it doesn't matter what they say about me; I just read the textures of the words.

I see everything that way, the surface of things, a kind of mental Braille, I just pass my hands over the surface of things. I think of myself as an American artist; I like it here, I think it's so great. It's fantastic. I'd like to work in Europe but I wouldn't do the same things, I'd do different things. I feel I represent the U.S. in my art but I'm not a social critic: I just paint those objects in my paintings because those are the things I know best. I'm not trying to criticize the U.S. in any way, not trying to show up any ugliness at all: I'm just a pure artist, I guess. But I can't say if I take myself very seriously as an artist: I just hadn't thought about it. I don't know how they consider me in print, though.

I don't paint anymore, I gave it up about a year ago and just do movies now. I could do two things at the same time but movies are more exciting. Painting was just a phase I went through. But I'm doing some floating sculpture now: silver rectangles that I blow up and that float. Not like Alexander Calder mobiles, these don't touch anything, they just float free. They just had a retrospective exhibition of my work that they made me go to and it was fun: the people crowded in so much to see me or my paintings that they had to take the pictures off the walls before they could get us out. They were very enthusiastic, I guess. I don't feel I'm representing the main sex symbols of our time in some of my pictures, such as Marilyn Monroe or Elizabeth Taylor, I just see Monroe as just another person. As for whether it's symbolical to paint Monroe in such violent colours: it's beauty, and she's beautiful and if something's beautiful, it's pretty colors, that's all. Or something. The Monroe picture was part of a death series I was doing, of

*International Velvet and
Alan Midgette in* * * * *
(Four Stars), 1966/67*

people who had died by different ways. There was no profound reason for doing a death series, no 'victims of their time'; there was no reason for doing it at all, just a surface reason.

I delight in the world; I get great joy out of it, but I'm not sensuous. I've heard it said that my paintings are as much a part of the fashionable world as clothes and cars: I guess it's starting that way and soon all the fashionable things will all be the same: this is only the beginning, it'll get better and everything will be useful decoration. I don't think there's anything wrong with being fashionable or successful, as for me being successful, well . . . uhhh . . . it just gives you something to do, you know. For instance, I'm trying to do a business here at the Factory and a lot of people just come up and sit around and do nothing, I just can't have that, because of my work.

It didn't take me a long time to become successful, I was doing very well as a commercial artist, in fact, I was doing better there than with the paintings and movies which haven't done anything. It didn't surprise me when I made it; it's just work . . . it's just work. I never thought about becoming famous, it doesn't matter . . . I feel exactly the same way now I did before . . . I'm not the exhibitionist the articles try to make me out as but I'm not that much of a hard-working man, either: it looks like I'm working harder than I am here because all the paintings are copied from my one original by my assistants, like a factory would do it, because we're turning out a painting every day and a sculpture every day and a movie every day. Several people could do the work that I do just as well because it's very simple to do: the pattern's right there. After all, there're a lot of painters and draughtsmen who just paint and draw a little and give it to someone else to finish. There're five Pop artists who are all doing the same kind of work but in different directions: I'm one, Tom Wesselman, whose work I admire very much, is another. I don't regard myself as the leader of Pop Art or a better painter than the others.

I never wanted to be a painter; I wanted to be a tap-dancer. I don't even know if I'm an example of the new trend in American art because there's so much being done here and it's so good and so great here, it's hard to tell where the trend is. I don't think I'm looked up to by a large segment of young people, though kids seem to like my work, but I'm not their leader, or anything like that. I think that when I and my assistants attract a lot of attention wherever we go it's because my assistants look so great and it's them that the people are really staring at, but I don't think I'm the cause of the excitement.

We make films and paintings and sculpture just to keep off the streets. When I did the cover for the TV Guide, that was just to pay the rent at the Factory. I'm not being modest, it's just that those who help me are so good and the camera when it turns on just focuses on the actors who do what they're supposed to do and they do it so well. It's not that I don't like to speak about myself, it's that there really isn't anything to say about me. I don't talk very much or say very much in interviews; I'm really not saying anything now. If you want to know all about Andy Warhol, just look at the surface: of my paintings and films and me, and there I am. There's nothing behind it. I don't feel my position as an accepted artist is precarious in any way, the changing trends in art don't frighten me, it really just doesn't make any difference; if you feel you have nothing to lose, then there's nothing to be afraid of and I have nothing to lose. It doesn't make any difference that I'm accepted by a fashionable crowd: it's magic if it happens and if it doesn't, it doesn't matter. I could be just as suddenly forgotten. It doesn't mean that much. I always had this philosophy of: 'It really doesn't matter.' It's an Eastern philosophy more than Western. It's too hard to think about things. I think people should think less anyway. I'm not trying to educate people to see things or feel things in my paintings; there's no form of education in them at all.

I made my earliest films using, for several hours,

just one actor on the screen doing the same thing: eating or sleeping or smoking; I did this because people usually just go to the movies to see only the star, to eat him up, so here at last is a chance to look only at the star for as long as you like, no matter what he does and to eat him up all you want to. It was also easier to make.

I don't think Pop Art is on the way out; people are still going to it and buying it but I can't tell you what Pop Art is: it's too involved; it's just taking the outside and putting it on the inside or taking the inside and putting it on the outside, bringing the ordinary objects into the home. Pop Art is for everyone. I don't think art should be only for the select few, I think it should be for the mass of American people and they usually accept art anyway. I think Pop Art is a legitimate form of art like any other, Impressionism, etc. It's not just a put-on. I'm not the High Priest of Pop Art, that is, popular art, I'm just one of the workers in it. I'm neither bothered by what is written about me or what people may think of me reading it.

I just went to high school, college didn't mean anything to me.

The two girls I used most in my films, Baby Jane Holzer and Edie Sedgwick are not representatives of current trends in women or fashion or anything, they're just used because they're remarkable in themselves. *Esquire* asked me in a questionnaire who would I like to have play me and I answered Edie Sedgwick because she does everything better than I do. It was just a surface question, so I gave them a surface answer. People say Edie looks like me, but that wasn't my idea at all: it was her own idea and I was so surprised: she has blonde short hair, but she never wears dark glasses . . .

I'm not more intelligent than I appear . . . I never have time to think about the real Andy Warhol, we're just so busy here . . . not working, busy playing because work is play when it's something you like.

My philosophy is: every day's a new day. I don't worry about art or life: I mean, the war and the bomb worry me but usually, there's not much you can do about them. I've represented it in some of my films and I'm going to try and do more, such as *The Life of Juanita Castro*, the point of which is, it depends on how you want to look at it. Money doesn't worry me, either, though I sometimes wonder where is it? Somebody's got it all! I won't let my films be shown for free. I'm working principally with Ronald Tavel, a playwright, who's written about ten movies for me; he writes the script and I sort of give him an idea of what I want and now he's doing the films as off-Broadway plays.

I don't really feel all these people with me every day at the Factory are just hanging around me, I'm more hanging around *them*. (Oh, those are great pants, where did you get them? Oh, I think they're so great.) I haven't built up a defense against questions that try to go below the surface, I don't feel I'm bothered that much by people. I feel I'm very much a part of my times, of my culture, as much a part of it as rockets and television. I like American films best, I think they're so great, they're so clear, they're so true, their surfaces are great. I like what they have to say: they really don't have much to say, so that's why they're so good. I feel the less something has to say the more perfect it is. There's more to think about in European films.

I think we're a vacuum here at the Factory: it's great. I like being a vacuum; it leaves me alone to work. We are bothered, though, we have cops coming up here all the time, they think we're doing awful things and we aren't. People try to trap us sometimes: a girl called up here and offered me a film script called *Up Your Ass* and I thought the title was so wonderful and I'm so friendly that I invited her to come up with it, but it was so dirty that I think she must have been a lady cop. I don't know if she was genuine or not but we haven't seen her since and I'm not surprised. I guess she thought that was the perfect thing for Andy Warhol. I don't resent situations like that but I'm not interested in subjects like that, that's not what I'm pushing, here in

America. I'm just doing work. Doing things. Keeping busy. I think that's the best thing in life: keeping busy.

My first films using the stationary objects were also made to help the audiences get more acquainted with themselves. Usually, when you go to the movies, you sit in a fantasy world, but when you see something that disturbs you, you get more involved with the people next to you. Movies are doing a little more than you can do with plays and concerts where you just have to sit there and I think television will do more than the movies. You could do more things watching my movies than with other kinds of movies: you could eat and drink and smoke and cough and look away and then look back and they'd still be there. It's not the ideal movie, it's just my kind of movie. My films are complete in themselves, all 16mm, black and white, me doing my own photography, and the 70 minute ones have optical sound which is rather bad which we will change when we get a regular sound tape-recorder. I find editing too tiring myself. Lab facilities are much too tacky and uncertain, the way they are now. They're experimental films; I call them that because I don't know what I'm doing. I'm interested in audience reaction to my films: my films now will be experiments, in a certain way, on testing their reactions. I like the film-makers of the New American Underground Cinema, I think they're terrific. An Underground Movie is a movie you make and show underground, like at the Film-Makers' Cinematheque on 41st St. I like all kinds of films except animated films, I don't know why, except cartoons. Art and film have nothing to do with each other: film is just something you photograph, not to show painting on. I just don't like it but that doesn't mean it's wrong. Kenneth Anger's *Scorpio Rising* interested me, it's a strange film ... it could have been better with a regular sound track, such as my *Vinyl*, which dealt with somewhat the same subject but was a sadism-masochism film. *Scorpio* was real but *Vinyl* was real, and not real, it was just a mood.

Jane Forth and Joe Dallesandro in Flesh, *1968*

I don't have strong feelings about sadism and masochism, I don't have strong feelings on anything. I just use whatever happens around me for my material. I don't collect photographs or articles for reference material, I don't believe in it. I used to collect magazine photographs for my paintings, though.

The world fascinates me. It's so nice, whatever it is. I approve of what everybody does: it must be right because somebody said it was right. I wouldn't judge anybody. I thought Kennedy was great but I wasn't shocked at his death: it was just something that happened. (Why do you look like a cowboy today, with that neckerchief?) It isn't for me to judge it. I was going to make a film on the assassination but I never did. I'm very passive. I accept things. I'm just watching, observing the world. Slavko Vorkapich was just telling you how to make movies his way, that's why I sold my ticket after going to the Museum of Modern Art to his first lecture.

I plan to do some more films soon, in 35mm: perhaps an autobiography of myself. My newest film is *The Bed*, from a play by Bob Heide that played at the Caffé Cino, in which we'll use a split screen, one side static of two people in bed and the other, moving, of the lives of these two for two years. All my films are artificial but then everything is sort of artificial, I don't know where the artificial stops and the real starts. The artificial fascinates me, the bright and shiny.

I don't know what will happen to me in ten years . . . the only goal I have is to have a swimming pool in Hollywood. I think it's great, I like its artificial quality. New York is like Paris and Los Angeles is so American, so new and different and everything is bigger and prettier and simpler and flat. That's the way I like to see the world. (Gerard, you should get a haircut, that style doesn't suit you at all). It's not that I've always been looking for a kind of Los Angeles paradise; I wouldn't be taken over by Hollywood, I'd just do what I always like to do. Or something. (Oh, hi, David.)

My Hustler was shot by me, and Charles Wein directed the actors while we were shooting. It's about an aging queen trying to hold on to a young hustler and his two rivals, another hustler and a girl; the actors were all doing what they did in real life, they followed their own professions on the screen. (Hello, Barbara.) I've been called: 'Complex, naive, subtle and sophisticated –' all in one article! They were just being mean. Those are contradictory statements but I'm not full of contradictions. I just don't have any strong opinions on anything. (Hi, Randy.) It's true that I don't have anything to say and that I'm not smart enough to reconstruct the same things every day, so I just don't say anything. I don't think it matters how I'm appreciated, on many levels or on just one. The death series I did was divided into two parts: the first on famous deaths and the second on people nobody ever heard of and I thought that people should think about them sometime: the girl who jumped off the Empire State Building or the ladies who ate the poisoned tuna fish and people getting killed in car crashes. It's not that I feel sorry for them, it's just that people go by and it doesn't really matter to them that someone unknown was killed so I thought it would be nice for these unknown people to be remembered by those who, ordinarily, wouldn't think of them. (Oh, hi, Paul.) I wouldn't have stopped Monroe from killing herself, for instance: I think everyone should do whatever they want to do and if that made her happier, then that's what she should have done. (There's something burning here, I think. Don't you smell something?) In the Flint heads I did of Jacqueline Kennedy in the death series, it was just to show her face and the passage of time from the time the bullet struck John Kennedy to the time she buried him. Or Something. The United States has a habit of making heroes out of anything and anybody, which is so great. You could do anything here. Or do nothing. But I always think you should do something. Fight for it, fight, fight. (There *is* something burning here! Danny, will you please get up? You're on fire! Really, Danny, we're not kidding now. *Now* will you get up? I mean, really, Danny, it's not funny. It's not even necessary. I *knew* I smelt something burning!) That was one of my assistants; they're not all painters, they do everything: Danny Williams used to work as a sound man for the film-making team of Robert Drew and Don Alan Pennebaker, Paul Morrissey is a film-maker and Gerard Malanga, a poet. We're going into show business now, we have a rock and roll group called The Velvet Underground, they practice at the Factory. I'm in their act, I just walk on in one scene. But anybody who comes by here is welcome, it's just that we're *trying* to do some *work* here . . .!

I think the youth of today are terrific; they're much older and they know more about things than they used to. When teen-agers are accused of doing wrong things, most of the time, they're not even doing wrong things, it was just other people who thought they were bad. The movies I'll be doing will be for younger people; I'd like to portray them in my films, too. I just tore out an article about the funeral of one of the motorcycle gang leaders where they all turned up on their motorcycles and I thought it was so great that I'm going to make a film of it one day. It was fantastic . . . they're the modern outlaws . . . I don't even know what they do . . . what *do* they do?

I think American women are all so beautiful, I like the way they look, they're terrific. The California Look is great but when you get back to New York you're so glad to be back because they're stranger looking here but they're more beautiful even, the New York Look. I read an article on me once that described my machine-method of silk-screen copying and painting: 'What a bold and audacious solution, what depths of the man are revealed in this solution!' What does *that* mean? My paintings never turn out the way I expect them to but I'm never surprised. I think America is terrific but I could work anywhere – anywhere I could afford to live. When I read magazines I just look at the pictures and the words, I don't usually read it. There's no meaning to

the words, I just feel the shapes with my eye and if you look at something long enough, I've discovered, the meaning goes away . . . The film I'm working on now is a 70-minute aria with the Puerto Rican female impersonator, Mario Montez, called *Mr. Stompanato*. I think the questions usually asked me in interviews should be more clever and brighter, they should try to find out more about me. But I think newspaper reporting is the only way to write because it tells what's happening and doesn't give anyone's opinion. I always like to know 'what's happening.'

There's nothing really to understand in my work. I make experimental films and everyone thinks those are the kind where you see how much dirt you can get on the film, or when you zoom forward, the camera keeps getting the wrong face or it jiggles all the time: but it's so easy to make movies, you can just shoot and every picture really comes out right. I didn't want to paint anymore so I thought that the way to finish off painting for me would be to have a painting that floats, so I invented the floating silver rectangles that you fill up with helium and let out of your window . . . I like silver . . . and now we have a band, the Velvet Underground, who will belong to the biggest discotheque in the world, where painting and music and sculpture can be combined and that's what I'm doing now.

Interviews are like sitting in those Ford machines at the World's Fair that toured you around while someone spoke a commentary; I always feel that my words are coming from behind me, not from me. The interviewer should just tell me the words he wants me to say and I'll repeat them after him. I think that would be so great because I'm so empty I just can't think of anything to say.

I still care about people but it would be so much easier not to care . . . it's too hard to care . . . I don't want to get too involved in other people's lives . . . I don't want to get too close . . . I don't like to touch things . . . that's why my work is so distant from myself . . . ∎

BLUE VALENTINE
KATHY ACKER

Kiss, *1963*

Until I started writing this, I had never realised how much Andy Warhol's work and ethos shaped my own writing and life.

In the last half of the 60s, I was living in San Diego, California: I was at undergraduate, then at graduate school at UCSD (University of California at San Diego). I hated it. My life. The hippy years had begun when I had still been at Brandeis University near Boston and they were now into full swing. People around me believed that they and hopefully all other people could and would only feel peace and love. Women wore granny dresses, became pregnant, and cooked healthy food. I felt isolated in this world, as if I was pitch black and everyone else, pastel.

I had one close friend, Melvyn Frielicher, still one of my dearest friends, who was also a literature graduate student and gay. I mention that he was gay because, at that time, just to become divorced was tantamount to expulsion from graduate school. For one had to be or become a fine moral product in order to teach Ford and Melville. And as for 'gay' . . . one didn't mention such things. (Gay men, at best, were supposed to hide their love in the bathrooms.) For hours Melvyn and I would listen to Warhol's production of The Velvet Underground and fantasize about living in a society such as that of Warhol and his friends, a society in which the two of us weren't outcasts.

In those times art, for me, the highest of all possible existences, wasn't so much what one did but how one chose to live. A moral even a religious commitment. I dreamed about New York City because New York City was Andy Warhol was that responsibility named freedom.

Two years later I was living in New York City and working in a sex show for financial reasons. I was now living two lives or in two societies: a society of sex shows and forty-second street and one of poets. The poets who were my age were hippies: they all slept together but, of course, had nothing to do with and despised the riffraff – whores, pimps, working girls of all sorts, drug-dealers, transsexuals and transvestites – the general population of forty-second street. Hippies were cultured.

*Viva and Louis Waldron
in* Blue Movie, *1968*

Francis Francine in
Lonesome Cowboys,
1967

In the forty-second street world, but not in the poetry world, I ran into the Andy Warhol crew. I was working at FUN CITY, a combination magazine and peep-show emporium and a (fake) sex-show theatre. My boss' nephew, who worked in this family concern as the video booth cleaner, was friends with Joe Dallesandro. He told me that he and Joe used to heist cars over the New Jersey state line until Joe had cleaned up his act and started to work for Andy. In fact, one of the lines in our sex-shows was that we were waiting to be discovered by Andy Warhol. We weren't entirely joking, but we were hoping.

Around the corner from where I worked, the woman who would become Lou Reed's wife was dancing at the *Metropole*. And so forth. For Warhol, in his early films, in the beginning days of The Factory, had united two distinct groups and classes: the uptown fashion and society world and the very gay riffraff of forty-second street, that group who at that time no decent person, even a hippy, would recognise as being human.

Warhol's early art, first of all for me, was revolutionary. Every revolution is political. He made the art world, then the United States generally, accept, even admire those whom they had formerly condemned: drag queens, strippers, young homeless kids, not hippy pot smokers but actual heroin addicts and welfare victims.

Warhol's art for me was proof that that art in which there is no distinction between politics and radical form, that art in which these two unite, is what is 'high art'.

In the 60s and early 70s, the Fluxus or 'Happening' artists announced 'Art is life'. George Maciunas, the self-appointed head of Fluxus, didn't have to make art to be an artist, according to him, he just had to live in a certain way.

But Warhol made art, lots of it, and helped other people to do the same. I remember when I first walked into the Whitney to see his cow wallpaper. Before entering the museum I had thought,

conceptually, O.K. it's interesting to challenge the 'idea' of art and the critics by showing wallpaper, endlessly and cheaply reproducible, as high and expensive art. What I didn't expect was the visual impact. What seemed to be a wall reaching up into a ceiling-less heaven, totally covered by unbelievably almost unseeably coloured neon purple and yellow cows plus background, hallucinated before or in my eyes. Here was artistic form in explosion.

Warhol's use of artistic form and genre to make a political statement and reality, his refusal in either

his form or content to distinguish between élite and scum, between high and low, in any way, his radical refusal to pay any attention to the notions of fine art taught by the academy, his amazing clarity and courage, and his overt proud homosexuality, his peculiar ability to listen to other people, to learn to watch – all these positions, for every artistic position is also a moral and political one, deeply influenced both me and my work. And I wasn't the only one. His later work . . . but everything and everyone, consciousness, changes ■

Alan Midgette and Viva in Nude Restaurant, 1967

THE BANANA DIARY

THE STORY OF ANDY WARHOL'S 'HARLOT'

RONALD TAVEL

**From *Film Culture*,
no. 40, Spring 1966**

Stars are always late. But, of course, O Lord, what a moment when they begin to shine! The shooting of *Harlot* was called for 3 o'clock, Sunday afternoon, 13 December 1965. Director Andy Warhol, all the actors and speakers, technicians, and the press were on hand on time. The star, Mario Montez, was telephoned at 3:30. Still in bed.

Sometime after 5:00, he emerged breathless through the studio elevator, make-up kit and costume luggage in hand, bleary-eyed, unshaven. The photographers converged. 'No pictures, no pictures!' he cries, 'until I have my make-up on!' 'Please, Mario, just one shot as you are now.' But he is adamant.

Mario retires behind screens (actually into the famous studio toilet, setting of the film *Clockwork*) to begin the long process of transformation. Photographers poke around the barriers, peek into the open door of the dressing room (the toilet has no light bulb and its door must be left ajar to permit the metamorphosis).

'Please, Mario, one shot now – you're half-way there.' 'No pictures now, no pictures!' The other *Harlot* participants wander restlessly in the silver-foil studio on East 47th St.

'Where's my razor? Where's my shaving cream?' 'One shot with your 5 o'clock shadow.' 'No, no, sorry. Wait till I get my wig on.'

The Wig looks like an ill-skinned white cat, the gown of yellow chiffon goes on over the square, strong shoulders of the lithely dark Puerto Rican. Pink make-up lightens his face.

An hour later, Mario is still struggling with his girdle straps and stockings. 'I think the strap-thing is on lop-sided, it's coming down the middle instead of on my thigh. Could you help me?'

I pull and tug and push up, Mario pulls down; we fall several times. I clamp onto the shapely thigh and stretch the double nylons as high as they will reach. Something embarrassing about my face in those thighs. A photographer giggles gleefully behind us: he shot his load.

'Oh!' sighs Mario, the perspiration streaming down his forehead, 'it's a drag to get in drag!'

Jean Harlow is a transvestite, as are Mae West and Marilyn Monroe, in the sense that their feminineness is so exaggerated that it becomes a commentary on womanhood rather than the real thing or representation of realness.

For this reason, the role of Harlow is taken by a man and the man-queen-star is comfortably reclined against a lesbian lover. The two 'ladies' have male counterparts positioned above them behind the couch. Harlow has a Mafia-type for partner, the lesbian a less formal, darkly handsome overseer as mysteriously motionless as herself. A large shampooed white cat is held in the lap of the lesbian's black evening dress. It will be the center of all idea.

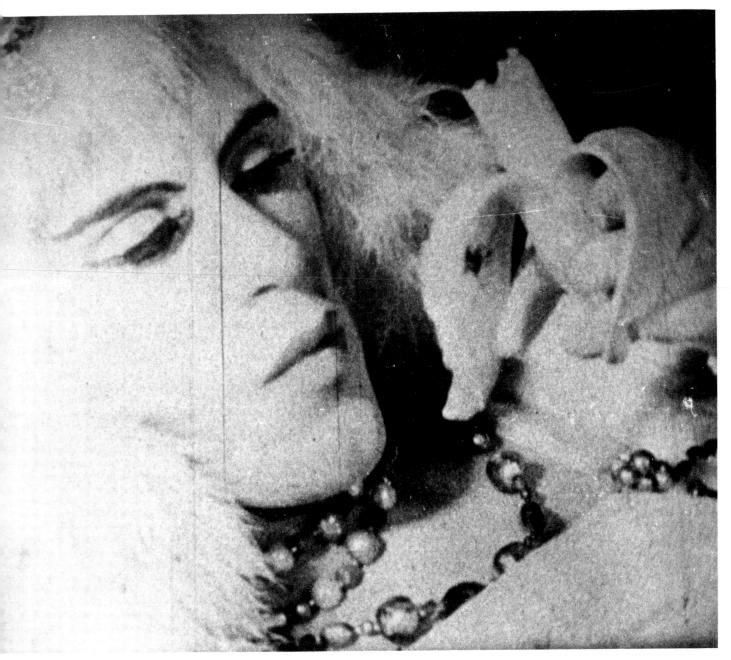

Mario Montez in Mario
Banana, *1964*

Harlow is the center of all movement, that is, after dutifully posing for the tableau vivant which opens the film. The initial visual impression is not so much a breathing tableau, however, as it is one of those stilted family photos circa fin de siècle. Except, what a family!

After the audience has had sufficient time for its ideas to come full circle back to where they originated, Harlow begins the epic adventure of her banana feast. The banquet will evolve into a near-orgy of banana consumption, but that will be virtually all there is to the action. The banana is tirelessly phallic in the fingers and the mouth of Harlow, finally along her legs, between her thighs, in her behind. They emerge from her cheap beaded purse, are fed to her by the Mafia lover, emanate from under the seat of the lesbian. Harlow takes the lesbian for granted, as part of the furniture, a permanent fixture. She acknowledges her existence only once, teases her briefly with a half-eaten banana. Midway in the film, Harlow takes the Italian into perspective. She flirts shamelessly with him, fingering her ungloved biceps, but not as if he were a particular, a personality; she substantiates in her seduction his face-value. At length, she stirs clumsily from her recumbency to kiss him. The kiss is awkward, loveless, perfunctory, trance-perfunctory. A hundred meanings depart in every direction from out of its meaninglessness. And Harlow returns to the satisfactions of her bananas.

The Mafia-type is stirred by her neglect. He engages in a game of cigarettes. How puny this phallus appears at first, how ethereal its smoke blown over the bananas. He looks for greater response from the motionless male at his side; the latter allows the unlit cigarettes to be forced sidewise between his lips, but lets them drop almost immediately. Our attention comes to home in this expressionless figure. He slowly wets his lips with the small tip of his tongue. Who is he? The lover of the well-dressed gangster? The lover of the mesmerized lesbian? At any rate, he emerges as the most sensual and seductive of the parlored foursome.

The conservatively gowned lesbian is so silent and wooden, she appears to be sleeping with her eyes open. She is forced into action by an unpredictable event: the cigarette smoke irritates the cat and suddenly, it struggles to escape. Without breaking her stare at us, the lesbian roughly grabs the cat at its nape, plants it squarely back in her lap; the cat capitulates. It nuzzles against Harlow's white wig, its skinned sister. The cat and the wig patiently compete for the star-billing.

Some love is lost between the lesbian and her gentleman admirer during an exchange of liquid dousings during the last moments of the film.

There is a gradual acceleration of event during the 70 minutes of footage, but few ideas or notions are allowed to generate without coming full circle back to their still immanence.

The Sound
'*The track sounds like 3 people talking on 42nd Street.*' Jack Smith

Director Andy Warhol approached me and asked, 'Would you prefer to be behind a screen where you don't see the filming, or would you want to watch the actors while you're talking?'

'It's immaterial to me,' I said, 'ask Harry what he wants to do.'

Harry was positive: 'Oh, no, we have to see what's going on.'

I agreed; ¼ bottle of scotch makes me agreeable; Harry was sober. Except for a beer with a scotch top. 'Alcohol makes me sleepy,' he asserted.

Harry and I are a gruesome twosome: I was not advised in advance he had chosen a third partner for crime: Billy Linich. I never saw Billy before in my life: indeed I had spoken to Harry Fainlight only 2 or 3 times previous to our assemblage.

While Mario dressed, Harry and I sat around

'feeling each other out' as Gerard thought. It was less that than coming to an uneasy truce. I discussed Sitwell's death; he had not heard, regretted my not having saved that surprise for the recording. Her death does come up on the track, but as a result of Harry's foreknowledge, it runs into a rhetoric of recently transitioned prominents.

About all we concluded previous to the actual take, all we planned, was that I should inaugurate the track with a story, preferably the 'marriage' story, Harry suggested. He seems to alter his opinion of the story's worth, however, as soon as it gets underway, interrupts it, and the result here is that it is continuously reintroduced, forming a sort of running theme ending with the grass widower narrator's actual search for a new wife. Alcohol may take the credit for that.

While the camera was being positioned and tested, we studied what positions would advantage the mike. There are two couches in the studio and low as the unstarred one is, it proved too high to pick up our voices. We placed the mike on a wooden carton, cushioned it against tilt, and tested 1, 2, 3, 4, can you hear me? 'Not well enough,' the sound technician decided. We would have to arrange the couch's cushions on the floor around the mike. Harry concluded that I should sit in the center, opposite the mike's mouth, with himself to my left and Billy to the right. This seating arrangement proved crucial. We tested again and the sound technician seemed satisfied.

In the meantime, the ingenious positioning of the set had been worked out. It is difficult to tell how long Warhol thought about the arrangement, or when or where. Did it occur to him when it occurred that the letters of his name are the same as Harlow's? Had it that kind of astronomy? Or was it decided in the ten minutes it took to adjust the sound?

We readied ourselves. Harry tensed, I had another scotch, Billy worked on a record catalogue. He was choosing a record collection for a friend of his. He continued to do so throughout the entire filming.

About the time when evening is securely settled, the shooting began. Swan Lake, a local favorite, pours dramatically onto the track, the tableau breathes, the pompous and preposterous are sublimely, idiotically at truce, Swan Lake trails off, and the speaking begins. Also the war of the speakers:

As soon as the tale of the star's marriage gets underway, Harry regrets it, interjects a series of associative puns and syllabic extensions in an effort to save it or redirect it; and Billy shoots down, wittily cutting into and often off whatever thread of thought is struggling to lengthen.

Billy knows the exact pitch at which to throw his voice, leans exactly toward the mike, pencil in writing hand, whenever he speaks. Harry is sometimes too far from the centre to be heard distinctly. And I had a tendency to purr too often, unaware it would cost the blurring of many an important line.

Incomprehension of my dramatics and a growing frustration over the failure of our teamwork, Billy's delight in testicle-slicing and a malice inherent in the punning leads to a near breakdown of concerted effort somewhere towards the ¾ mark on the first reel. Considerable argument is whispered between us under the pickup, furious sign language, and a good deal of instruction to each other delivered in the guise of dialogue. Harry's good temper flags, he pulls back and announces he's going to piss – the pullback obscures the line and a recondite remark follows: 'Where are you going? The toilet is right here.'

Actually, Harry was using a displaced toilet as his backrest.

It is at that point that the unique in sound tracks occurs. Inspired by a near empty scotch bottle and self-pity for his loneliness, the grass widower finds Billy 'appealing' (Mario has been lecherously peeling bananas) and puts the make on him. The line, 'I find even the hair around your nipples appealing' is not imaginative. Ill-advised fingers had just made that discovery. The press suddenly finds the speakers more photogenic than the actors and a rush across the studio endeavours to record the incident. Billy is taken completely by surprise and his response does not make the extracurricular activity clear on the track. Indeed, he puts forth unbecoming innocence, the I-don't-know-what-you're-up-to bit and whatever-it-is-you're-making-a-mistake. The widower was indeed 'making a mistake.'

A quarrel ensues, an anger over predilections, and Billy is confronted with the specific, 'Well, just what kind of trade do you cater to?'

He defends himself as being strictly an amateur. And this feeds the last clear pronouncement of reel 1, fortunately caught just before the footage ends:

'Well, I think they should get the amateurs off 42nd Street!'

The shooting of the second reel began about 8:15. The press was gone, the studio quieter. Harry decided the 'prima donna' seat would be occupied by himself for the last half and that I should take the toilet position. He asked that I let him lead at all times from then on, and that Billy no longer shoot down. The second reel belongs to Harry, is decidedly more literary, if not dramatic.

Here, we three turned our attention more directly to the actors. There is a detailed examination of Harlow, the way she looks, what she is doing. This leads to a concern with bananas that will rarely flag. As the actors become more and more suggestive in their activity, the speakers warm up to a verbal libidinousness bordering on the vulgar; only the genuineness of their avidity converts the prurient to the delicious. And Harry at least achieves the transport he has awaited, inaugurates a banana peon that will carry the track to a feverish climax; the ending of Swan Lake whelms out of nowhere, Harlow achieves her most sensual-sensitive movement yet, the speakers cry against the dying of

the track. Then – marvelously – the music breaks, there is a calm center, and everyone is caught with his pants down, the flashlights on his ruddy rear. Bewildered, thoughts go round in circles, intermittent grabs at straw. . . .

It is this break that makes the ending so powerful, so aesthetically satisfying, so in keeping with an underground and out of keeping with Hollywood.

Then the storm of music resumes, the actors and speakers, having been thoroughly mortified, resume courageously, ridiculously after the fact, the banana peon returns as if nothing had cut it, and everything o everything has cut it, and with the cries of 'bad banana, bad banana, bad banana,' being answered by the hysterical plea: 'Eat me! Eat me! Eat me!' the reel circle-punches white and ends.

No one knows that poor Billy answered the 'Eat me,' except of course, the 3. He said, in perfect down-rhythm, 'Rotten! rotten! rotten!' but the footage cast the die against his accurate sliding pond and nothing records that 'happy ending' except this page.

A good deal of love was lost among the oralists. Harry would feel on the hook for days, Billy retire to his unconcerns (to his disc catalogue), and I announce nothing immediately per usual personality. The camera had tilted during the break between reels and the lights were never focused identically for the second half. We wondered what the results would be, how divergent the last 35 minutes. Our fate was in the hands of the gods, is, in a film whose technique is never to edit.

Carol threw on her coat and split the second the camera stopped. Philip came out of the actor role into all the business of winding and rewinding lights out real toilet scene. Mario hastened to disdrag and return to a wilder fantasy world, to return to a fantasy world. And Andy moved calmly about, occupied, processing, fingers crossed. By 10:00 the studio and set were settled down to celluloid and waiting for Monday.

Monday was losing no time. The footage was

converted to a reversible and ready by Midnight. Gerard, Philip, Harry, Andy and I made for the studio at 2:00 after the New Yorker cleared out; Andy nervous, Harry a wreck, Gerard confident, Philip and I curious.

We decided to screen the second reel, since the hour was late; but ended by needing to view the whole. Harry relaxed, felt off the hook re his participation, everyone was impressed by the visual accomplishment. Andy thought perhaps too much went on; there was a jerkiness in part: true, but it would iron in, is that ingredient of awkwardness, the child-did-it-in-his-trouserness that is the hallmark of a new cinema, a greater pain.

A sneak preview the following Tuesday morning at the New Yorker proved the miracle: not a boring moment! The point was well taken, you could watch forever. Why? I do not know exactly, except that a Warhol film is the world itself which we have and must watch; he proves we can watch and let the idea of the 'destructiveness' of Warhol's art play around with that for a while. If his movies seem to scream their attack on the nature of the cinematic art, seem to have no purpose other than to undermine it, bring it to the blank walls; then their creation lies in a totally disarming area nearer afield: the plastic of our earth itself. His films accept it. The cinema shall rebuild closer to its material after this director has stampt it.

The Actors

1 Gerard Malanga was introduced to Andy Warhol the first week in June, 1963 at a party given by Willard Maas and Marie Menken. He recalls the artist's silver hair, white skin, dark shades, and outright nervousness. Gerard had just curtailed his formal education at Wagner College and was 'desperately in need of a job'. Andy was in need of an assistant to help with the production of his silk-screen paintings.

Gerard began working for Andy at what was then his studio, a condemned hook & ladder company located on 87th Street, between Lexington and Third Avenues. The city had sold the building to a real estate agent at an auction, and Andy was renting the entire building for $150.00 a month, until such time as he would be asked to vacate the premises.

Andy and his new assistant began working almost immediately on the silk-screening of a portrait of Elizabeth Taylor on a canvas prior prepared with a background of silver spray paint. Gerard says the messy part of the job came later with the varolene cleaning of the screen.

The two printed four or five 40″ × 40″ canvases, after which they repaired to Andy's home and Gerard scrutinized his employer's photograph collection, while 'Sally Goes Round the Roses' spun. The photos were an odd assortment of car and nature lovers. Gerard realized that the photos were the actual subject matter reproduced into silk-screens.

Gerard Malanga was born in New York on 20 March 1943. His lineage is Neapolitan. When a teenager, he was a 'regular' on the Alan Freed Big Beat TV Show until the payola scandal shut up its viewings in November of 1960. Along with Baby Jane Holzer, he introduced the 'Gobble' for Ed Sanders' Fugs. He is Sanders' 'Playboy of the Month'. He has appeared in almost two dozen underground films.

Gerard is said to be the most widely published young poet in America. His calmly worded and rhythmed poems with their unabashed indecipherability, their frank echoes of all the verse of this decade, his fashion exercises and his ready-mades are extremely important comments on the poetical tone of our most recent times. The significance of his contribution lies in its reverberations rather than in the print, somewhat like the unacknowledged significance of Marilyn Monroe's singing, and not altogether unlike the statement of Warhol. He is archly contemporary, and so inextricably and innocently so, that his achievement is as yet recognized by very few.

His poems, interviews, articles, and book reviews appear in virtually every important magazine, including the *New Yorker*, *Kulchur*, *Partisan Review*, *Film Culture*, *Fuck You: A Magazine of the Arts*, *Filmwise*, *Silo* (Bennington College), *'C' Magazine*, *Lines*, *The Minnesota Review*, *Poetry Chicago*, *The Sunday Herald Tribune Magazine*, *Wild Dog*, *Nomad*, *Elephant*, *Graffiti*, *The Sinking Bear*, *Art & Literature*, *Locus Solus*, *The Lugano Review* (of Switzerland), *Ex* (Rome-Milan), etc. etc.

From 1962 to 1965, he edited the *Wagner Literary Magazine* and in 1964, he was an editorial associate of *Nadada*. He is currently an official staff interviewer for *Kulchur*.

2 Philip Norman Fagan is as illusive in actuality as his role in *Harlot*. The darkly handsome, Mexican-looking adventurer is actually of Yankee and Irish stock. A seaman by profession, he was born and raised in Fort Worth, Texas. He is an accomplished motorcyclist (who has competed in important races) and a deep-sea diver. His single recall of fear was the claustrophobic sensation produced by diving helmets. He explains that they are too roomy to feel like clothes, roomy enough to give the impression of tiny, trap-like chambers.

While in the Navy, he put time in in Japan. He loves Orientals, considers his Asiatic experiences to be 'innocent'. The Orient still makes strong claims on his imagination; his eyes turn this time toward Hong Kong. The legendary heat of Hong Kong invites him as much as its exotica. 'The hottest day last summer was my most comfortable in New York.' No, Texans are not amused by the cold.

In the past few years, he traveled extensively in Central America and Mexico, mostly hitch-hiking. While in Mexico, he studied under El Hundaro (the Alan Kaprow of Latin America), helping him with the execution of Happenings, and learning mime at the same time. He claims mime has to do with body expression rather than facial; and that therefore, his miming in his close-up performance in

Screen Test I was out of place.

He adheres to the Panic-Philosophy, as exemplified by Little Richard, but offers few elucidations on the subject.

His favorite color is black, an immediate complement to his cynosuric skull-on-wings tatoo as well as his raven hair. And the tatoo is equidistant between the claims of marine and Pop Art.

He plays Cupid in Gregory Markopoulos' *Illiac Passion*. He is the prototype of Markopoulos stars. His longest film is *Six Months*, literally a study of Philip aging over a six months' period.

Philip's performance in *Harlot* is very much the person he is. He stares at us (by several inches the image farthest from the camera) with the direct simplicity and intangibility that seems to be his composition. Possessed of an intuitive intelligence, its quality is agonizing to the analytical mind. He looks out at us from the screen with as much curiosity as we return to him. His delightful business with the cigarette-exchange, its unnerving ambiguity, is delicious torture. The care with which he waters down the female he oversees has the ironic, cynical effect of a balm passing over our agitated ganglia.

Standing to his pale-face, black height, he seems destined to star in Cowboy-Art films: an inevitable, on-the-horizon expression of the New American Cinema. In the final, psychologically maneuvred minutes of *Screen Test*, he suddenly conjures the almost anima of an Aztec sacrifice. We are quickened by the prospect, by the remembrance, of the offering of his heart to the Pagan Sun. And he? while he? turns his liquid eyes toward a bombast of brine, toward Hong Kong, Asia, or the Orient of the Sea, where, if he is not before some grinding celluloid or screen of our thoughts, he is now.

3 Cathay-born, convent-bred Carol Koshinskie, for contrast and cleavage, appears in *Harlot*. She fancies The Beatles, The Rolling Stones, and The

Pretty Things. She admires Fred Astaire flicks, the New Yorker Theatre, Dietrich flicks, Horror flicks, Deanna Durbin flicks, and Truffaut, esp. *Jules and Jim* and *Shoot the Piano Player*. She loves Jennifer Jones, Joseph Cotton, Hedy LaMarr, The Marx Bros., Charles Aznavour, James Mason, Phyllis Calvert, Joan Crawford, Bette Davis, Geo. Brent, Joan Fontaine, Torin Thatcher, Cameron Mitchell, and Freddie Bartholomew.

Carol owns an alleycat named Pussy Galore. 'White Pussy' is therefore a step up for her in the world.

Carol also owns forty-five pairs of patterned stockings.

She draws caricatures.

She is the Margaret Dumont of the Pop Cinema. She wants to be a star of New York, New York.

She continues the tradition of DeHavilland Montez, and other of the more sensitive movie ladies by writing verses. A sample:

Rats have pretty faces:
    All they need are Braces,
On their protruding fangs,
    Their lack of beauty hangs.

They're wistful fangèd cuties.
    If bathed, they would be beauties.
Do you think you'd be a flower,
    If you could never shower?

Carol describes herself as feeling as if she were on the crest of a wave. She loathes nature; the great outdoors overwhelms her. She is a child of the city and likes her nature tamed: Prospect Park, trees rooted in cement, incarcerated house plants, weeds in a vase, dried flowers as bookmarks. But the 'country' is 'too much'. She finds woods and undergrowth, the green and brown and gold scary. The fresh air makes her dizzy. I.e., she is psychologically well suited for a Warhol flick.

She would love to be Marlene Dietrich, so she could drape herself in feathers and spangles and sorrow two inches thick. She dreams of that buttery spotlight on Dietrich's upper lip.

Carol tolerates a description of herself as an unambitious female. She takes life as it comes. She lives a very day-to-day existence, but takes exception to persons who survive on an hour-to-hour basis. She is black and white in her attitudes: she loves or hates, is never in-between. She blames this on the Zodiac: she's Leo.

She claims she wasn't born in Cathay – or in Mongolia or Istanbul. (Press releases are negative truths.)

Carol wishes she weren't born in these times (perfect movie psychology). She is uncontemporary – prefers a birth-date circa fin de siècle, or Edwardian – or 1930s (perfect Harlow psychology).

When considering her own writing, she thinks of Tom Wolfe, her favorite scribbler. She loves him because he is so awful and inaccurate and because he tries so hard and works so hard and writes and writes. When he's finally good, she says, He Is Great!

She claims she is the only person in New York who doesn't even KNOW Baby Jane Holzer.

When Andy Warhol approached her for *Harlot*, Carol exclaimed, 'Great, I'd make a wonderful Jean Harlow.' Then he informed her that she'd play Harlow's girlfriend: she envisioned herself sharing a Coca Cola with Harlow at the neighborhood sweet shoppe. She comments: 'It didn't turn out that way. Boy, was I naive.'

Carol had mixed emotions after viewing the completed film. She thinks she watched it too objectively, but states that she had to or would have become hysterical. She feels that she looked best during the first reel, although she was quite uncomfortable throughout the shooting of that and 'under great physical strain'. She thinks she appears neckless and 45 in the second reel. She believes she adequately contrasted 'all the wild things that were taking place and figures Andy had

her stare into the camera and not move for just that effect'.

She feels White Pussy was great and holds no grudges against its undirectability. She finds Mario a genuine superstar, terrific in this film. She thinks some of his intrinsic sweetness shows through and that he really pulls off a Jean Harlow very well. She says he makes a better Harlow than Carroll Baker: more believable. And prettier.

She found difficulty in explaining to her parents that *Harlot* will not make the Loew's or RKO circuits. She tried to describe the film to them: 'Mario eats five bananas; Philip pours a glass of water over my head.' No good.

Carol Koshinskie's real contribution to *Harlot* is the thousand subtle, all thousand nearly escapable expressions that emanate from her 'still' face. It is altogether possible to view the film by concentrating on her face alone, and to come away thus viewing with most of the flick under one's eye.

Miss Koshinskie still thinks she would make a wonderful Jean Harlow.

If Andy ever does a flick called *Jean Holzer* à la Jean Harlow, she would like to play Baby Jane.

If Andy ever does a flick called *Bette Davis* à la Jean Harlow, she would like to play Baby Jane.
4 White Pussy is a pet, property of Mario Montez. Part Angora, part Alleytom. It was luxuriantly shampooed prior to its performance, walked about the studio in clean discomfort. It is friendly to strangers, is not temperamental. But it objects to company smoking, and offers that by way of excusing itself for the jumpiness that added the inadvertent symbolism to the film.

White pussy is naturally clean and so proved by tongue-bathing itself at various points while the camera ground.

Pussy's politics are right up the center.

Mythology
Hollywood is the mythology that Americans have in common.

Gerard Malanga, Philip Fagan, Mario Montez and Carol Koshinskie in Harlot, 1964

It is not an exaggeration to claim that the historical product of Hollywood functions very much as the Greek myths for old Greece. Hollywood embodies the ambitions and daydreams of the American populace and, more importantly, its peculiar interpretations of the complex cosmos surrounding it. Hollywood is as scientific as the earliest Greek myths, as Mother-Aphrodite, as Earthsoil-Helen, as sunrise-Apollo creating the trees on the horizon, Daphne, and, in its chronology, almost embarrassingly historical. This explains why stars have always been more important than directors – they are our gods and goddesses, our clutter of glorious Apollos and blonde Venuses. Who remembers the creators of the Mediterranean allegories? And meaning by allegory an imposed, often postured, significance printed over a bewildering collection of facts.

Hollywood, then, is the background and material for the *art* of the New American Cinema, much as Greek mythology was the subject matter-at-hand for the art of Homer and Sophocles. *Harlot* is not a travesty on Jean Harlow films; it does not recognize her work as traditional creativity; and it is certainly not concerned with commenting on earlier oeuvres. *Harlot* circles about the *idea* of Jean Harlow, the current, suddenly palpitating cult whose insignia is best sellers, TV interviews that have undusted 30s forget-me-nots for defense and scandal. And *Harlot* handles the freakernalia of Harlow instance with the art of a wicked unmasquerade.

But there is an endless feed-back between Hollywood and America. The hairstyles in a popular costume-drama are thinly veneered coiffures of the moment the flick is shot, yet the period gowns are sure to affect next season's fashions. In the end, it is near impossible to tell apart the language of the average American from the dialogue in the cinema that reflects and directs him.

In the same way, recent scholarship suspects that Homer may have invented almost as much mythology as he employed. That 'poet' may have

been as effective a sectist as Luther or Calvin or Joseph Smith. And the New American Cinema may not elude this news of Homer either. For one thing, it lacks the objective use of myth that the artifice Frenchmen like Cocteau, Anouilh, and Giraudoux manifest – which may be to its compliment. It has a way of holding faith with Hollywood for all its savageness, a manner of burning off the superficial tinsel to touch the incredible essence of that body of belief in order to press it forward, in order to carry in triumph on shoulder-height, in order to insist on its promise and perhaps foster its fulfillment. That the promise is the sham and its product sheer horror seems not to mitigate the naivete of the New American Cinema. It is, yes, 'new', but it is still an 'American' cinema. It is not really thinkable that this artist faction will ever produce a *Marienbad*, *Hiroshima*, or *La Notte*. But something on the order of *Les Enfants du Paradis* may be in the offing.

Cinema has its crucial position in American art because it is so intuitive (were not most film classics created by idiots?), as opposed to, say, epic literature, which requires education. Without education, and I see no education on the foreseeable American horizon, our chances to compete with European novelists and playwrights must remain slim. We shall go on producing stylists of the highest order and critics who wallow in polished prose, but absolute perfection of style is as much the earmark of the second-rate writer as his limited vision. We have managed to cough up (against every effort to destroy him) a single William Burroughs, the exception that proves the rule. But note how in the arts that require no intellectual endeavor after the ultimate sphere of human comprehensibility we stand strong along our competitors, if we do not forthrightly pace smartly ahead: what country, with any honesty, may be said to have made music more cogent than ours in this century? And New York's flowering since the war into the art center of the world is so much to the point that it requires no further comment.

Which, by way of parenthesis, contributes somewhat to explaining the almost pathological concern with lyric poetry in the hitherabouts. And, by way out of parenthesis, a glance at our new poetry brings us back to the cinema. The hysterical insistence on lyric solus is a throwing up arms in the face of any systematic determination, a retreat on the advocacy of its impossibility if not an outright ignorance of its ever-existence; cerebration is about as natal to new America as the Beckett trilogy; and the numerous references to Beckett as the poet of contemporary poets is its condemnable evidence. Yet, if the Chinawall of American artistic Power lobbies down to the last row in its audience, lets William Burroughs sit materially unexplainable-away against it, he is sitting in the last seat of that last row, and it appears a pew because of that.

The New American Cinema held solid ground in its incubating days, the time of its silence. Who has not, at one time or another, groaned for the filmic classics of the pre-*Jazz Singer*? Movies were a marriage of painting and dance. *Potemkin* was felt to be the exemplary comprehension of the film art form. But the sound track was invented, and it is as useless to insist on the singular status of the silent screen as it is to want to give the country back to the Indians. Time, in its semishame guise of Progress, marches apace. Cinema, since *The Jazz Singer*, has participated in the possibility of the farthest reaches of art. That it has sunk, in the states, to the lowest form of stage play is all to our discredit, but not to the discredit of the sound track. Our formatic material seemed beyond the harness of our imaginable ambition. Yet, the attempt is upon us and all about us. *Marienbad* comes first to mind as a major essay at the use, perhaps equality, of sound. It fails rather glaringly; except for odd inspirations, the sound is distracting and oppressive. But there are glaring reasons for this: the arty-farty Frenchy narration as well as the philosophical orientation of the scenario, which is to wallow in The-Without-Meaning. And words,

unfortunately, are meaning. One wanders from illumination in trying to imagine what Resnais was thinking of in this self-defeating project.

But words with their new literary freedom, their just-got Americanness, stand their first chance these days to carriage flicks to the last posthouse, though their patience is near its end. It is to that which is viably unprejudiced in the New American Cinema that they look, and it is for the New American Cinema they intend their rewards, shall they but be given the breath they are so urgently capable of.

The Film-maker

The authenticity of this film-maker, Andy Warhol, is evinced in the unflagging interest of this film. It is himself. It is impossible to imagine anyone else succeeding in a project like this. Witness the un-edited *The Queen of Sheba Meets the Atom Man*: no noted routine of its remarkable players, no pornographic trick in the Lower East Side bag, was overlooked, and yet this effort is tiresome from beginning to end. What then is the secret to the endless absorption of *Harlot*, as well as Warhol's other movies? Simply, that every moment is invested with the actual reality of its creator, the turning of business into art, of publicity into poetry, of mass media into human meaningfulness. He protests, he testifies that his films are boring, that he loves the emptiness of their endless hours, that he has never bothered to sit through most of them. But our attention is riveted to the apparent vacuum, to the inventory of vacuum and such an inventory extends into timelessness. The harlot and her company of the couch pose on forever, just as when we first see them, they seem to have been even so situated since the orientation of their possibilities.

Warhol's art of his inattention to significance carries, just that, the significance itself. He would claim to want, with his special and extreme handling of Pop Art, to lobotomize the public. Yet this operation-theatre he brings us to and in which we at first resentfully feel ourselves to be the patient, suddenly actualizes as the real and traditional theatre: we are audience as always, suddenly alive and watching, horrified after amused, scholarly after ennuied. And alarmed. The 'destructive' artist proves again the prophet and makes of his life a stunning cry, withal keeping his mask-distance of laughter and contempt. He emerges gentle from a warehouse of Brillo boxes, having stated his bleak vision, as social an artist as any 30s fiend could ask for.

Tomorrow finds us thankful to move.

Continually inspecting the act of locomotion.

Warhol says: 'I was in the subway once. Terrible place.'

Speak to him, work with him, have dealing with him: it is all very like the films. Courteous and reserved, he is as adamant a quiet man as ever I hope to meet. Instinctively intelligent, rather than calculatingly so as his public image would have it, his eye seldom errs albeit it can not be applied to every object on the assembly line. He is also in the continuous act of studying, although we catch ourselves in the study of his films before we realize him in the study of the plastic. It is intriguing to eat with him, the only time he isn't working or contracting, and wait in abeyance for his study. I remember netting him only once; something over my head, on the wall in back of me, required his attention:

I turned around and looked up. There was nothing there.

He shall be remembered as long as histories of art are compiled. His position is one of the major statements of our century. He whose art declares there is no art, who turns no-art into a presented art, he who refuses to touch his art, who will have nothing to do with it, who turns his back on it.

There is death in the films, the films are death, the movie *Henry Geldzahler* is the peeling, frightfully stagnant, unflecting mirror of death. Nothing is more upsetting. But art is not art if, like

fate, it does not close one door without opening another. In this destruction is the rejuvenation. For one stares at this spectre until he realizes he has never really looked at a human face before. He has learned every pore in the skin and returns to other movies with a lengthy education applied to a few-second frame of an actor's face, applied to the people opposite him in the train.

A cleansing is the other coin-face of the lobotomy. And from the blank creation, art begins anew. The simplest gestures emerge from the once unmoving figures, the briefest lines from the silent mouths. A half-dozen sound films later and (in *The Life of Juanita Castro*) a complex of absurdity is achieved, an absurd play is wrought, absurdity being the molecular foundation upon which refinements, possible logistics and orders, or greater chaos may emanate.

The Flyer

The flyer for the opening of *Harlot* read as follows:

ANDY WARHOL
presents
MARIO MONTEZ
as
HARLOT
with
★ Gerard Malanga
★ Philip Fagan
★ Carol Koshinskie

introducing
'White Pussy'
sound track by Ronnie
Tavel ★ Harry Fainlight
★ Billy Linich ★
The New American Cinema
World Premiere Monday, Jan. 10th
9:00 & 11:00 pm Cafe au Go Go
152 Bleecker St. Admission $2.00

Drawn up by Gerard Malanga, it is an historic

document. In and of itself, it inaugurates the star system in the New American Cinema.

Previously, in the tradition of all good art movies, the director's name was the pull, the interest. Now there are two attractions. Mailed all across the country, within a week hundreds, and by now thousands, of people wanted to know who Mario Montez is. Suddenly, there was money in his name. Soon, competing studios would vie for his talent. Delicious and nutty, the stairway to stardom reopened in New York. Dozens of starlets besieged the directors, writers, and hangers-on for walk-ons in any flick whatsoever. Several studios toyed with the idea of having the actors fuck their way into the flicks as means of cutting down on the applicants – and as a means of reaching greater heights of reckless humor. Audiences now applaud the stars' first second on the screen, their names on the credits. Stars pull star-bits; they come shrieking off the set refusing to carry on when the shooting disturbs them; they become choosey about scripts; they scour movie rags for mention of their names; they sue publications that use unflattering photos of them. With every passing month, it becomes more and more difficult to take them seriously – and more and more difficult to deny their existences.

And something else is noteworthy concerning the flyer: its inaccuracies. It says Monday, Jan. 10th: that Monday was the 11th. Also, the all-important price: the Go Go charged $2.50 – an unheard of temerity at the time.

These flyer errors are the badge of the New American Cinema: its actors who stare into the camera suddenly as if about to wave to relatives, its blank overexposed footage, its purposeful amateurish put-together, its humanness.

Harlow

The first public reference to *Harlot* appeared in the magazine section of the Sunday Herald Tribune three weeks after the film was made. It said, among other things, that *Harlot* was a travesty on the currently raging Jean Harlow cult. Warhol's movie relates to the actual woman when the spotlight is turned on her in the following ways:

The Blonde Bombshell of Metro-Goldwyn-Mayer is hurtled into our year as the white heroine of a dark age, a Depression beyond innocence, a time we can readily associate with, but one which was merciful enough compared to our present condition, and which can console us with a bit of balmy delusion. The facade of the hard-boiled cookie, the therefore oblivious to the treacherous world, the Sex Goddess Supreme, the therefore orientation at the level of want and desire in a time of chaos and denial, the comedienne of frivolity, the therefore traditional America turning its back on the facts, the slippery sensualist, the therefore literally slipping through and out of the vise of circumstance, Jean Harlow is a ready-made contemporary rallying-point.

A preoccupation with her biography is all to the interest of the New American Cinema as well as the country in general in a time of the relaxing of censorship codes. Her advocation as a foul-tongued tart, a street-stalking werewolf bitch, a Madame de Sade, and an egotistic talentless boudoir Angora athlete, is so much part and parcel of the underground movement as to need no elaboration. And to credit Harlow with having never known the eroticism she aroused in her public, is to give her an indelible brand-mark dearer to our Yankee Doodle Dandyism than to our professional Europeans putters-down.

The lady drank, gambled and dissipated. She painted Mexican border towns red. She was she who is what-else-can-we-do-in-our-predicament? And she was the extreme symbol of White, white from platinum head to silver-coated toenails, white pushed to the point of American Neurotica, to the preposterous and the condemnable.

Jean Harlow was born Harlean Carpentier (Carpentier – Biblical symbol and complex needing no comment). Her parents had prayed for a male-child, had held in readiness the name Harlow, after the maternal grandfather. What a disappointment when the first-born proved a girl! Parents caught on the wrong color of the gambling cloth pressure genetics; and the bewildered offspring often make inroads toward compliance:

Harlean neglected her dolls, she detested frill feminine dresses, she refused to play house, jacks, skipping ropes. She took to lengthy hiking over the Kansas flatlands, she endeared herself to dogs rather than cats, she became an expert horsewoman. (I cannot help recalling the brutal Anglicism, 'The Cuntless Horsewoman'.) At the age of 16, ostensibly to escape the authority of school, she married a 21-year-old alumnus of Lake Forest Academy – her first lesbian act. She would later marry twice and have endless affairs with authority figures: pitiful attempts to resolve the conflict that carried her faster and faster along her sado-masochistic path to death.

Is any devotee of the underground cinema really in need of a *Who's Who* to Hollywood lady-stars who have walked this same sad bisexually chaotic mile?

In the current defense of her reputation, associates unwittingly reveal that she was 'undersexed'. They cannot understand how a girl so extraordinarily endowed could evince so little capacity for its employment. These same associates will go to their graves never understanding if white were really white, black black, why black looks white or what a horsewoman is. Harlow continuously worried about her looks (what actor can afford not to?) – but hers was the preoccupation that is the spokesman of sexual uncertainty, and that rationalizes weight-losing into ceaseless sets of tennis. They cluck cliché-ishly that happiness always eluded her. To be happy, one must have some inkling of what he wants.

She maintained a miniature menagerie (one of the symbols of the cat in *Harlot*) – a trait so common in Queens of the Silver Screen – a trait so common in people who cannot deal with the complexities of human beings.

She frequented art galleries, attempted long conversations involving verse and prose masterpieces, she carted about a satchel of poems to study between takes – she sounds like Marilyn Monroe; she sounds like several dozen other freaks Hollywood so repetitively molded.

Her most retailed scandal, that of Paul Bern, her second husband's suicide, needs no exact decision of facts to make its point. It was murder any way you hold the mirror. Harlow murdering Harlow, Harlow murdering Bern, Bern murdering Harlow, Bern murdering Bern, Harlow murdering Harlow most of all. It seems impossible to believe that either partner was ignorant of his motives or potentials or incapacities. But that is because the two are others for us. Did we share in their nightmare, it is more than likely that even in this enlightened distance, we would be as self-ignorant as they.

And her death. They chatter it resulted from damaged kidneys, which resulted from the masochistic beatings she craved. Does that detail matter either? Death she craved, and death is the screen siren's dealt. Some have managed to swallow it in dosages spooned out to their seventies and eighties; the more dramatically inclined have satiated (I hope) our lustihoods with their youthful Aztecian sacrifices.

What else is of note in Harlow re *Harlot*? She enjoyed a good joke. She told a good joke and listened to a good joke. She laughed frequently and the crowd rode with her. Mario Montez brilliantly projects the siren-comedienne. The hypnotism of the image is in good part due to its continual humor. But the joke was always on Jean Harlow, and her present disinterring proves a good joke never grows stale. And that, too, is the grim discomfort that greeted the first screening of *Harlot*. The New American Cinema has failed to elude the extension of its mythological essence. (Was it doomed to its comment inevitably?) The spokesmen of the movement tell us that they will evade the destruction Hollywood trades in, the use and exploitation of the human element and the rapid using-up of it and casting it aside. Yet, Mario Montez in his tiara of morticians (professional mummies they finally appear, in their stilled slow macabre gestures) is the Movie Queen all over again, is the would-be imitation that wounds us to the quick because nothing has been imitated or genuinely travestied: *Harlot* has succeeded in repeating the madness that is America. Whatever is inadvertent and innocent in Hollywood becomes intentional and artful in the New American Cinema, but it is the same story all over again and we are the same Americans. The nightmare is merely sharper in Mario Montez, and if there is any hope for our expiation, it lies in our being unable to avoid the tragedy of this boy.

Finally, when the excitement of the newness of being open about Harlow's lesbian affairs has passed, they tell us about a certain evening that Jean Harlow spent in a brothel. She requested a meek-mannered man for partner, proceeded to tie him to the bed and pet him in his particulars. Then she divested herself, rolled all over him, and, striking a match, lit the corners of the sheet he lay upon. While the flames rose, she applied all her 'knowledge' of love-making to invest his attention. However long his erection lasted, it wasn't long before his screams for help were heard. The madam came to the rescue and 'quenched the flames'. Harlow stood abashed and whispered: 'Passion failed, the Harlow Passion failed!'

What flames did the madam quench, we wonder? What passion failed? What was Harlow Passion? I suppose it is better to leave the situation in the corniness of its own speaking, rather than to pander for tears here. But, unless the warning that the all-reflecting Screen repeats to us, the Wicked Queens about Snow White, is taken seriously, we shall follow the Wicked Queen to the cliffside as surely as we do the white-hatted cowboy and the villain. If there is no 'knowledge' in our art, may we not, at least, standing apart from our creations, awaken?

Jean Harlow said: 'I believe Hollywood stars owe the fans everything. Yes, even the right to crowd around the entrancces of cafes and theatres with autograph books, and to have the letters they are kind enough to write answered, and to ask us to pose for their own cameras. I don't know how others feel about it, but I love their attention, and I'll never get over the thrill and flattery of knowing they like me well enough to do all these things.'

Mario Montez loves you, too.

Harlot Plays

Harlot premiered at the Cafe au Go Go still smarting from its obscenity suit re performances of Lenny Bruce. I was amused to learn they had not screened it, wondered if they would be outraged when they saw it themselves for the first time at the opening, and had visions of a new law suit. I was not amused at their shocking, public-be-damned attitude after the nerve of charging so much money, wondered if *Harlot* could ever again be shown commercially following the fiasco at Go Go. A capacity crowd showed for the opening, college professors, writers, Hollywood actors, play directors, schoolteachers, artists and reporters from a score of magazines. Conscienceless, the Cafe carted out a third-rate projector with a near-dead light bulb and focused the first reel on a tiny wrinkled bedsheet; no one was amused by the television impression of those first moments. And the screening was silent. The proprietor seemed impressed to learn that *Harlot* was a talkie: his machine would not carry sound. Furthermore, the showing began an hour-and-a-half late. Lines of celebrities shifted restlessly around the cafe. The speakers made bleak apologies to the prospective audience that had come from Connecticut and Philadelphia, possibly farther. The wise requested rain-checks.

The Cafe had been offered a good sound projector days in advance, and had turned it down. The employees of the Cafe greedily

Carol Koshinskie, Mario Montez, Philip Fagan and Gerard Malanga in Harlot, *1964*

counted the dollar bills.

At 10:00, Gerard Malanga left in a dither to scour the Lower East Side for a system that would carry the film. He arrived with a group of near-hysterical people at 10:45, with promising equipment. But the Cafe lacked an extension cord to its power hook-up in the back! *Harlot*'s second reel ground out weaker lighting yet, and an inaudible sound track. Only Harry Fainlight's shriek, 'BANANA!!' was comprehensible.

Blessed are the faithful, for a good part of the audience took the fiasco good-naturedly, called it a pop happening, did not even ask for their money back, and went away thoughtfully. Yes, the New American Cinema screws up again, but they are willing to give it another, several other, chances.

Go Go made no public apology, satisfactorily pocketed their outrageous take. And the Village Voice did not attack the Cafe, despite the angry protestation of one of its reporters that it would.

For the next few days, I anticipated that the crew of us should be run out of town; but further bruit of the affair was not sounded. Operations to license *Harlot* got underway following the developments of two more prints, but it was turned over to the Film Co-op in March for immediate showing, non-profit all the way down the circuit.

In January, a Swedish museum lent out a print and gave the film its European opening with favorable results.

Two months later, the print arrived in Paris. Suggestions were offered that it be given French subtitles . . .

Life goes to a Harlot opening
Amongst the august at the Cafe premiere was one Shana Alexander, the Feminine Eye of *Life* Magazine, and her 2 ¢ worth appears in the 29 January 1965 issue of that publication.

One gathers that the feminine eye turns away from underground flicks, but does so with disarming disclosure of its motivation.

Miss Alexander saw fit to put in a put-down of Warhol as prologue, palm off Pop as a money-making practical joke, and proceed to a squimish brickbat over the Co-op in general. But her piece is perfect because she tells why.

She came away from Go Go thinking everything had come off as planned. Such paranoia is native to her psychology. She was also bored, her self-satisfaction not allowing her the possibility that all flicks are not as boring as the eye that witnesses them, the Feminine Eye.

Scorpio Rising, *Flaming Creatures*, and *Candy*, as well as Debbie Reynolds (Warhol's favorite star), are also insufferably boring and 'ineffably sad'. Her ineffably sad disclosure of where she's at consciences a gentleman to pass her by without comment. But one good turn deserves another.

She agitates for a new Mrs Grundy; she claims pornography never corrupted anybody (?) but that it is distasteful; the new Mrs G. would spot 'fake artists' and 'pretentious critics' and prevent Ford Foundation grants from going to inventive souls. This self-styled defender of the public's morals is confused by the 'legal shelter under the wide umbrella of the First Amendment'. Let us hope that the bomb-shelter her popular viewpoint may eventually make usable is not as confusing to her.

Actually, she aided the underground movement. Had a woman with her mentality passed well on *Harlot*, the potentially interested should have dismissed the flick as unworthy of their attention. And the disinterested should have taken it to be something like the well-meaning art flicks from the continent and also dismissed it. But as it is, her condemnation stirs curiosity and film-makers, theatres, and museums all over the world have perked up their ears because of it.

As if that abstraction were not enough, succeeding issues of *Life* have featured articles concerning Warhol, these either noncommittal or favorable; and the N.Y. *Herald Tribune* and N.Y. *Post* have followed suit.

Further talk of critics involves only the most obvious clichés. Every new movement must meet it. Few in an audience ever seem to adjust to the endless pattern. Stirred from our habitual attitudes, we moan peevishly. Older artists, set in their careers and art-directions, are often more faulty than the public. Money is involved. Their money. Monopolies tremble at each incursion. And personal pride is always offended.

A birth is painful to the hospital.

The Star

A press release in the permanent files of the Co-op offers some ten startling lines on Mario Montez, strictly à la Hollywood, that leaves little to add. Except that nobody believes it.

They say, in effect, that Mario Montez feels that Miss Yvonne deCarlo has tried futilely for fifteen years to replace the original La Montez, that she has had more than enough time, and that he believes he can step quite well into the wedgies of Maria Montez and adequately continue the great tradition.

The tradition in question is the presentation of the perfect visual phenomenon: the actor or actress who can make real the experience of viewing shades on a two-dimensional sheet. French critics have argued time and again that one never has the illusion of reality in the cinema. They return to the theatre. In theatre we have real people on a real platform before our eyes. They speak and move as persons in the pale beyond the play. When they achieve a certain accuracy corresponding to our perception, our agreement that they are performing falls apart and they snap into our acceptance of the actual. In that moment, we become the hero and experience his trials. We enter the actor, as if by osmosis; and, shed of our physicalness, rise to the pure contemplation of his/our condition. Therefrom, we arrive to the revelation, catharsis, rejuvenation, or whatever you want to call it.

But the eye betrays such amenability as we bring to the screen: the brain revolts and repels the information as not so. And yet, it has happened that on rare occasion the most incredible assumptions *have* been made digestible; made, through illusion, real. There is a missing link.

That link is the nature and presence of the actor; the he who on the screen actually thinks it is so and precipitates thereby, to those caught up, his reality as an acceptable reality; and who fosters an illusion toward a pinnacle experience somewhat akin to that known for milleniums to exist in the theatre.

Maria Montez is perhaps the most glaring example of this desiderated link to illusion. And Mario has not inappropriately adopted her name. At first, this adoption seems preposterous. But it works. The obviousness, the silliness, is soon forgotten. And so does he work, to a lesser extent of course, as his namesake did. Make no mistake about it: Mario Montez believes he is the Queen of the Silver Screen. The entirety of *Harlot* rests on his belief and its success is supported almost solely by his extraordinary belief. There is deliciousness in his gestures that passeth understanding. His coy rising to and sinking against the back of the couch when Swan Lake suddenly swells up at the end of the film is a piece of intangible truth that bridges our deepest ganglia.

Stars of this nature can be created. They are created by directors who wish to statue a vehicle for the expression of themselves. Mario Montez is a creation of Jack Smith. He formulated him at his Cinemaroc Studio, first as Dolores Flores; and, later, when his development became undeniable, as Mario. Smith fed Mario his vision, his psychology, his dream. Mario cleansed his dream, and Smith refilled it. Mario took on Smith's vocabulary, his costumes, and his fantasy. He moves in the circles of circumstance his director chalks.

And, true to form, the procedure includes much danger. Smith said stars are the Alexanders the Great of the 20th Century: they think they are God. Which thinking goeth before a fall. Mario has rapidly come to being choosy about his scripts, has already turned down vehicles composed especially for him, refuses to shoot certain scenes not to his taste, etc., etc.

The drag queen, natal to cinema, is especially pertinent in 1965. Movie studios all over the world are the festering nests of transvestites. (Include Ancient Greece, the Elizabethan Theatre, the Chinese and Japanese Theatres.) The New American Cinema has taken the mask off rather than put it on. The New American Cinema smacks of Cinéma Vérité in almost more ways than can be counted. The souls of the beings we view are enlarged before us, even to the point of snapping out of character and blinking into the camera; an instance more and they would be waving at us. That these souls are so often wretched, which means our souls are wretched, has brought the accusation of brutality and sadism against the movement. Yet who among us, in his own life, escapes the complex of sado-masochistic chaos or finds his way about in a commodiousness less than brutal?

And the drag queen is all over our year. 'No sex in '65,' I sometimes think. The Beatles and their horde of imitators, the dances where partners never know each other, the bewildering and willing stagnation somewhere between male and female, the surrendering of sexual psychology to the physically, supposedly inappropriate opposite, and any number of instances where the relaxation of the sexual definition produces relaxation, all tell the same tale. The drag as the symbol of our time marries the drag as the visual phenomenon; and the New American Cinema becomes somewhat more interesting than the European avant-garde.

Esta R. I dubbed him when I first met him. He talked about Taylor in *Cleopatra*, wondered if they would allow the scenes where her breasts are exposed. He listened with patience to everything that was said. I discussed quantum physics and the vector theory with a professor friend. And he listened to all, as if absorbing it all. He was.

In the street, he donned a raincoat and rainhat, shades, affected a walk more masculine than a diesel. I used not to recognize him when he first came into a room off the street, so complete was his disguise. I would pass him by. He would remove his hat and say, 'It's me.'

That slightly mysterious accent you hear in his later sound films is what you suspect, Puerto Rican. He holds down the most banal office job: he pigeonholes. And that is enough irony for one book.

Mario's rise to stardom nonpareil in underground movies was so traditionally Hollywood as to again defy belief. He was introduced as a Spanish dancer in *Flaming Creatures*, where his role was but a few moments' dure. But it left an indelible impression. Everyone wanted to know 'who that brunette was' as they have wanted to know 'who that blonde was who just walked through' in several other historic flicks. Added to this was a mystery. As late as '64, some important reviewers of *Creatures* still could not figure out if the dancer were male or female. One critic claimed the point of the film centered about the question. In '63, he appeared in a somewhat longer role in Ron Rice's *Chumlum*, but with name credit at the bottom of the list. The nature of *Chumlum*, however, does not call attention to the stars; photography, editing, and superimposition were the stars. A bit here and there in '64, and *Harlot*, made him one of the more talked-of personalities connected with the movement, but for the moment, attention had shifted to two or three female stars in ascension.

Then, with the screenings in the second week of February '65 of both Warhol's *Screen Test II* and Smith's *Normal Love*, it happened. Little doubt was left that underground films had a great star on their lots. He is the answer to a director's and writer's prayer. And his lot, his problem, is his stardom.

People sometimes ask me what Mario wants to do – 'I mean, other than what he has.' Mario wants to charm, to be, in his own word, a 'cockteaser'.

Aside from the director's wonder, his innocence only charms father-figures, cloaking him in protection.

The truck driver has not seen, and is turned the other way.

Soundtrack of Andy Warhol's 'Harlot'

with Ronald Tavel
   Harry Fainlight
   Billy Linich
Soundtrack begins with a few bars from the beginning of Swan Lake.

Fainlight: Hey . . . hot-rod.
Tavel: I was married to the star of this film – did you know that?
Linich: I've heard that story.
Tavel: It was a marriage of convenience. We were working on another film and she was to be the reward for my helping to make it; I took a look at her, she took a look at me. I thought it was okay, she thought it was okay. We made it.
Fainlight: What kind of marriage was it?
Tavel: A social function, a marriage of convenience.
Linich: THE ACADEMY AWARD.
Tavel: Well, what do you think of marriages that are made that way?
Linich: Oh! I usually don't think of such formal situations.
Tavel: Who will take the place of Edith Sitwell:
Linich: Hermione Gingold.
Tavel: Would you bet on a marriage like that?
Linich: I rarely invest and I never speculate.
Tavel: William Bendix is dying today.
Fainlight: Oh yes, I heard about that.
Tavel: Gilbert Roland, Roland Gilbert, he died yesterday. There was something wrong with his voice; he couldn't make it in talkies.
Fainlight: Who are these photographers?
Tavel: Why are we pinned and wriggling on the wall?
Linich: Wire.
Tavel: Must writers and poets be subject to photographers?

Linich: Roasting. Yeah, and everyone gets skewered.
Fainlight: Star is rats backward.
Tavel: Fiddles are made of cats' guts.
Fainlight: Stars' guts backwards.
Linich: No, the first is on the cat's guts. The second fiddle. What is that made out of?
Fainlight: Sears backwards.
Tavel: Who will take the place of Edith Sitwell?
Linich: Not Hermione Gingold.
Fainlight: Smoke gets in your ash.
Linich: arrgh.
Fainlight: Man, is this a . . . . a. . . . . .
Linich: Try to be a photographer. This uh . . . intimacy.
Tavel: Do you want to know about the divorce?
Linich: I'd like to know about it, certainly.
Tavel: It was a matter of communication.
Linich: Things are usually a lack of communication these days.
Tavel: There was a telephone – I had to call between jobs, and nobody on the other side knew whom I wanted to speak to. I said, 'THE STAR'.
Linich: 'Beyond the Twelve Mile Reef.'
Tavel: The funeral of the grammarian.
Fainlight: Horrible species of insect abroad.
Tavel: It's called the pipes and the photographers.
Fainlight: Go away, please!
Tavel: I remember that she used to say to me that he wanted to photograph us as we really are.
Linich: Did he really want to?
Tavel: No, he wanted to photograph us as he really was.
Linich: Wanted to . . . photograph us.
Fainlight: Cash their checks.
Linich: And that's as he really would.
Tavel: What? Really?
Fainlight: Bad Banana!
Tavel: I've seen Miss Norma Vincent Peal.
   What will she do with the banana after she strips it?
Fainlight: She's a vegetarian.

There's a meat shortage in the situation.
Tavel: But, maybe the divorce came about because I did not want to be known as the husband of
Linich: What did you say that marriage was?
Tavel: A marriage of convenience.
Linich: The cat is a cat of convenience.
Tavel: Pussy de convenance.
Linich: It's a white lie.
Tavel: What is a white lie?
Linich: I don't know.
Tavel: A lie told by dash.
Linich: There are implications.
Tavel: Awake! Awake! Take oh take those lips away that were so sweetly formed.

Afterwards, I considered marriage on the basis of love only.
Linich: I resign.
Tavel: Afterwards.
Linich: Aye.
Fainlight: Banana tempting.
Tavel: But then there was so liggd little variety in the act of kind.
Fainlight: So vegetarian.
Tavel: The act of kind?

And I said, where would we get our carbohydrates from?
Fainlight: What's a person called who eats only fruits?
Tavel: A protean – a protean eater.
Linich: A prude.
Tavel: A non-Hindu.
Fainlight: A fruit.
Tavel: Look at her jewels. What would you give to be that cat right now?
Fainlight: Bananahood.
Tavel: Actually, bananas remind me of Carmen Miranda.
Fainlight: Maybe if you put the banana into the pussy.
Tavel: The lady with the tutti-frutti hat.
Fainlight: Hey, put the banana into the pussy.
Tavel: And there was something else between us. It

was the fact that my beauty marks on my cheeks were real – on both my cheeks. I don't know if she ever forgave me for that.
Fainlight: Look at the cat looking around.
Tavel: Perhaps if we called them birthmarks we could blame the former generation.
Fainlight: Turning the other chick.
Tavel: There was a bone of contention between us. But there was a social problem – our friends did not agree. The sort of problem you have to face in a marriage of convenience.
Linich: She?
Tavel: She knew nothing – remember that. We gypsies get blamed for everything.
Linich: General welfare.
Tavel: How much cash do you get for your cheeks?
Linich: Indoors or outdoors?
Tavel: Outdoors on forty-second street.
Linich: $2.98.
Tavel: $2.98? Don't you realize you're compromising the trade?
Linich: No, I don't.
Tavel: What particular trade did you accommodate?
Linich: Not in your hand.
Tavel: I got fired because of Earthy Kitt's record of Yummy Yummy.
Linich: I Muy, Muy.
Fainlight: Goody.
Tavel: I'm still trying to remember what came between us.
Linich: I still don't realize.
Fainlight: Is the banana still in camera?

She lift up her foot and that's a banana skin slipped on her foot.
Linich: The skin on the ground.
Fainlight: The cat is wrestling for the skin. It's an ol' banana condom.
Linich: Your banana skin or your life.
Fainlight: Ever slip on a condom?
Tavel: I am a can opener.
Linich: She's a banana skinner.
Fainlight: Gotta get –

Tavel: Do you think we can still get together? I think maybe we can.
Linich: If we're very very very still . . .
Tavel: If you can't get Aunt Jemima in the box, get Maxwell House in the can.
Tavel: Listen to me, Harry, we belong to a tradition. Some people are born free. They can do as they choose. But upon what we do rests the reputation and happiness of everyone now.
Fainlight: Condom maker.
Linich: Nation.
Tavel: Which nation?
Fainlight: Male Salems.
Tavel: Sabu would have had trouble with a spider, too.
Linich: What am I supposta make out of that?
Fainlight: Spiders stow away in crates of bananas.
Tavel: Spiders aren't the same shape as a bunch of bananas.
Fainlight: A yellow widow.
Tavel: I'm a grass widow.
Fainlight: Damn you.
Tavel: Sabu had to deal with the spider; he had three wishes, remember?
Linich: Rub. Rub. Rub.
Tavel: Always remember that bananas have to ripen on the very very tropical equator.
Fainlight: Limerick.
Tavel: On the afternoon of the day she died, Carmen Miranda called Havana and she said, prepare everything. I'm coming for a vacation, not to perform this time.
Linich: Havana, she said, Havana, come here.
Fainlight: Speak in tongues.
Tavel: If I skinned the cat . . . many ways to skin the cat.
Fainlight: Unpeel the cat.
Linich: I can make you a violin string.
Fainlight: One is an oral experience.
Linich: Or-really.
Tavel: Harry, Harry. Did you touch on the Atlantis when you crossed back and forth on the Atlantic?

Fainlight: Yes.
Tavel: What did you think of Atlantis? How did you anchor, in mid-ocean?
Fainlight: I was trying to be a seagull.
Linich: Don't try to change your name.
Fainlight: Get drowned.
Linich: Always doing something, Harry, always doing something.
Fainlight: I wet on the setness.
Linich: I sit on the witness.
Fainlight: Throw me your old juice banana skin.
Linich: Baby.
Tavel: Save your used banana skins, for the South will rise again.
Linich: Again all your sins.
Tavel: Again all your sins? I find you very appealing and I still do.
Linich: We've got to have something.
Tavel: Perhaps we can talk this over.
Linich: A Tar Guard.
Tavel: Why don't you relax?
Linich: It's a replacement for the guitar of the traveling troubadour.
Tavel: What are you holding?
Linich: You're going to give or take a few inches.
Tavel: I find you very appealing.
Linich: Put your arms around me (singing).
Fainlight: I'm going to take a piss.
Tavel: The toilet is right here.
Linich: Wind it tight; well, maybe I'm yellow.
Tavel: I find even the hair around your nipples appealing.
Linich: I don't know what you are trying to do, but you'd better cut it out.
Tavel: I think we're being caught in the act.
Linich: What did you say your name was?
Tavel: Antinen.
Linich: I think you're right. Antinen.
Tavel: What is she taking?
Linich: If you go further, it will be electrical. (laughter)
  Get a charge out of that, huh?

Tavel: I'd like to get you.

Linich: You'll getta kick out.

Tavel: on a slow

Linich: boat China China China . . .

Tavel: Who will replace Edith Sitwell?

Linich: I will.

Tavel: Shitwell.

Linich: Automatically.

Tavel: Have of what? But you're recognizable, your legs, anywhere.

Linich: Thin 18m on the other side of the —

Tavel: Why do you spend an hour in the Tasse?

Linich: Tasse?

Tavel: Because you have beautiful legs, you may be there. But what kind of trade do you cater to?

Linich: Amateur.

Tavel: Well, I think they should get the amateurs off forty-seventh street.

Linich: Catering has to do with professionalism, which I never become. Service is O.K. with me.

Tavel: Thank you. I shall take good advantage.

HARLOT – SECOND REEL

Fainlight: I just realized that cat skin's head.
    You think the cat must have grown on the skin?
    We're all being good here.

Tavel: There's a bruise on the banana.
    (long pause of silence)

Tavel: She used to speak to the monkeys of Argentina.

Fainlight: But she's already done that.

Linich: Didn't she already do that?

Fainlight: Well, you see, folks, there are these monkeys throwing things over their shoulders they're so hard to deal with.

Tavel: They won't let a female monkey out of Africa. It is said that monkeys are sometimes excited by human females.

Fainlight: It's the way bananas are bent – it has to do with Learned Hands and Well Hung.

Linich: Thank you.

Tavel: How are you fixed for bananas?

Fainlight: How are you hung for tropical fruit?

Tavel: There are seeds in a banana.

Fainlight: Well, in the Golden Bough – it's getting very learned.

Tavel: Her bent legs and the bent banana, my wife, my sometimes mistress.

Fainlight: Talking of banana brains, what about that . . .?

Linich: That no doubt would we undergo change.

Tavel: I would say so.

Linich: Say so?

Tavel: Why does she use the cat to cover her head; did I not cover her well enough?

Linich: Do not ask me questions.

Tavel: Peel me a banana.

Fainlight: Banana-eater.

Tavel: Well-hung.

Fainlight: BANANA!!!!!!! (Schreeeeeeched)
    Banana split.

Tavel: Because it was too tight.

Linich: Too many scoops.

Tavel: She used to speak about the monkeys in Argentina.

Fainlight: Baaah!!

Tavel: And if you came from Argentina, would you be as interested in bananas, as you are now?

Fainlight: Excuse this vicious brew.

Tavel: But the dictator of Argentina had a film actress for his wife.

(PAUSE)

Tavel: He was sent back to Spain very recently when he tried to disembark in Uruguay.

Linich: Uruguay?

Tavel: She had bananas for her husbands.

Linich: Because she was under the couch.

Tavel: That is because Spain wants only poets for her ambassadors. What would you do with the banana if you ate it?

Linich: My God! I guess I would – I'd shove it right down my throat.

Tavel: Who will replace Edith Sitwell?

Linich: I will replace Edith Sitwell.

Mario Montez in Screen
Test No 2, *1965*

Fainlight: Well, the movie camera's making crazy noises.

Tavel: Take down his drawers.

Fainlight: That's a skinned cat going up and down the middle showing a face.

Tavel: I prefer that they face the pillow.

Fainlight: It's almost irritation it's getting so ticklish.

Tavel: The banana looks like a French Tickler.

Fainlight: Old lushed-up cat . . .

Tavel: If I tickle your feet, would you put the pillow in your mouth?

If I tickled the pillow, would you put your feet in my mouth?

Tavel: If I undid her garter and threw it to the bald-headed row, would you eat your banana?

Fainlight: Pussy-scalp!

Linich: Banana looks?

Tavel: There's a cock-teaser around here.

Linich: What? What?

Fainlight: The fierce Southern whites for bananas. Slave ships reeking with bananas.

Banana slave! I WAS A BANANA SLAVE!!!

Illuminate us BANANA.

Tavel: Well, maybe I'm yellow.

Linich: Better yellow than red.

Fainlight: I wonder if the souls of banana flip through the night.

OH GERRY – MR BANANA VAMPIRE!!

Tavel: You'll wonder where the yellow went when they drop the bomb on the Orient.

Fainlight: Red cheeks in the Communist furnace.

Tavel: Miss Normal Vincent Peal.

Fainlight: Peel your John. Go into the John and peel your Vincent!

Linich: Joan Vincent?

Fainlight: I've cost the media mud, here!

Linich: You've paid the price.

Fainlight: This is an exercise in banana Yogi.

Tavel: What would you do with the seeds of the banana for an encore?

Fainlight: I'm passing into banana trance, stage one.

Linich: Is that Jean Harlow?
Fainlight: Oh, forget it, she's dead.
Fainlight: You are the head head!
Linich: I investigated it.
Tavel: O yeah, man?!
Linich: I know all about *that*. Yeah, I was there when that happened. I investigated it if that's what you mean. I investigated it.
Fainlight: Off the peg! Off the peg!
Tavel: These gypsy microphones get blamed for everything.
Fainlight: Phoney Mike!
Tavel: Mike? He was one of my former husbands.
Fainlight: You and your band of hussys!
Tavel: Hussies? It was all legal – consecrated by the church and everything else!
Fainlight: Get that banana.
Tavel: Oh, the harlot! the harlot! Let her put it in the crouch of her knee.
Fainlight: 'The knees.' That's why she's called Denise.
Tavel: Let her put it in the garter of her stocking.
Fainlight: Jealous banana trees bending down in hurricanes of rage!
Tavel: After all, I know more about her than you do. I was married to her.
Fainlight: Old banana peel you used to be real.
Tavel: Here we go 'round the banana tree – you and me!
Fainlight: I object.
Linich: Objection overruled.
Tavel: Old bananas for new. Oh, bananas for you.
Fainlight: I really want to say something about bananas and I can't.
   And all this is binickering . . .
Linich: . . . is making you yella.
Tavel: They show bruises.
Fainlight: Evil bruises. She's getting down to the nitty gritty.
Tavel: Use 'KY' before I die.
Fainlight: I think we should all make a public apology to bananas.

Linich: I'll have nothing to do with them.
Fainlight: How can we make it up to bananas for all we've done?
Linich: I'll not recognize them; I'll not talk upon the subject; I'm going to squeeze it right here.
Fainlight: Maybe if we glued them back on the trees. Make it our life's work. It's all in the head. Oh . . . oh . . . get back to the trees. That's our trouble, folks, this has been all recorded on Forty-seventh Street.
Tavel: Oh banana!
(music begins, screams, shrieks)
Tavel: Do something!! You banana bitch!!
Fainlight: Hey, dance the banana waltz. You bloated-broken banana.
Tavel: The calm after the storm.
Fainlight: The banana storm – all banana trees swaying in the crouches.
   Oh, peace is banana isle, bananas gently swaying – their crouches;
   Oh, banana bliss! Oh pulp! pulpy dreams . . . O, O, O, O pulp.
Tavel: You are a bad banana and will not be eaten.
Linich: Bad banana. Pick a banana.
Tavel: Peel me.
  (pause)
Tavel: Eat me! Eat me!
  Eat me! Eat me!
Fainlight: Abandon banana. . . . abandon banana.
Tavel: Eat me! Eat me!
  Eat me! Eat me!

The Speakers
In a rather natty, hostile, in-joke review of Warhol's films, *The Nation*, whose reporter was present at the shooting of *Harlot*, notes that three Tangiers-type poets huddled together out of camera range preparing to speak the sound track. Two of the three in question have never been to Tangiers and one is not a poet. The gentlemen were:
1 English poet Harry Fainlight, born in New York City in 1935. He was educated at Cambridge University and has taught in Rome, Paris, London

and New York. His sharp British accent was heard over the BBC Third Programme of the Arts and he has been published in *Encounter*. His poetry also appears in the PEN Anthology, *The Listener*, *C Magazine*, *Floating World*, *Nadada*, and *Fuck You, A Magazine of the Arts*.

Harry Fainlight has made several short 16 mm films, the first of which was financed by a grant from the British Film Institute's Experimental Film Fund. His movies have been screened at the City Hall Cinema and other New York houses.

2 One of the most striking things about Billy Linich is that his daily conversation is a continuation of the *Harlot* sound track. The associative punning and staccato rhythm comprise nearly all of his normal speech.

Billy Linich was born in Poughkeepsie, where he claims the great influence on his life was the fact that his father was German and his mother Italian. He was educated by Dorothy Podber and did the theatrical lighting for more than a dozen performances seen at the Judson, The American Theatre for Poets, and the Tent Theatre. He starred in *Haircut*, versions 1, 2, and 3, *Dinner at Daley's*, *13 Most Beautiful Boys*, *50 Fantastics* and *Couch*. He is a barber and adviser, and a 'very becoming photographer'.

Billy has traveled in California and Italy and was a maneuateur for The Floating Bear and on the board of directors of The Sinking Bear.

3 Ronald Tavel, whose family derives from more than half-a-dozen countries over Europe and Asia, was born on Amboy Street and raised in Gravesend Bay, but the country most closely associated with his name is Morocco.

In second grade, his teacher named him the Pied Piper for his practice of luring other pupils away from their ball games with his stories and readings. At this time, he began composing his first narratives in the form of illustrated comic book adventures set in the African forests, the Indian west, Southern plantations, South America, etc. During his Junior High School days, he was featured on radio panel programs where some of his comments on current situations were so unexpected that they were quoted in *The New York Times*. He was a child actor with the Originals Only Company, appearing in *Aegean Fable*.

Ronald Tavel studied and worked in Wyoming and after leaving the universities, traveled over most of the United States, Canada, Cuba, Mexico, France and Spain. His lengthy sojourn in North Africa provided the setting for his major novel, *Street of Stairs*, sections of which have appeared in the 1964 issues of *Chicago Review*. Samples of his scenarios are published in *Region* and *Clyde Magazine*. His plays and poetry appear in *Tri-Quarterly*, *Chicago Review*, *Anthology 5*, and the Harcourt Brace College Text of Contemporary Poets.

He has worked on almost a score of films for Andy Warhol and Jack Smith, as scenarist, prop-man, and actor. In the summer of '65, he became the first playwright of 'The Theatre of the Ridiculous'.

The Author

At a reception for *Harlot* held at Warhol's studio, Mario Montez introduced me to Isabel Eberstadt. 'I have to be on my best behavior and think of what to say exactly,' Mario stated excitedly, 'they say some nut is here who's going to write the book on Harlot!'

'I am that nut,' I said quietly to Mario ∎

DRAGTIME AND DRUGTIME
OR, FILM À LA WARHOL

PARKER TYLER

From *Evergreen
Review*, vol. 11 no. 46,
1967

Dragtime

Pop Art is a cultural misnomer. It was really studio phenomena that went Pop, by way of comic strip drawing and advertising layout, so that 'Pop Art' became a commercial article patronized by a section of the sophisticates who go in for art collecting. If we hope to do justice to a distinguished art world personality such as the Andy Warhol who makes films, we must abandon all the film-poetry cant of the Underground cultists and look at his work and its motives in a much more realistic light. Warhol, at first letting it out to friends that he wished to make 'bad films', served fair enough warning of his own. Granting nobody consciously wants to do or be 'bad' (why should bland, nice Andy Warhol want to do anything or anybody harm?), he must have meant he planned to make films that were 'bad' *as films* but 'good' as almost anything else, including the fun-potential based on the success of Pop.

In 1963, when Warhol first set up his sentinel camera, it wasn't original to ignore the hard-won title of 'art' that had been historically attached to film. It was already a confirmed, and in fact celebrated, habit of the new American avant-garde to practise an art-economy motivated to some extent by the economy of production costs. For many years, *Cinéma Vérité* and the *Nouvelle Vague* of France had been impressing film fans over the world with the virtue of informal manners, uncomplicated photography, spontaneous fancy, and texts taken unpretentiously from contemporary life. For all I know, the *Nouvelle Vague* to Warhol was only a name. However, he was brought along to a private screening at the office of *Film Culture* by Charles Henri Ford, whom I had asked to attend. Getting there a heavy load of the current Underground style of reeling around on the reel, Warhol also seemed to get the idea that nothing was easier than to make an impression with the medium of film. Film, after all, was even more untouched by human hands than the technical means Warhol employed for his graphic works. His intuition turned out to be very shrewd. His first films, *Sleep*, *Eat*, *Kiss*, and *Haircut*, aroused the fervor of the dominant New York Underground film group, whose magazine, *Film Culture*, proceeded at once to give him its Sixth Independent Film Award.

Pop is a cult of the ready-made re-processed for the uses of camp entertainment. Its parody idiom stretches from the puritanically strict to the bohemianly brash. A lot of rough stuff in the home-movie style (played, as in *Flaming Creatures*, for pathos camp rather than camp laughs) was then available as models. Yet, in an instinctive gesture, Warhol chose to exploit a minimal rather than a maximal animacy, and to limit his subject matter accordingly. His first move, metaphorically speaking, was to nail the feet of his camera to the floor. He might have decided that the camera was a

*Viva and Louis Waldron
in* Blue Movie, *1968*

Candy Darling in Women in Revolt, *1972*

least as talented as Gertrude Stein and deserved every single second of its liberal say-so. The consequent unedited footage was as fetishistic as *musique concrète* except that, as *cinéma concret*, its silence, for a while, was unbroken. He himself knew nothing about the film camera, was probably frightened of its famous pyrotechnics, and so began by treating film as if it were a tentative extension of his still portrait variations, such as the multiple Marilyn Monroes.

It seemed to work wonderfully with the unaided image of a sleeping man. Here was a living organism in which unconsciousness is the more spectacular in that, when wide awake, man is, without a rival, the most intelligent among the animals. True, his reputation has seriously declined in this century, but in the six-and-a-half hours which Warhol devoted to this specimen breathing blissfully along, man as such tends to regain a certain appealing, even monumental, innocence. God knows who, in the eyes of the general audience, the sleeping man is, but he proves that an adult can sleep like a baby; and not just any baby, but a Pop baby.

The *précieux* among cult connoisseurs were not slow to stress the exquisiteness of displaying the simplest, most ordinary happenings at an unvaried pace, to unprecedented lengths of time, and from a viewpoint with the fixity of a voyeur's if without the voyeur's dividend; the aspect of the early subject matter is prim, not scandalous. Other spectators, more permanently and loyally acclimated to the variety and skills of the film art, found Warhol's dragtime film much more replete with nullness than with nuance. Nevertheless, we must note, nuance had appeared with some real success in the film-maker's Pop paintings.

The multiple Marilyn Monroes show the actress's head in poster colors via the Warhol simplified-photography method, but each of these images is subtly varied so that we get very much what, if it were transposed to film, would be a series of frames cut from a film sequence in which colored lights had been passed around Marilyn's head. As Allan Kaprow once pointed out, the subject's facial expression varies from unit to unit so that a fluently moody Marilyn is created. Such an effect (Warhol repeated it more dramatically with variations on Jacqueline Kennedy's head) is indeed 'human' when compared with the static rows of those poker-faced soup cans. Later, Warhol converted the red-and-white Campbell's Soup color scheme into arbitrary 'psychedelic' spectra, related to the fluent kaleidoscope of his Velvet Underground projector.

Whatever value, market or aesthetic, may be placed on Warhol's Pop paintings, they do not demand the passive attention of a fixed (that is, seated) spectator in a film theater. This is what makes the viewing time required for his films into a drag exquisitely nuanced or excruciatingly redundant. Once you take an attitude, it's not hard to decide which of these responses is yours. But suppose you don't find it easy to take an attitude, to judge the thirty-three minute *Haircut* after three minutes or the forty-five minute *Eat* after five or ten minutes? Suppose a sort of hypnotism emanates from the screen so that you begin to feel rather like a rabbit being fascinated by a snake? The 'freeze' is not only on the subject, and the camera swallowing it, but on your own morally committed attention.

I am analyzing a likely spectator-response. After all, it's the ritual habit of a film-goer to enter, sit down, and relax. Does any film-goer avoid this habituation? Film-seeing implies the most passive psychological state of all the visual arts because the theater seat itself is habit forming, and because while watching plays, on the contrary, one shares a certain tension with the live performers. Stage actors themselves speak of rapport with the. audience: a feeling that cannot exist for film actors. The very decision to applaud is incubated from the first in the theater-goer and stimulates his attention. Both mind and eye, in the theater, feeling more responsible to the spectacle as a living thing, are the more alert. On the other hand, deep within the principle of film action (and thus film time) is something 'not living': a self-starting independent mechanism, a kind of *perpetuum mobile*, that relieves the watcher of his maximal mental cooperation.

A part of Warhol's negotiable charm as a modern entertainer is his work as applied art-naiveté. There is something both perverse and violent about pasting the camera eye on a limited field of vision with limited action inside it, and asking the spectator to paste his eye over that, and just wait. The ensuing charm, I should say, is more than a trifle masochistic. But take the contrary view. A high pulse exists in the modern temper (I mean everybody's temper) for elective affinity with occupations that dissociate themselves from the ugly spectacle of war, and lesser lethal agents, as forms of cut-throat competition. The very peacefulness of just watching a man eat a mushroom (even though, as if on purpose, he takes forty-five minutes to bite, masticate, and swallow it all) has its exclusive charm: an exclusive charm that makes it easy for the watcher to feel both chic and restful. The idea of peace, I mean, is directly related to the ultra-passivity of the pre-conditioned, relaxing film-goer.

Obviously, too, the chic feeling relates to the Pop ambience of the vulgar made precious through parody. The Pop cult is a cult of reassuringly minimal irony; the more it blows up actual scale beyond natural proportions, the less room there is for bothersome irony. Warhol, incidentally, liked to give his early films 'art projection' (magnified 16 MM) on ordinary interior walls. A pair of kissers then look like an animated mural, billboard size. If overwhelming reality *must* invade our privacy and peace, let it be screened, at least, at the door, and only amusing versions allowed in. As we know so well, certain scales in Pop painting, especially murals, simply giganticize the scale of advertising art, often literally as large as, or larger than, life.

Warhol's first film gambit was to giganticize with *time* instead of *space*. Doing it with time (in the film house there is no inevitable sense of the actual physical magnification) made it necessary for him to choose subjects just as obvious and commonplace as those of his paintings.

For many years now there has been a school of film thought of which film à la Warhol is Pop parody. Its theory may be conveniently termed (in the late Siegfried Kracauer's phrase) 'the redemption of physical reality'. This school believes that the true function of film was not to produce and maintain a new art form, but to provide a super-investigation of mere physical reality. To struggle with this theory on the basis of whether art *is* a mirror, and film a *representational* art, would waste time in this place. Warhol's (probably unconscious) parody of 'the redemption of physical reality' makes such an aesthetic argument pointless. The living organic world we see in *Sleep*, *Eat*, *Haircut*, and *Kiss* has a visually implosive force whose burden we must bear or else heave off. Warhol's point is exactly that what we see should reveal nothing new in proportion to the quantity of time required to watch it; indeed, his object might be to portray a deliberate 'vicious circle': a closed process with no progress whatever, only an 'endless' self-engrossment.

Inevitably, all mental interest and visual attention are governed by an economy that establishes a self-sustaining rhythm. Experimentally, Warhol matched the pulse beat of the camera and the respiration of a sleeping man (the mastication of an eating man, the osculation of erotic couples, etc.) with the pulse beat of the spectator's available interest. If these don't match in the film house, the spectator's boredom will take over. At the same time, the film-maker's strategy was to make a direct appeal in line with the automation atmosphere of the film. The temptation for the watcher (the pre-conditioned individual I mentioned above) is to be automated along with the camera's automation as this is rhythmically adjusted to the basic physical drives of eating and kissing. It is 'good' to eat. It is just as good, or better, to kiss. How could either occupation make a *bad* film? Such commonplace activities are universal and thus very easy to 'identify' with. The film, Warhol plainly says, is no 'better' or 'worse' than what it records. Result: the plastic medium that creates 'filmic interest' and 'film art' becomes the victim of another Pop put-down.

That a number of filmmakers in the Underground movement, as well as a brace of art connoisseurs,

Ondine in The Chelsea Girls, *1966*

fell prostrate before the Warhol Pop film tells us something tangible about the current state of the American avant-garde in film and elsewhere.

Dragtime (the superficial tempo of Warhol's primitive films) might be said to have more than a mite to do with drugtime and the magic beauties of an expanded time assisted (as it is in *The Chelsea Girls*) with overt psychedelic decor. Theoretically, the Warhol devotees suppose that a definite beauty exists in his reductio ad 'least' absurdum of progress in objects.

The same reduction seems less absurd if we expose it to a light to which it might seem to aspire. We know a great deal about the chemical change of witnessing organisms that much expands time-lapse as measured on the clock. The well-publicized 'psychedelic experience' is all we need to be informed that the agent of such wondrous expansion is a variety of drugs, having a range of effects on time-awareness and the appearance of objects, but all peculiarly improving the rewards of sense perception. I recall how, as long ago as pre-WPA days, certain Village brahmins would speak of the marvelous thrill to be had from smoking marijuana. A cat would cross the room; that was all. And yet not only was this something that seemed to go on forever, but also it produced a fantastic sort of pleasure: a pleasure which looking at a cat crossing a room when one was in a normal state decidedly failed to produce. The later Warhol films suggest that he divined in the physical accumulation of screen time a potential hypnotic effect on watchers which nothing else but drugs could guarantee. I think that his primitive films can be called experiments in dragtime which logically predicated an innoculation of the unwinding reel with drugtime.

Drugtime

Warhol was still a rather esoteric quantity as film-maker till his latest film, *The Chelsea Girls*, which climaxes his self-maneuver out of his original styleless style into something like profession-pretending film-making. The purity of the original eventless films was first modified by *Blow Job*, an erotic conceit that begins with the opening of a fly

Edie Sedgwick in ∗∗∗∗
(Four Stars), *1966/67*

and ends with closing it. In between, with only the passive subject's face in the unswerving camera range, we are treated to a process which actually, since it leads to an orgasm, is also a progress with a ready-made mounting interest. Here the psychological element of a *tiresome* progress, an *exhaustible* drive, was significantly, in fact fatally, hinted.

Even the sexual act is something in which a boredom-potential inheres. At the same time, sex has an indispensable organic suspense: the climax may be irritatingly or profitably postponed; the very physical labor may unaccountably grow wearisome; still the great end, psychologically and physiologically, stays in view. Referring *Blow Job* to the preliminary sexual activity of kissing, one notes that *Kiss*, which lasts fifty minutes and holds numerous pairs of kissers, does not fail to show signs of tiring its subjects and forcing them to fresh prodigies of osculative style to justify, it seems, the camera time being spent on them. Here already was a flagrant 'impurity.' The human subjects involuntarily betrayed that a sort of theater was present, a 'show' which felt obliged to sustain the 'interest.'

Hitherto, Warhol's subjects notably seemed indifferent to being watched, to (so to speak) having to perform anything with a 'program' or a 'script.' For all that suspense or expectation is involved, *Haircut* or *Eat* might be totally outside time in a vacuum like that of far space. When, for example, we are asked by *Empire* to watch a famous landmark ('the world's tallest') standing quite motionless, with the camera equally unmoving, while the sun is allowed to take all of eight hours to go down and come up, we are being asked to submit ourselves to an endurance test; that is, to the opposite of an entertainment form ... unless (which is, I think, the point) it should occur to us that this quantitative time, spreading out its minutes in a morgue, is merely the abstract proposition for a much more entertaining, specifically psychedelic, time. The latter provides a

dramatically decisive change not in the object, but in the one viewing it. *Drugtime is the other pole of dragtime.* However unconsciously, Warhol began playing with this interpolar tension as if it were a new toy (which in a way, being a camera, it was!) His social milieu already contained these same two polarities and their vibrating rapport. Another ready-made subject awaited his Pop ministrations.

Narcotizing is very close to Narcissizing. The only distinction is that with drugs, the gazer's own image is not the object of fascination; rather it is the image of the world transmuted by a chemical change in the gazer's perceptive faculties. Narcissus' image *has become* the world and the resultant rhythm of merged awareness is, exactly, drugtime. It is the time of sublimated leisure: *all the time in the world*. Warhol's *Vinyl*, his first film with 'progressive' social action, came along as a documentation of people in the mixed throes of narcotizing and narcissizing; also for the first time, there were credits for the title, the idea-man and the leads; otherwise, as usual, the film was titleless. A group of young men, watched by a motionless female odalisque, are got up in a way to suggest exotic Leather Boys while their behavior (sado-masochistic according to the shadowy script) suggests the dazed performers of an impromptu, faltering charade. We are witnessing a snail-paced fantasy in which familiar homosexual sadism, enhanced by drug-time, is putting on some kind of an act. Warhol still holds up a still, small mirror to nature, but now nature, by all the signs, is narcotized narcissism.

One hears that Warhol's productions have a way of being group-groomed. Logically, then, his function became a parody of the Hollywood 'genius' producer who decides everything and delegates the execution to others. However valuable another's contribution, the Warhol label is the only thing featured. A curious accident took place in the next film, *My Hustler*, aligning it with the objective hazard of the Surrealists. Not only does this film fall apart into two sections of very unequal aesthetic caliber, but the accident seems to have been caused by the studied inattentiveness to form typical of Warhol's *cinéma concret*. A rather flossy homosexual, with a handsome, freshly picked hustler as guest at his beach cottage, is in a tizzy that marauding male or female will grab him away during his lone sunbath on the sand; this is the gist of the clumsy screen sequences, badly framed, casually intercut, amateurishly acted, indistinct in sound and altogether home-movieish, that comprise the first section. The second section is a small miracle, not the less miraculous for seeming just as ad libbed and 'unprofessional' as the first; once more, the camera is without so much as a tremor to disturb its voyeurish solitude.

A dark-haired hustler, an old-pro, has appeared at the beach cottage and has evidently decided, on his own, to help initiate the blond, a newcomer to the trade. Cozily flank by flank in the cottage's tiny bathroom, the pair engage in some beautifully deft verbal sparring. The hush that can sound like an interminable desert of silence in Warhol's films is here as precisioned into tense pauses as the most carefully crafted dramaturgy. One has a notion the directorial genius that makes everything in this true-life put-on look utterly right is a real objective hazard; I suspect it was due simply to the perfect understanding between the two performers as to just what was involved. Adagio, sotto voce, it leads into a veiled proposition from the old-pro – tactically prolonged through an endless shave and wash-up – that the blond, in return for the other's invaluable list of tried customers, must first render up his body to the07 old-pro himself. The charade idea is built into the ready-made material, which is as sober in tone, as ordinary in rhythm, as the action of *Haircut*. Here, too, is the old faint-away stop: tantalizing because we don't find out if the wary neophyte accepts the proposition or even if he's faking his alleged puzzlement over what the proposition really is.

Then came the expanded-keyhole variations of *The Chelsea Girls* suite, which, as I write, has just been promoted to art-theater status. Some confusion among fluttered commentators has been created about whether the film is 'dead serious' or a horrendous 'put-on'. Whichever it is, they like it as much as if it were a homemade *La Dolce Vita*, which is what it is. The fact should have wider currency that nothing can be so 'dead serious' as a 'put-on' by Warhol Super Stars. Super Star is a category which some of his actors claim and to which all have the legitimate right to aspire. Fame, sheer fame, has a way of stirring up its favorites and would-be favorites with the force of, at least, amphetamine. The whole cast of *The Chelsea Girls*, seen for 3½ hours in a series of sometimes overlapping rooms, has the habit of loitering before the camera with looks half drug-dazed, half glamor glutted, and for super-measure, more than half bold with nonchalance. Without nonchalance, they could hardly 'perform'. And sometimes – it is Warhol's big step toward 'theater' and 'story' – the actors here do perform.

Not only do the actors before Warhol's cameras seem, now, really involved with something, his camera itself is involved with what it sees. *All* tend to freak out. Intermittently, in contrast to some steady-eyed close-ups, the camera pointlessly starts zooming with the push-button ease of an addict launching on a rhythm kick. No longer is it a stand-in for the beautifully bland, impersonal, kind and so tolerant gaze of a transfixed watcher immune to boredom. Now it is as perambulant as some of the guests at a (supposed) Chelsea Hotel who pay each other cozy, more or less friendly, visits. The dragtime, with its monotonously circular non-progression, is much tightened, though still distance-going. The subject is, in fact, peepshows, and the show is, nearly always, intoxicated persons (even beer is one of the intoxicants) doing their stuff under bright lights with the dazzling intimation of coming publicity. It is for intransigent critics or in-group gossip to say whether the performers are really drug addicts, or just pretending to be. The inside myth is, I take it, that they are, and thus that Warhol's camera has grown daringly, shockingly candid.

The truly shocking thing, in terms of the previous Warhol, is the new sort of violence: the violence of sadists and masochists freed into their desired domain by courtesy of a stimulant such as amphetamine or an hallucinogenic such as LSD. Yet, while there is a dedicatedly dreary scene in which a hustler lolls around in bed with his male patron, spitefully upstaging him, there are no wild orgies even approaching Sadian eroticism. Because of the pacifying effect of the drugs, apparently, the sadistic impulse, like the erotic impulse, is rerouted and held in a kind of narcissistic trance in which the monologue takes command. Here is narcotized narcissism in full, unimpeded, leisurely stride. As a sadistic bout, it seems best suited to Lesbian delusions of grandeur; for instance: the Amphetamine Amazon on the telephone and Hanoi Hanna in her straight-camp TV parody, during which, on the side, she persecutes two of her weaker mates. Not that cinematic skill or theatrical form have materially altered Warhol's primitively flat style. At best, *The Chelsea Girls* provides some scenes that, properly trimmed, would look like respectable *Cinéma Vérité*. But that is the limit of Warhol's homage to the film art, with the sole exception of a color sequence where his sliding Velvet Underground lights project the interior of an addict's trance. This sequence has quality but within the context of *The Chelsea Girls* it is only another form of Olympian self-documentation.

Curiously enough, however, the 'self' has become schizoid here: both in some of the actors and in the camera. Through most of the film two screens (or 'rooms') exist side by side. Dragtime/drugtime is itself a split plastic 'personality' and this is reflected in the alternate aspects of a character seen simultaneously in different psycho-physiological states in different rooms. Crudely handled as the device is, it is intrinsically interesting, especially as to its possibilities. Warhol's invasion of hallucination as promoted by drugs poses a procedural dilemma for his future film-making. The formal restrictions super-exploited by his primitive style (the dragtime) imply an almost puritanical detachment from life: reality's fabulous deadpan dream. Now he has chosen to grapple with that peculiar collective secession from normally rational society that implements drugs to achieve its isolation. He has not tried to use hallucination as a device of creative film-making; rather he has shown, almost exclusively, the *outsides* of those seeking hallucination as means of rescue from sober, everyday reality. Has this 'behaviorism' of hallucinated subjects always been Warhol's Underground motive? Did he always intuit the psychic tension between dragtime and drugtime and gradually begin manipulating it?

This seems certain: The anti-heroic film marathons he calls *Sleep, Eat, Haircut, Kiss,* and *Empire* can be conceived by dedicated audiences *as if* they were drugtime – that is, as inexplicable wonders of eventfulness. As I say, Warhol has translated into quantitative minutes on the screen the magical *durée* inducible in watchers by marijuana and other drugs. Psychologically it is possible for quite sober persons to grasp the physiological principle lodged in drug-taking and transpose its consequences, in terms of visual perception, to some film *objectively laid out like a 'trip.'* Hence the primitive Warhol films might function as dialectic antitheses, demonstrating how what is excruciatingly tiresome and commonplace cries out for the right conversion-formula in the witness – not the intermediate witness, the camera, but the final witness, the audience. Warhol may have moved in some mysterious way his wonders to perform – those wonders so filmic and yet not filmic! ∎

THE SEXUAL POLITICIAN
STEPHEN KOCH

**From *Stargazer:
Andy Warhol's World
and his Films*,**
London, Marion
Boyars, 1985

. . . the dandy's beauty consists above all in the cold appearance which comes from the unshakable resolution not to be moved; one might say the latent fire which makes itself felt, and which might, but does not wish to, shine forth. Baudelaire

Exactly. The description of cool. But far more than latent fire is immanent beneath the cold appearance of Baudelaire's dandy, and more than latent fire lights Warhol's peculiarly disembodied image. Warhol is the greatest living inheritor of that creature of style Baudelaire so flawlessly described, but both are more than the Image to which they wish to reduce themselves. The dandy refuses to be moved; he will not respond. The passions are mute but immanent within him, and Baudelaire's immemorial metaphor for those passions is fire – consuming, destructive, and feared. Baudelaire describes a man who lives only through an image of himself. The dandy is an *envisioned* man; in the ideal moment of his existence, he imagines himself, his life is coolly transfigured by that repressed, unconsuming flame. He is one for whom the fire of existence ignites only when he is able to see himself and repress that fire. He imagines himself as a being with the properties of another. So it is with Warhol. That image of the Self that Warhol has so masterfully created looks isolated and luminous, an image on the silver screen. But there is no image of the self that does not entail – invisibly, perhaps, out of frame – the image of others. And the dandy's narcissistic isolation is haunted by the specter of others. It is against them that his 'resolution not to be moved' acts with a power defined by mutism, passivity, visibility. Yet it is real power.

But it is almost never the kind of power he supposes it to be. As we shall see, his pathos derives from seeking a vision of the wholly autonomous self; his blindness consists in failing to understand that there *is* no self without others. Warhol's image has its purity, but its specific gravity impinges on us with the solemnity of an existential errand, an effort to define being. That image forces us into a consideration of the relations to others it embodies. To understand its power, we must understand – we must *hear* – its silences, hear to whom, and to what, those silences are directed. We must define the politics of Warhol's experience.

We are dealing here with the image, not the man. I will be speaking of the politics of masculine narcissism, of the metaphors locked within its flesh; referring to its dynamic structures of need and being as they alternate between coldness and adoration; between voluptuity and the refusal to give or be touched; between the slap of lust and a drifting revery of autonomousness. A warning: Though Warhol's world is decidedly homosexual, it is the strategies of narcissism and not homosexuality that have my attention here.

*Ed MacDermott and Paul
America in* My Hustler,
1965

Homosexuality is not an existential dilemma in the sense in which I understand the term: it is simply a way of conducting one's sexual life, happily or unhappily as the case may be. It can and does at times confront the dilemmas and impasses I will be discussing. But they are dilemmas that move in deeper regions than sexual behavior.

Nor do I mean by narcissism merely the adoration of the self, merely the rapture of the boy at the reflecting pool. I mean narcissism as a form of relating to others. I do not mean to define it clinically; I do not mean to enshrine it philosophically. I merely want to sketch the structure of an experience, in the hope of understanding what it has to say about love.

'Frigid people really make it.' – AW

The face of the adolescent fills the mirror, and he suddenly feels flooded with a new rapture, he has made the beginnings of a discovery. The bliss of the narcissistic *frisson* is a life force, the first discovery to one's own *power*. I am tempted to think it the *sine qua non* of that discovery. The child in his dependence suddenly sees in the glass one to whom love's sustenance is not arbitrarily dispensed by others, one to whom a new kind of attention can be given: This being is not a child, not dependent. For the first time, he rapturously feels that the person in that mirror is beautiful, capable of separateness and strength. Inscribed in that face, those features, those limbs, is whatever human power it is that makes one 'Some One', makes one a being with something to say about the terms of self-esteem, a being no longer a childish suppliant, one capable of commanding attention and caring, one to whom love's sustenance is not arbitrarily dispensed by others; one capable of exercising that autonomous existence necessary to make oneself loved. Or feared. Or felt.

This discovery takes the form of a search; a deep attitude of scrutiny is its *tao*. But scrutiny is not enough. After the primary intuition that that 'Some One' exists, one proceeds to discover its continuing existence by living. Suppose that 'Some One' is never found. Suppose the narcissistic intuition becomes only the further pretext for division and weakness. Suppose the face in the distance of the mirror becomes the very image of the self divided. A vicious circle initiates itself. Eros is alive within one, demanding its gratification, hungry for others, insistent. Yet the self is not strong enough for the encounter; very often the Other means something very dire: the self feels too weak to confront the threat. To feel this weakness is in itself humiliating, and so desire awakens not the prospect of gratification, but the anguish of self-hatred, along with the threat of humiliation and degradation, all of them joining in a conspiracy of anxiety, which is in turn an agency of repression. Desire itself comes to be felt as a variety of pain. (That 'pain' may be further disguised as 'boredom,' or 'contempt,' or 'disgust'.) Yet Eros will have his season. He turns his warmth on the one object he is capable of confronting: the isolated self. And anxiety and the threat of humiliation resolve themselves into serene rapture. For a while.

Fearing both others and the self, the ego returns compulsively to the narcissistic surge for confirmation, seeking to tap again that delicately overwhelming intuition of strength. But the face in the mirror is a stranger's. It reawakens not the sense of strength but self-hatred. And in the effort to rid oneself of that hated self, one begins to love the attributes of the image that make it seem to be a stranger. The self can only be bearably envisioned as another. And in the throes of hatred for the self, one falls in love with that image of self as other. Now, this image of the self-as-other has one very noticeable attribute, its 'personality' has something special about it. It is loved for itself alone. It does not relate to others.

Baudelaire's vision is born.

The narcissistic intuition of strength, of the power

to live and relate, is replaced by a drifting, self-protective revery of self-sufficiency. The image in the mirror is eroticized but remote; beloved but unapproachable; needed but incapable of being possessed. And these attributes become the precise terms of the narcissist's existential description of himself. The nearness and farness, the presence and absence of the divided self are eroticized. For itself.

This turning inward is famous for its sweet pathos. We know that the boy hovering so breathlessly over the reflecting pool will never embrace himself. He wants himself – wants with a vast, sweet ache of yearning that cannot be assuaged. His dilemma is tender. But tenderness is not quite the whole story. He wants himself because he does not possess himself. His ache of yearning is also the ache of pain. Inevitably, his desire is imperious and all-consuming. He wants to live, but cannot; he correctly intuits that possession of himself is the One Thing Needful. Other people remain insignificant to him so long as the crucial, essential being eludes him. He is bereft, nothing matters but redemption. His pain is terrible. *He experiences himself as an absence.*

But his tenderness is cold. He is in deep complicity with the absence, and it is because of his complicity that fullness eludes him. For he wants only a self that wants only others. He wants precisely that self that the adolescent so rapturously perceived might have the power to live with others on his own terms. But that self does not want the narcissistic kiss – it humiliates and insults. He wants the joy of living, understood as relationship. But, through some injury or delusion, that joy seems unbearably threatening, and is mercilessly scorned.

So narcissism means dividing the self to obviate the threat of needing others. All its energy, all its eros, all its sweetness, all its rage, are directed toward this repressive end, which is almost never recognized as repression, because it is a repression that takes the form of desire. One thinks of desire and gratification as following a sequence. But narcissistic desire is simultaneously its own lush gratification and its own savage frustration. It is desire *as* frustration.

The narcissist yearns for wholeness because he feels himself to be divided, and his self-division finds its very image as he stands before the mirror. His divided autonomy is preferred to a wholeness of self. Yet that wholeness – obscurely intuited, loved as another is loved, mysteriously, elusively immanent in the mirror – is also his most dire image of self-obliteration. This is his dilemma: He desires only what he utterly refuses to possess. And so he is damned.

Those who have not known this damnation cannot understand how simultaneously seductive and terrible it is. R. D. Laing has said he is amazed only by the fact that more people are not raving mad; gibbering in the streets. To feel a desperate need for others that drives one inward rather than toward contact is to feel simply crazy. To feel oneself refusing everything one most deeply desires, to experience desire as a form of refusal, is to suspect one's own sanity. Love is ferociously scorned. Self-esteem mercilessly despised. Meanwhile, eros saturates everything in a vast desert of disinterest. Yet these seemingly mad transactions occur with utter conviction and every appearance of complete necessity. It is indeed miraculous that its victims do not rave and scream, that they find themselves instead washing the dishes, showing up at work on time, and smiling to the cashier.

A word or two more about some characteristic ways of experiencing this conundrum. One such way, motivated by a refusal to permit the other his distinctness, habitually confounds the experience of desiring with the experience of being desired. One feels a baffling incapacity to sense the crucial distinction between the two, feels a peculiar blindness to the fact of their separate occurrence. Another modality requires that all emotion be self-

Blow Job, *1963*

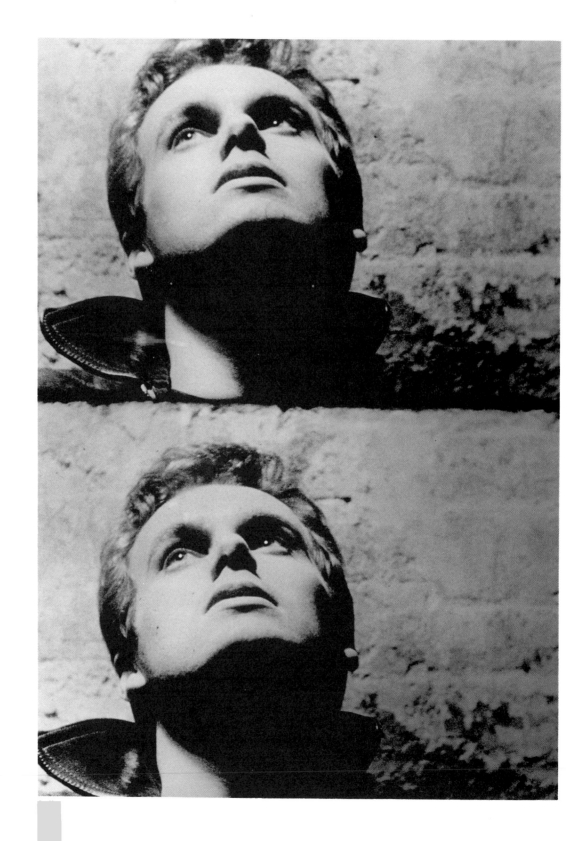

reflective in order to be experienced at all. This self-reflective dimension may or may not be the grounds for a superior consciousness (though it often is); but, in its pathological form, it seeks to evade the immediacy of forbidden need by reducing it to the innocuousness of a spectacle in which one is both actor and audience. Outside the arena of this spectacle, emotion is simply not felt. It becomes impossible to desire in any simple way, impossible to tolerate being desired with that simplicity that calls for a frank return of feeling or rejection. Desire may wholly dominate the personality, but always as a means for assuring that actual gratification does not take place. One can adore – alone. For in one's adoration, one is 'lovable'. One can be adored – alone. For in one's indifference, one is invulnerable. But, in either case, abandoning an essential solitude means vulnerability to a love worse than death. And so one alternates inexplicably between abject adoration and a terrible *froideur*.

But to return to Warhol.

> *I think a love affair can get too involved, anyway, and it's not really worth it. . . . You do it like you watch a movie made for television.* AW

Narcissism lives in the theater of itself; theater is its refuge. Warhol's early critics were fond of pointing out that his is a primarily theatrical as opposed to plastic gift. It is indeed a virtually metaphysical dimension of his identity. The narcissistic mind is likely to have a peculiarly deep commitment to the strategies of the unreal because the unreal gives permission for experience and emotions that are otherwise forbidden or unbearable. Condemned to passivity and repression, the imperious need to *act* still exerts itself. And so one 'acts', theatricalizing a role or identity not one's own. Forbidden emotion is given permission to emerge by virtue of the falsity of the role. Yet it is real emotion. That is *its* sweet pathos.

There is a breach between the need and the permission: the space between the real and the played, the distance of theater. It is also the space between the boy and the surface of the reflecting pool. Or, to subdue the discussion to Warhol, it is the distance of Warhol's stare, the distance between himself and the world he transposes beneath his aestheticizing gaze. But, in the voided, empty spaces of this distance, the Thing Denied is need. Need is humiliation; it is loss of self; it is death. Of course, denial does not make need go away. The obsessional transaction becomes this: a search for permission and repression at once – a search for permission *as* repression, repression *as* release. It is only in the narcissistic revery, only in Baudelaire's elsewhere, that these antimonies can be resolved. One enters the theater of that elsewhere in order to trigger a permission that will be as full as it is unreal. Now, Warhol *is* permission, he *is* theater; he creates around himself that aura of the unreal that is also the space within which he cannot be touched, not ever literally touched. There Warhol gives permission for the sexualization of his eros. That sexualization is something very different from the liberty of sexual desire as it craves others: that liberty can never be granted. It must always be taken, assumed in that very act of taking that is forbidden to the narcissistic mind.

The distinction I am invoking between sexuality and sexualization rather resembles the famous distinction between style and stylization, and is both as shadowy and as crucial as that concept. Self-reflectiveness is, of course, the key to both – just as stylization is so often named as the besetting vice of highly narcissistic art. But I am less interested in a normative definition than in a certain experience of emptiness, an eroticization that touches everything in one's experience except the wellsprings of gratification; a sexuality in which everything is permitted except *being*.

The central reality in this theater of the unreal is the

body. What is the meaning of nakedness? Warhol is obsessed with it, he scrutinizes it endlessly, it is another of the mysteries he ponders over, staring. The flesh does indeed incarnate a mystery, but it is the mystery of desire itself, the mystery even of what desire is, and how it can be released. The body incarnates the mystery of the real. But for Warhol that mystery remains impenetrable. Nakedness is innocence, vulnerability, desirability. And so nakedness is scrutinized in search of all these things, none of which the narcissistic mind can afford or tolerate. One's own flesh is adored at the

Gerard Malanga, Kate Heliczer and Rufus Collins in Couch, *1964*

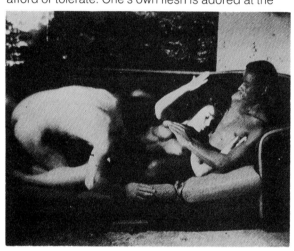

distance of one's refusal to tolerate what it is, or what it represents. The endless scrutiny of the naked male body that constitutes the central erotic concern of Warhol's late work and all of Paul Morrissey's is a search for the wellsprings of feeling itself. The rapt, drenching attention given to those bodies is a search for release, an effort to discover the liberty to take and be – to take and be real – to have substance – that the flesh embodies. Nakedness is a search for permission. But its nakedness is covered, the search is false, the game rigged. In this theater of permission, permission *is* denied. The theater can only be entered because it is innocuous and unreal. It is an arena in which the

flesh glows with the mystery of its absence, enhanced by an eros that denies substance to what it truly desires and that lives only in a theater that denies life to what it gives liberty.

These paradoxes are desired: What's craved is an unreal experience of liberty – understood to be free *by virtue* of the fact that it is unreal. This is an eros that sexualizes and theatricalizes need so completely that desire seems to drown it. The result can be the familiar but still bizarre paradox: a completely sexualized personality unable to say anything at all about what it wants. In Warhol's world, this is the eros of the hustler, the transvestite, the superstar. Animated by adoration and indifference, desirability confused as desire, glamour confounded with self-hatred, this eros makes people shine in the peculiarly unreal way Warhol has made famous. It is also the eros that makes people jump out of seventeenth-story windows or swallow thirty Nembutals. Its pathos is the necrophilia and impotence of the star and sex idol, to which the Warhol ambience is so deeply addicted; the pathos of Valentino and Harlow and Monroe and James Dean. But it is also the pathos of the utterly dispossessed. And it is a dilemma to which Warhol, in another of the brilliant moves that make up the strategies of his own cool narcissism, has made himself the utterly absorbed and uncaring witness.

Warhol's own solution to the narcissistic dilemma is so simple that it is positively breathtaking. It has been to absent himself as conspicuously as possible. He has joined the dandy's strategy with that of the voyeur, and elevated the conjunction to a principle of being. Predictably enough, as the ultimate voyeur, Warhol has surrounded himself with exhibitionists. His strategy is far more successful as a repressive tactic than theirs: In his voyeuristic compulsion to absent himself, in his refusal to be present within the circle of love, Warhol acquires a 'capacity not to be moved' that is far more complete than the exhibitionist's dream of having the world at his feet, adoring and enthralled. The exhibitionist dreams that, if only he were adored, he would at last feel substantial and autonomous, beyond risk, *real* within the glow of his fame and beauty. Haunted by invisibility and inexistence, his compulsion is to become visible, known. This compulsion insists upon incessant and extravagant renewal. Like the junkie, he must have his fix. He is wholly dependent on his dream of autonomy. He is going to shine, be untouchable, he is going to be a star. That is *his* pathos.

That's the thing I'm always thinking about: Do you think the product is really more important than the star? AW

By making himself the prime witness of this pathos-ridden and pathetic dream of autonomy, Warhol has achieved his own airtight image of autonomy. We're correct to speak of superstars, all right, but it is the merest flattery to give the name to Ingrid or Ondine or Viva. Warhol is the superstar. He has entered that pathological American dream and enacted it in reflective terms that provide him with a peculiar immunity to its dangers and disasters. Or at least so it seemed until Valerie Solanis appeared. As a master of passive power, Warhol *is* the self-esteem of his hangers-on; *He* is their fix. The results of this absolute dependency can be terrible: The annals of the Factory include not the rhetoric but the reality of madness and suicide that is like a heartbeat. As of this writing, the latest victim is Andrea Feldman, who, in the fall of 1972, leapt from a seventeenth-story window clutching a Bible. She had recently appeared in *Heat*. It is from this hysteria and dependency that Warhol seems so coolly immune. He can rest still within the hall of mirrors, unthreatened by the rising and shifting specters of the unreal, those prismatic flatterers that can become so cruel. Every suicide must be its own story. But surely those of the Factory must include

some terrible conjunction between the incapacity to reach desire, the thirst for an authentic action, and the desire to *make it stop*. In his complete surrender to the demons of the divided self – withdrawal and passivity – Warhol discovered his autonomy, his power, and what once seemed his immunity. But, if he was able to make his peace with inauthenticity, others could not.

Warhol's avenging demon turns out to be not suicide, but murder.

Still, for a time the strategy seemed flawless. His conspicuous withdrawal allowed him both his image of autonomy and the gratification of being *seen* on a scale known to few artists in history. His psychological game of presence and absence is intimately related to the Duchampian logic he raided for his capacity to act as an artist, and film gave him the means to hypostasize that condition with a fullness and variety previously unknown to him. Combing the psychological and aesthetic strategies, Warhol discovered the key to becoming the complete master of his narcissistic compulsions, and, by using both of them to diffract and dissociate those compulsions, he provided himself with a kind of horrible strength and liberty.

Finally, Warhol has brought the dissociation of sensibility to the most pathological elements of the American desperation – such as stardom – and subdued them to himself. Divide and conquer. As the word proclaims, stardom is a metaphor. He will shine. He will be remote, majestic, untouchable, simultaneously adored and self-contained. That's a contradiction: *the* narcissistic contradiction. Perhaps it is also a metaphor. As we know, Warhol's style is dissociative, which is what kept him out of Hollywood – and, as for metaphors, one of his principle artistic procedures is to untie the knot of metaphor. And he has untied the metaphor of the star to become one who is seen because he sees, one present because he is absent, a star who is in fact a stargazer. And, in this reflectiveness, he has discovered his fame and his life ∎

RIO LIMPO

'LONESOME COWBOYS' AND GAY CINEMA

MARK FINCH

Fundamentally, being gay in the 60s consisted of refusing to be anything else. Self-assertion – the refusal to play straight – was the dominant political tactic; the problem was, what to be? If the two options for being homosexual were being camp or in the closet, what was gay? In 1967 Stonewall – a night of riots, the yardpost for the start of the gay movement – was two years away, but lesbian and gay communities were already organised; the set menu for political activity was street-based zaps, marches and sit-ins. Yet there was always this problem of what to be, or, specifically, what to wear. Gay politics rested on making the invisible visible, a metamorphosis enacted largely at the level of the representational – hence radical drag. Increasingly, moustached men on marches would appear in slingbacks and jockstraps, fishnets and bikers' jackets. Drag – the couture culture of passing for the other sex – has a long tradition with gay men and women, but radical drag had less to do with masquerade and was more about a reckless mix of gender signs, about being neither straightforwardly masculine nor feminine. This male-led spike-heeled costume excluded women, who for reasons of history can't get – and probably don't want – the same shock value from polyester suits and button-down collars; nevertheless, radical drag became a marker for the later 60s liberation, even spinning off into smaller all-drag posses, like The Sisters of Perpetual Indulgence (bearded nuns on a mission of mercy) and, in theatre, San Francisco's The Cockettes, and the New York troupe Hot Peaches.

Beneath this make-up and political playfulness was an awkward refusal: we're neither ordinary men nor women, neither invisible nor one of the old stereotypes. This is a problem too for cinema: how to represent homosexuality? The difficulty is that there is no 'natural' representational vocabulary, just as there is no 'natural' way to be a homosexual. What there is has been invented, like Hollywood's repertoire of sissy queers and butch bar dykes, and the gay slang of camp. Underground and other non-realist film-makers are in a good position to gain some leverage on the problem. Warhol's non-narrative films – like any of the avant-garde – have never found favour with a broad gay audience, and there's certainly no reason why they should have done in the late 60s. But it seems to me that, almost despite themselves, Lonesome Cowboys and the gay movement of its time get the same flavour of refusal from pretty dissimilar ingredients.

There are lots of arguments about what constitutes gay cinema. On the one hand, is gay cinema a history of openly gay artists, like Fassbinder and Cocteau? Or is gay cinema an engagement with Hollywood's homosexual images, or a more subtle search for subtextual traces (Whale, Arzner, Garbo)? And then there's the 'by, for and about' argument – that gay cinema is by, for

Paul America in My
Hustler, *1965*

and about gay people, which lassoes gay pornography but little else. Arguably, *Lonesome Cowboys* rides over all these concepts: described by Richard Dyer (the only critic to exhaust underground cinema from all gay positions), Warhol is probably 'the most famous openly gay artist who ever lived'[1]; *Lonesome Cowboys* certainly isn't Hollywood but it does take cues from mainstream conventions, as well as joke about the Western's habit for homoeroticism; and at the same time Warhol well knows how to produce something that looks like porn, even if he doesn't want to.

Nevertheless, *Cowboys*' gay bite comes from outside of these categories. This is not to say that Warhol's Western isn't other things also, or that it is therefore somehow progressive, but that there's something about the film's floundering form (and, within that, its languid gestures) which fits with the form and feel of late 60s North American gay culture.

Cowboys doesn't lay any claims to being a political statement. Essentially the film is a series of loosely connected confrontations between individual members of an outlaw gang and the

Joe Dallesandro and Tom Hompertz in Lonesome Cowboys, *1967*

town's trio; they drink, fight, but mostly talk. To suggest Warhol might have intended any conscious political message would merely raise a weak smile from anyone who's had to sit through some of *Cowboys*' more excruciating stoned-out scenes; at times the experience is like being trapped, teetotal, at the fag-end of a sodden, bad party. Distractedly the camera picks up on certain details often unrelated to the garbled, drunken conversation; these might just as easily be a beercan as a bare chest. Yet, *Lonesome Cowboys* originally comes on like porn, to a pacey, inapt title song. With the camera static, Viva seduces blonde-haired trailhand Tom Hompertz; fully clothed, they kiss passionlessly. Viva fumbles with Tom's fly, and he has problems pulling off her trousers, but they persist. She entreats him to part with his shorts ('If I don't do it now I'll never do it') and finally they start to fuck. I say fuck, but after a vigorous start Tom lies slumped at an angle while Viva thrusts her hips desultorily, at a distance from his body which makes genital contact fairly implausible. It's neither simulated sex, nor *simulated* simulated sex, a parody of porn; Viva and Hompertz and Warhol suggest they can't even be bothered to go through the act of pretending.

From tawdry to tundra: after the Times Square titles we're in a one-street Arizona outpost, with a grab-bag of genre giveaways and what even seems like the start of some character detail. Viva, the town's prostitute 'Romona', and her nurse, Taylor Mead, zig-zag drunkenly across the street in search of boys as, in the distance, a band of horseback outlaws mosey towards them. Excited and panicked, Mead suggests to Viva that they 'pretend we're used to people being around in this place'. With the cowboys foreground, Warhol cuts between their expressionless close-ups as Mead and Viva dish deadpan, voice-over: 'I think they've got mascara on', 'He has false eyelashes', etc. The Sheriff – Francis Francine – arrives, but is clearly bored by the gang leader's protests at this verbal

assault. The scene peters out in a post-synched conversation over Romona's sexual appetite.

The point is its pointlessness, of course. But more than that: *Lonesome Cowboys* shows that it can be clever – it can ape porn (the first scene), or Westerns (the second), but really doesn't want to. The sense is not of Warhol trying by failing, but of someone who can't even be bothered to pretend. It's not that the film is failed porn; it just doesn't want to bother (in an unusual burst of energy, Viva and Tom Hompertz later play-act at sex with a chairleg and other props; but to his suggestions 'let's really do it!' she parries the punchline 'Fuck off' and the scene ends)., Strikingly, *Lonesome Cowboys* comes up with a scenario that America's new gay porn industry was about to grow rich on (bored straight boys with nothing to do but fuck) and then walks away from the game. Early on, the outlaws argue, scratch, piss, throw beer at each other, and then set upon the especially irritating Eric Emerson with scrum-like cries of 'Brand him! Brand him!'; by the end this uptight machismo gives way to scenes like cowpokes Hompertz ('Julian') and Dallesandro ('Little Joe') discussing eloping to California, maybe. In as much as it offers any momentum, *Lonesome Cowboys* – unlike the sex films of a Warhol contemporary, Pat Rocco (*Mondo Rocco*, *Marco of Rio*, *Sex and the Single Gay*) – moves from camaraderie to coming out with barely a grope.

Even the comparison with late-60s softcore porn gives the film a trajectory which it languidly declines. Similarly, to talk about *Lonesome Cowboys* as a kind of Western gives it a spurious shape. Aside from its title and setting there's only a mean sprinkling of key Western moments: the ride into town, the love scene, the walk into sunset. When the gang is first filmed in close-up the voice-over of Mead and Viva ('Maybe they're real men', 'He's cute') proposes a witty take on the genre, like two movie queens overheard in the back row. But Warhol foils any sustained satire with cuts to doped-out Viva (visibly not part of any familiar Western *mise en scène*) and through drowned sound. Again, it's as if *Lonesome Cowboys* were showing its capability, but then announcing that it's too bored to continue.

If *Cowboys* refused to be porn or a Western, there's a more interesting way in which it also refused to be an underground film. In the 60s, other underground gay film-makers like Anger, Markopoulos, Jack Smith and the Kuchar brothers slipped into the pool of sexuality, but each in a different fashion. Anger may have (in 1967) just left behind the charged montage of *Kustom Kar Kommandos* and *Scorpio Rising*, but his magical films are just as driven; likewise, Markopoulos' yoking of mythology with wedding cake structures of sound and image is strongly motivated; and Smith will scream and scream at the camera until you don't know what's right or awry with the world, and certainly till you don't care. Broadly, each has a rigour because each needs a form for its introspection; *Invocation of My Demon Brother*, *Blonde Cobra*, *Twice a Man* and *Hold Me While I'm Naked* are all – with degrees of irony – about getting at inner states. *Lonesome Cowboys* couldn't care less about anyone's psyche. Various characters make gestures – Eric has a droll monologue about narcissism ('You're out here so much you have all this love in your body, you get lonesome and build up so much love for yourself for so long that you can't find anybody that you love as much as yourself . . .') which could function as a key moment in the film but which trails out in contradictoriness; Viva kills herself after having the best achievable sex, but it's a joke. No one is interested in explaining sexuality, not least the film-maker. At a fundamental level there's an ambiguity about the cowboys' object choice; the town's residents – Mead, Viva and the Sheriff – have a rough idea of what they like (men, and dressing up), but the out-of-town boys seem equally interested in each other and Viva and nothing at all. There is a rape scene, of sorts, but it's even more desultory

than anything before it. Viva is set upon by the gang but her assailants are really more into horsing around with each other. Whereas Anger and Kuchar often bandy about examples of 'good' and 'bad' sexuality – the first, preparatory part of *Scorpio Rising* versus the later wild party; *Hold Me While I'm Naked*'s unrepressed extras versus Kuchar's self-mockingly plugged-up protagonist - Warhol proposes no schema (although, as Richard Dyer notes, the opposition of townspeople and outlaw gang offers this potential[2]): his characters are not just psychically and sexually amorphous, they're unclassifiable.

On the film's London re-release in 1984 reviewers in the gay press talked of the film's eroticism, which is surprising, because even at the level of being into the boys' bodies, Warhol can't be that bothered. Exceptionally (and specifically) Tom Hompertz is rather eroticised; he's the most muscular and tanned of the outlaws, and is also the newest (Eric Emerson bitches about him). In the fitful first scene it's his rear that occupies most of the frame, and at one point the camera moves in on his back muscles; later there's a long-held silent shot of Julian washing his face and chest. Aside from this, it is Viva who is the film's sexual centre; narratively (as the prostitute who has slept or will sleep with all the men) and photographically (her white emaciated body is the counterpoint to Tom's; she is nude in at least half her scenes). Of course, nudity isn't the only entrance for eroticism, but the meandering 'plot' is well-met by an unfocused sexual gaze.

Another tactic of the 60s underground is to *show* everything. There's two senses to that: to go to far degrees in the continuum of 'explicitness' (Brakhage's childbirth home movies; Anger's fellated Christ), and to put on a show (Dwoskin's uncomfortable long-held snapshots; Ron Rice's *Chumlum* and Jack Smith's *Flaming Creatures*). With *Cowboys* (unlike, say, *Couch*), Warhol refuses to *show* (explicit sex) but gestures that we can look anyway. It's not a well-what's-your-response? voyeurism; rather, it precisely questions the function of that provocation. On one occasion Warhol's troupe get energised and put on a show – the Sheriff, more sober and less drugged than other characters, drags up for one of Romona's client's; the other boys try on dresses and fool around for a few minutes – performed and filmed like a stage number; but the rest is about as showy as watching someone get stoned (which is what they do, persistently).

What I'm describing is the film's refusal to be

something other than what it is, although the word refusal suggests a rigour belied by its languid quality. *Lonesome Cowboys* is something like a chaise longue in the scene of gay cinema; whilst porn, political diarists and other undergrounders get to grips with the chances in political formation, Warhol sidesteps everything and reclines. If *Lonesome Cowboys* has a consistent quality, it is limpness. The cowboys slouch, their horses dawdle into town; Julian can't get it in, let alone up; the soundtrack shambles in and out of audibility. This is crucially not the same as limp-wristedness – it's Limp, not camp. Camp is a familiar but contestable strategy for gay cinema; on the one hand it can be

seen as an authentic expression from gay culture, a vocabulary and attitude which ironises everything; on the other hand camp has been described as simply self-oppressive or, more complexly, arbitrary in its post-modern playfulness (what's real? what's behind camp?). There are other problems with camp too; it has to be seen historically and culturally (camp may have been a subversive language in 50s New York, but what does it mean in 1980s Newcastle?). The point about camp is that – like all forms of irony – it is predicated upon knowledge; to be camp you have to be 'worldly'. To be limp you just have to be what you are.

It's not that Mead and Viva and Emerson aren't camp (God, no: 'You heard of the James brothers?' 'The *Jane* brothers?') but that the film's form – and forms of refusal – fits more closely with the just-say-no (or what-to-wear) strand of gay liberation I touched on at the start. Even apart from this textural coincidence, there are other points of resonance (Eric's stoned-to-camera song: 'I want to stay by myself in the sun . . . and here I am, being myself'), but these are more easily explicable as gay and drug culture jokes. What makes *Cowboys* exciting and difficult to write about at the same time is the absence of easy links between the film's form and this crucial moment in civil rights politics. In Warhol's brimming history, *Lonesome Cowboys* clearly isn't unique; but for gay cinema it kicks up a key question of how such a tight coincidence can come about. By the end of the 60s the gay movement had stemmed its dilemma through both separatism and a less controversial message ('we're just like you'), all of which made Warhol look anachronistic and silly, but the question still stands: what is the relation between the messages of the gay movement and the shape of gay-authored art? ■

Notes
1 Richard Dyer, *Now You See It: Historical Studies in Lesbian and Gay Film* [working title] (London: forthcoming Routledge and Kegan Paul, 1990).
2 Ibid.

'THE THIRTEEN MOST BEAUTIFUL WOMEN AND 'KITCHEN'

PETER GIDAL

From *Undercut* **no. 1, March–April 1981**

The question of a filmtime which *contradicts* in its machinations that of dominant cinema, both fiction and documentary. The unstopped duration, the concrete material passage of time 'upon something', foregrounds the lack of edit.

But this is not therefore 'more real', it is the particular, concrete, i.e. the remnant, that which is cut from the rest. It doesn't stand for the rest, is thus not a symbol or metaphor. And it doesn't allow you to be in a position of knowing the rest from it (logical deduction, rationalist truth, etc.). It presents itself, its apparatus, as one *extreme* function (therefore as arbitrary), choice, a selection, a part, a difference. A relation, thus, between the time of the film's passage through the projector and the time of the film's passage through the camera, *and* the time of 'the' film's reception (thus) by the viewer. Thus a concept which proposes the existence of 'shot' in cinema as dialecticisable.

It (unending duration) positions the viewer in a place of seeing, i.e. perception, without conflating that into knowing (as it is one extreme function, not *the* whole), without mixing the two up. The separation of the two underlies avant garde film practice from Warhol on.

So, each moment, each film-moment, is a specificity, inseparable from the mechanism (of its reproduction) and from one's relation and thought (and unthought expectations) to it. The filmapparatus, in other words, can't be metaphysically subtracted from the film, from the effects produced, which are given, here, as specific transformations of and in film and film-meaning. This opposes conventional film fiction or documentary which always necessarily disallows a production of effects presented. In such film we are in an imaginary space, and imaginary time, a seamlessness, a whole, in a position of our seeing equalling our knowing, 'science' and 'fantasm' becoming one, etc.

Of course always each effect is a specific effect of film in film. But Warhol's work here is a begin to such problematic being *engaged*. (I am overreacting further into the problematic than any one Warhol film singularly does.)

I am talking of the film as a work with its problematics, in the context of what (other films) we are about to see, as often advances help elucidate the prior, which may have had certain aspects submerged in certain other, at the specific historical time more dominant readings (such as with the Warhol films, the specific profilmic event; though in *form* that problem is constant. The different profilmic *contents* take on differing orders of importance in different historical moments).

Thus for example the subject matter of Warhol now seen with a difference, or even a distance, compared to the early 1960s, which does not deny what the film's mechanisms were instituting materially. It isn't as if each moment in history (an

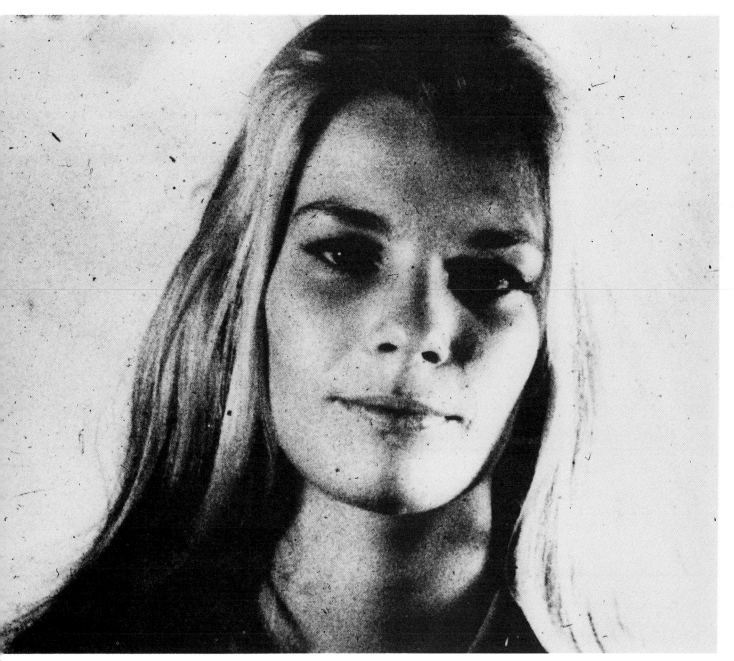

The Thirteen Most
Beautiful Women, *1964*

interruption, or a production), has a different set of contexts and meanings with the film becoming yet again mere pretext for the most suitable. A film, a production, has concrete effects. Opposition too aware of context can become formal play – opposition unaware easily irrelevant (i.e. retrogressive). Leave to later questions of what their final determinations are, and by what they are finally determined.

Problematics in the early Warhol *The Thirteen Most Beautiful Women*: duration, frame, character, viewpoint, illusionist/imaginary space (depth),

The Thirteen Most
Beautiful Women, *1964*

sound. The silence, durable, brings itself forth versus the possibilities of (imagined) offscreen sound. This 'imagining' is not some poetic act on viewer's part, but rather, the imagining constructed by cinema in the sound-cinema epoch. Any vacuum established, any 'timelessness' that is produced as a thought or feeling from this film is thus in opposition to something else, something not there, sound. Thus a constant defence against a difference, and a constant problematisation: why this not that (these questions do not come up when the dominant given conventions are fully utilised, there are then no absences, always nothing as part

of something, always something as part of something. Always a fullness perceived in that other system (consciously or unconsciously in the way one is positioned, finally, in knowingness). The vacuum established in that noiseless period of duration is full as the noise in so many other Warhol films (*Kitchen*), machines rattling, banging, moving, cups being moved, people, appliances, etc. In *The Thirteen Most Beautiful Women* silence makes discrete from whatever else there 'is'. Again and again it brings one back to the film, its concrete abstractions: concrete, as in a specific series of effects, images, relations . . . abstract, as in meanings, philosophical materialisations, inseparable from the material unreeling. Limit is the film's 100 ft. 'end' (or 1200 ft. 'end') not ontological and necessary but a convenience given as such (enough is enough, philosophically and materially).

The image in *The Thirteen Most Beautiful Women* is a head staring back . . . the question of the given line from your eye through the camera-person's, the cameralens, through to the subject to be identified into, who, looking back, becomes the object of your viewing, but this as in all cinema, only here foreground, made (un)clear . . . specifically resituating the viewer *from* that line. The shift for the viewer, for his/her identifications, takes place: am I, viewer, as behind and through the camera-eye therefore film-maker, identified (by the apparatus or by my self) with (in this case) him, or with some person in the unseen space? The subject of the film looks into that space; our identification mechanism would allow that. In fact where is the justification given to make that clean decision of identification into the one or other, or are we not constantly undermined in our knowing where that identity is, placing us in unknowingness. Inability to grasp the truth of a representation, and the problem of sexuality in the making of that 'truth': wherein is sexuality the emanation of a biological given: in *The Thirteen Most Beautiful Women* is any facial enactment feminine and if so, how is that act ingratiated, the character producing it constituted by it? Is it not, conversely, visage as visage, the voyeuristic camera-stare which premises a (repressed or not) stare back. This latter would be an obsessive engagement with staring and staring back predicted on the materialism and the specified historical moment given: two stares.

The above points to a realism, but one not of reproducing a series of meanings, or even questioning them, but of *enacting* a *procedure* inseparable from the mode and process of film and cinema. The determining factor historical not eternal is the process of attempted reproduction, i.e. the cinematic apparatus. Also, in *Kitchen*, sexed positioning always is an enactment taking account of the camera to whom it is addressed and to film which in its unceasingness makes demands, aggresses by its refusal to abstain. Sexual role-playing within the script in *Kitchen* is imbricated with this apparatus cinema which is one point in the circle as opposed to a viewing-plane here looking at a viewed plane of theatre there. Little is left when the process is ended. It might do to remember that in most cinema much is left, most of the meaning is left, retained, extracted, the process long having been concluded, and it might do to remember that surplus meaning, that value retained, is precisely surplus value in meaning, expropriated, resultant from extreme division of labour. So there is a political question in the aesthetic which too must be answered: in whose interest is this exploitation of surplus for consumption (as opposed to institutionalisation of production)? Production is a discourse not a religious 'moment'.

I won't discuss here the more overt parodying of sexual role, and the equation of impotence with male sexuality, and obsessive repetition in compulsive act and speech-act with the active female sexuality, both as parodies of existing conventionalised forms, without an interior logic sustaining the characterisation, no *a priori* whatever. Sure there are economic, sexual,

ideological deteminations but they're not to be historicised away from *this process*. Sexuality and sexed positioning as convoluted, (and hysterical, hysterically funny) disallows the holding on to type, biological or otherwise, Lacan's constant rememoration becoming thereby a memoryless carrying-on, never though in an anarchic forgetting of the closures awaiting each position and the concomitant oppression; thus the next move is motored. The real, as residue, nothing else left, no choice, this material all: such politics. (Note: not anti-psychoanalytic or anti-analytic, just anti-evolutionising to *another* process.) Are we not constantly undermined in our knowing where identity is, placing us in unknowingness. Inability to grasp the truth of a representation, not able, disabled, from our being placed in the position of and in an imaginary fictive or documentary 'real'. Now this could be political if such placing of the viewer is political. If it is not it is not.

A psychologistic interpretation can never be totally voided from any production, and with the Warhols the nihilistic formulation is evident in the movement towards stasis, the constant running out and down, towards entropy, unpleasure principle and deathdrive. Possibly this persistence of movement upon that which moves less produces such a nihilistic stance. But the machine (camera, projector) as unstoppable, durable, and unendurable. *And* 'the cinema' as machine.

In *The Thirteen Most Beautiful Women* any deep-space centre point out from the film (frame) is problematised that is to say it doesn't situate you comfortable within a convention of normalcy in relation to image, narration, etc. . . . you find yourself placed easily with difficulty, somehow recouped by the representation yet viewing it without an end (no narrative which can be followed and no implied narrative which can be phantasmed ahead and then retrospectively justified, made straight and even, technologically) and without end, the moment to moment movement of it always in reference to the moment to moment movement of you, viewer as separated, precisely not co-opted; viewer and viewing as not excised or repressed.

The problem is that from this one could conclude: unrepression. As if there were this blanket or veil which once lifted could betray the (everpresent) truth, whilst the point is precisely not that but the present in a non-metaphysical (i.e. non-eternalised, semiotic, *impossible*) sense: each concrete labour has effects and produces effects and the viewer's incorporation (as a term of relation for that process) is a specific effect which in *Kitchen*

and *The Thirteen Most Beautiful Women* is problematised by not being given as natural and prior to and free from that which constitutes it. Material relations from the 'I'. As such, then, there i no present, as the signifier signifies each moment something not-here.

If the observer is part of the system observed (inasmuch as such words then can have a meanin no forms can precede the perceptual activity, yet course they do (the acetate with its recording of light, producing images) often in early Warhols a stasis through lighting which allows space only to

The Thirteen Most Beautiful Women, *1964*

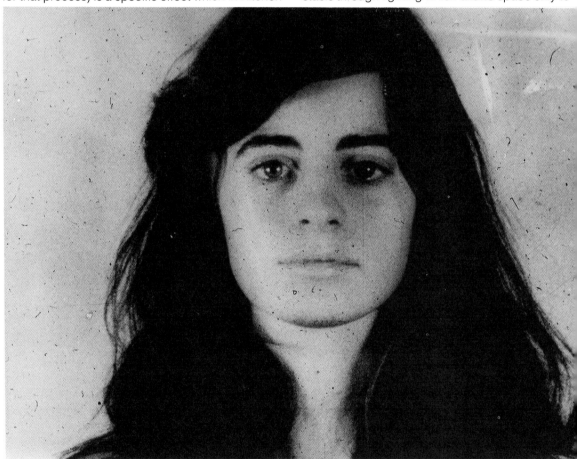

be constituted in and through action, not separate as a 'real representation'. At the same time since ideology resides in all representation, and the viewer is embedded in the ideological, the primary materialist function can hardly be ascribed to the (conscious or unconscious) viewing subject. Here the difficult problem of ideology (in certain interests we are positioned in certain ways) versus the phenomenological comes forth. The short way out of this must be to see the ideological as constantly placing the 'I', a cipher, contradictorily, and oppositionally though not only when a politics of opposition is *chosen* (the contradictory objective placing through ideology may always include oppositionality but the latter for various historical reasons of each individual in relation to what ideology in fact is, is usually repressed not to say suppressed). Ontology and epistemology are not divorced but seem so, – the phenomenal must be seen as the non-existent but phenomenal. Self as cipher as effect of apparatus' ineffable stare (duration): and as cause which in turn is an effect of another, political, apparatus. So in fact all film practice a negation practice, not a constituting different practice which can then be fetishised difference, fetishising difference, as substitute for stylistic.

No intention.

The actor's role 'vis-à-vis' or rather *in* the film image ('acting') and the question of any represented self as opposed to a character taken up and dropped and not even that by some 'one' but by a 'one' inseparable from those characterisations which destroy not only narrative but character. Thus the unfixed locus of the actor's presenting of self, the support structure for the 'aura' 'of' 'the image' is in Warhol's early films fragile and constantly re-situated, a series of poses, all of which are given as a series of poses, none of which are given as poses which could be dislocated from a real underneath. Thus an anti-psychological notion of character.

Note on *Kitchen*: Characters in and outside the film are constantly almost 'caught', held in by the reflection of the mirror played with by Edie, which (through prior knowledge) we realise is capable of freezing an image or framing one which may not be the 'right' one for the scene; a tension is set up precisely because of the mirror's capacity as active term, rather than mere reflector of that which is given as correct or purposeful. Edie's playing with the mirror reflects from within the space though alluding to a without which could not be the space of the audience but is (impossibly) 'there'. The viewer's identification into that space becomes problematised as Edie's view wavers from the interior space to the cameralens and viewer to those behind. This is all play, a chattering down to silence, remembering of lines then resuscitated by copies of the script . . . impossible to nail down the 'real' dialogues, monologues, etc. Same goes for the sudden changes of mood, in high camp. The film thus also a learning instrument, didactic, a procedure presented, a dialectic of/in film as to its possibilities: redundant in the natural's constant capitulation to labour.

Roles and masks are never metaphysically united in a body: spirit or essence are not found to reside anywhere at all. The residue of all this is politics and ideology, material history. It is as if such work were the process of a culture which no longer necessarily reproduces the bourgeois, thus the work is in advance of the present. Such work is also to remain unseen, denied, elided, unprocessed, etc., as the contradictions increase and their 'author's' position increasingly has a different objective (meaning). Andy Warhol is not the work, is of no interest to the work, though producer. Conflict even there, as in the contradiction in the films between the material support of film as physically foregrounded and presented (duration, grain, light/dark, focus, frame, camera-movement, stillness, etc.) and the fixing or impossibility thereof of whatever representation it is that is 'filmed' ■

WARHOL WAVES
ANDY WARHOL AND THE BRITISH AVANT-GARDE

A. L. REES

'I said to Sitney at dinner in July: I have found your structuralists, P. Adams, and they are in England. Complete to the diacritical mark, influence of Warhol, the whole number.' Hollis Frampton, 1972

'The formal direction of much recent European work was already initiated before the American influence, and certainly before Sitney's American structuralists were heard of in Europe.' Malcolm Le Grice, 1977

The influence of Andy Warhol was felt by two waves of British avant-garde film-makers separated by a generation; the first in the 1960s and the second a decade later. The earlier movement, in the period of the 'structural' film, had the more theorised response to Warhol, interpreting his work in a distinctly European context. The more recent trend, which like its predecessor began on the fringes of youth culture, showed a new interest in Warhol's exotic and baroque aspects, thus assimilating him back into the milieu of Jack Smith and Kenneth Anger, from which structural film theory had tended to divide him.

Warhol's influence has been exerted less on the films and more on the ideas produced by film-makers, in both of these epochs. The ways in which they saw Warhol explains something about the ways in which they saw themselves, perhaps more than is usually the case when influence is at work, because Warhol's own anti-interpretative stance allowed for what Harold Bloom calls 'strong misreadings' to be made.[1]

A further reason for Warhol's essentially theoretical impact was that his films were – and still are – rarely shown, with a few exceptions such as *The Chelsea Girls*. Near-illicit prints still circulate, the rarity of his films adding to their quasi-underground allure; they are still better known by report and rumour than by being seen.[2] What survives from this mixture of high status and low visibility (perhaps shared in the early part of the structural era by the Straubs and Vertov) were the ideas and implications the work arouses.

In so far as this is true, it backs up the claims made by most of the earlier English film-makers that their own movement in the 1960s had found its direction before the American avant-garde were widely shown here, their point being to stress European autonomy from American domination. The claim was important, and strongly tied to a highly revisionist (and ultimately narrow) account of the American avant-garde, but primacy is not the only issue. Understanding Warhol's British reception reveals something new about his work, just as it maps out the major moves of British avant-garde film-making.

The more recent generation shares several things with the earlier one against which it rebelled, including a taste for Warhol along with a dearth of his work and the awareness that he is better known

...erard Malanga in
...ifferin, 1966

as an artist and stylist than as a film-maker. But this also accords with a revived interest in image-making among the younger group, replacing the structuralists' concern for Warholian ideas such as the long-take or deliberate inaction. Through his style and imagery, therefore, Warhol has filtered through the generation gap into this later wave of film-making; perhaps returned to his roots, but also arguably less radical.

The leading structural film-maker and polemicist Malcolm Le Grice summarised the key tenets of the early movement in his 1977 book *Abstract Film and*

Berlin Horse, 1970 by Malcolm Le Grice

Beyond. Le Grice's account is not impartial, but is a closely argued defence of formal film and contemporary British film-making. Admitting the 'undeniable influence' of the underground, he also proleptically claimed that the European formal tendency was 'already initiated before the American influence, and certainly before Sitney's structuralists were heard of in Europe'. Only after 'the new movement was under way' were underground films widely shown.

David Curtis' pungent and vivid 'Chronology' of the British avant-garde (first published in a film issue of *Studio International* in 1975) supports this view, with his first-hand evidence in programming

for all the major venues of the period, from clubs and bookstores to the still active workshop at the London Film Makers' Cooperative (LFMC). But eve though the bulk of US films only arrived in 1968 – deposited by Sitney in the wake of a major European tour – Curtis also notes that the English were aware of the American movement, and Warh had long been a staple of the colour supplements The key question is how this work was understood rather than what came first. Le Grice recognised Warhol's 'provocative, neo-Dada' aspect, but (like Stephen Koch) largely dismissed it. The European preferred to cultivate their own forms of aggressio (some of which, especially in Germany and Austria had a Dadaist side), as in the hard-line rigour of Kurt Kren or the Heins as well as in the openly raw and random films and performance-work of the British. All saw themselves as beyond anarchism, an era dominated by protest at the Vietnam war. A similar partisanship occluded English vision of the native anti-Hollywood core to the American avant-garde, including Warhol's own mirror-image paroc of the Star System. The fiercely anti-narrative Britis avant-garde perhaps had no need of this distinguishing mark of the US avant-garde, having its own innate hostility to commercial film product of all kinds. But the result was a somewhat undifferentiated view of American culture, in which its avant-garde was blurred in with a general attac on US imperialism – cultural and otherwise.

If Warhol's Hollywood relations were undervalued here, his place in the art world was n ignored. Like the British movement itself, Warhol had turned to film-making as an expansion of painting and live performance. Warhol thus confirmed the British tendency to see itself as 'struggling for new cinematic form . . . referring to other areas of art than cinema', as Le Grice put it. An exact counterpoint is given by the only British-based writer alive to Warhol's very American involvement with the Hollywood image, Stephen Dwoskin, who states of the US avant-garde that 'reference to the arts gets crossed with the more traditional cinema'.

Dwoskin's unjustly neglected book *Film Is* (1975) is unique in the British context for an even-handed enthusiasm that encompasses both the underground and the structural film. It opens with Joan Adler's free-form evocation of Jack Smith's anarchic milieu, which overlaps with Warhol's. In his section on the underground, Dwoskin develops the theme that American film-makers were Hollywood's children: 'the movies had been part of the environment, as much as Campbell's soup.'

New generations now saw them on TV (in Kenneth Anger's *Scorpio Rising*, a leatherclad bike boy watches roll-bar Brando to a rock soundtrack).

For Dwoskin, Hollywood gave the US avant-garde a 'shape of thinking', a play of real and unreal, emptyness and fulness, which can be seen in films by Ron Rice (*The Queen of Sheba Meets the Atom Man*), the Kuchars (*Hold Me While I'm Naked*) and Andy Warhol (*Tarzan and Jane Regained, Sort Of*). The same shape is detectable in the cult of superstars (Ingrid Superstar, Maria/Mario Montez) and Monroe. These aspects were of little interest to Le Grice's account of the period, but they underpin Dwoskin's internationalist vision.[3]

To Le Grice, Warhol was important because he opened up in his films the fundamental question of time, 'film's primary dimension' – a 1978 definition which accords with Dwoskin's statement, 'it is *time* which is film's quality', a phrase he used when discussing Warhol's 'purest of films', *Empire*. Le Grice saw Warhol's extra-long-take films, of which *Empire* is the best known, as part of a historical break; 'he showed that the experience of duration as a concrete dimension could be achieved simply by the prolonged exposure to long periods of inactivity, and, by relating it to the commonplace, robbed it of any romantic, epic implications' (i.e., it was quite distinct from Brakhage's 4½-hour introspective epic *The Art of Vision*, which Le Grice criticized for its subjectivism while affirming its 'procedural' and structural side).

Warhol's 'temporal economy', his organisation of time, was also of interest beyond its anti-subjectivist bias and its overt challenge to the montage tradition in the underground cinema. The 'one-to-one' relation of shooting and viewing time (as in *Couch*, *Kiss* and – most notoriously – *Empire*), however Dada-tinged, led in Le Grice's view to a breakdown of illusionism through 'functional boredom'. The result was a 'new cinematic concept, that of representational equivalence in duration', the only 'counter-act to illusion in the representation of time'.

In these ideas were summarised some unique features of the British avant-garde. To this degree, Warhol helped it find its voice and some of its formal characteristics. Le Grice candidly mused that he doubted if Warhol himself understood all the implications of his work, and in this respect – the way in which it was given a British twist – he may be right. David Curtis points out that some of Warhol's most striking and remarked innovations, such as the sudden flash-frame of the 'strobe cut' or his very long takes, were beyond the means of his British admirers. What was more directly ripe for expansion, however, was Warhol's emphasis on the sheer physicality of film, including his blatantly simple joining of one roll of film to another, flare and fade included, to make up a sequence.

Warhol's emphasis on the material qualities of film is clarified by the different ways in which Dwoskin and Le Grice look at the photo-realist or quasi-documentary aspect of his work. Heir to Maya Deren's belief in the accuracy of the photographic image, its bedrock 'authority' (her word), Dwoskin states that in Warhol's films 'things are simply as they are'. To Deren's iconic argument (in which photographs resemble their objects to record, as she says, 'the way things are'), can be contrasted Le Grice's indexical understanding of the medium: 'as a direct physico-chemical extension from the events which it records, the photographic element of cinematography should be considered as a material rather than an illusionist factor.'

Le Grice's interest in the physical substrate of film went beyond its rendering of the image, and here he parts company with Dwoskin's claim that 'it is being photographically actual that is film's property' (just as time was 'film's quality'). From 1966, when he built his first home-made printer, to the period a few years later when professional printing machinery was installed at the LFMC, Le Grice was among many British film-makers who argued that film's primary material (emulsion, grain, surface marks, framing) should not be privileged over the image it yields. This position was open to them since, unlike their American counterparts, British film-makers applied a direct 'hands-on' principle to production, which included manipulating the print itself.

Several issues are raised here, which show that Warhol's ideas were elaborated in very different ways to his own practice. Direct work on the print, extended duration and expanded 'camera-procedures' all affirmed the fine-art origin of British work in the era of conceptualism. Like the informal nature of many early screenings, the stress on raw materialism and experiments with multi-projection (obliquely linked to Warhol's light-shows) pointed to a new equalisation of artist and viewer through 'exposing the device' and breaking down familiar cinematic values. Le Grice found a literal figure for these ideas in the equation between a film's shooting time and its 'performance' in projection time.

Just as these were distinct from Warhol's more ironic stance in relation to the reworking of film form, so too the British gave his films a social interpretation which differed from Warhol's ambiguous critique of US mores. Eliding or extending film duration was seen to challenge the social determination of time, from office, school, home and factory to the 'standard length' of the commercial movie. Warhol had shown that the massive expansion of time could give a genuine shock to the system. It was only the most overt instance of an attack, promoted by the British, on the idea of spectatorship and on traditional hierarchies and values. An assault on the assumed 'passivity' of the spectator, and an attempt to raise the act of viewing to self-conscious apperception, was shared by radical groups across 'party' and political divides (including, by the mid-70s, the Co op, *Screen*, and the Independent Film-makers' Association).

The post-Warholian British stress on film as a process in which maker and spectator both participated had as its symmetrical flip-side the literal 'processing' of the material by the artist. Warhol's dictum, 'I set up the camera and walked away' – was transposed or reversed into the European notion of predetermining the film's shape by visual scores, camera movements, time-lapse, angle of shooting and choice of location (as in many early films by Le Grice, William Raban, Chris Welsby, Kurt Kren and others).

If these factors, which questioned the received role of the artist, pushed film into the forefront of the advanced arts in the 1970s, it was also linked to a contemporaneous interest in 'primitive cinema', or film before narrative. In the American context,

Warhol's primitivism asserted itself in the simplicity of his means of production coupled with the camp and parody of the Factory, which stressed personal regression as a form of play. Self-conscious regressive fantasies had been explored in the underground from Brakhage's psychodramas to Jack Smith's infantile persona in *Blonde Cobra*. British work, with the rare and vivid exception of Jeff Keen, ignored this and concentrated on formal questions, leading to what Deke Dusinberre called its 'ascetic tendency'.

Messages, *1981–83 by Guy Sherwin*

The interest of the avant-garde in a new history of film, especially of its earliest and most mutable period, was shared by Brakhage, Le Grice, Klaus Wyborny and others (among the much older film-makers, Hans Richter, Stefan Themerson and Sidney Peterson had also explored this uncharted zone of cinema history). Fragments of early film often strayed into their works (as in Le Grice's *Berlin Horse*), but the more general impact of primitivist values is seen in a 'back-to-basics' philosophy of film-making. Together with the unstated urge to reveal one's own origins, and a very much stated impulse to expose the process of production, the British adopted primitivism as a politico-ethical position, well attuned to the craft-based ethos of the English art schools as well as the most recent debates about minimal art. Only Peter Gidal has perhaps kept aloof from the primitive-film, partly because of its realist illusionism. His unique reading of Warhol is expressed most recently in his book *Materialist Film* (1989). Like Dwoskin, Gidal had spent time in the Factory during the 1960s, and in 1971 had published the first study of Warhol's films.

Rather than Le Grice's materials-based account of Warhol's film-making, Gidal characteristically stresses the level of difficulty – of 'decipherment' – in watching the films. This deliberate art of difficulty has been cultivated by Gidal himself in films that range from *Upside Down Feature* in 1972–3 to his recent *Denials* (1985) and *Guilt* (1987–8).

In *Kitchen*, for example, Warhol 'plays constantly on the actors' awareness of the camera, of seeing and being seen', so that a stable identity for the characters is never established. Warhol's sexual parodies have no recourse to metaphor, his stars and personae are always 'in process or fluctuation'. Warhol thus becomes exemplary for Gidal's stringent attack on all forms of presence in film, of which the illusionist narrative is sign and symbol.

He thus retains the British ethico-political critique and applies it where it might least be expected, since Warhol's films have usually been

seen as records of direct self-exposure (from *The Thirteen Most Beautiful Women* to Ondine in *The Chelsea Girls*). In *Couch*, Gidal argues, the viewer's voyeurism is revealed and turned back on itself, made self-reflective. Other films undercut normal patterns of identification and memory in film viewing. The sparse style and fixed frame enforce a direct presentation of cinema itself. The effect of Warhol's films is iconoclastic; under the exposure, there is no self.

As with the near-arbitrary assemblage of sequences by the joining together of standard-length rolls, Gidal finds a similarly unsettling and disturbing aspect of Warhol's counter-narrative cinema in the opening three minutes of *The Chelsea Girls*. Again the example is surprising, taken from a film with cult status. Nico's askew close-up reveals for Gidal a complex play of fictive against real space, and is thus at the core of the anti-narrative project. Like Walter Benjamin, the argument asserts that the ambiguity of meaning forces a self-reflective state in which fixed forms are dissolved and certainties are questioned.

Throughout the 1970s, and up to the present day, Gidal has remained a vocal theorist and film-maker. If, as David Curtis says, Warhol's impact on the British scene was largely co-extensive with Gidal's arrival in London, so that Warhol's formal innovations arrived 'as already codified by Gidal', his consistent argument has been to reveal Warhol's radicalism. During the 1970s, he became almost a lone voice for 'structural-materialism'. In this period, not coincidentally, Warhol's impact faded. Interest turned to new forms of narrative, while for several of the post-structural film-makers the example of Warhol was combined with the cubists and abstract expressionists (Will Milne's *Christ or Feathers*, Nicky Hamlyn's *Guesswork*) or seen in relation to Anger and Genet, as by Jayne Parker in, for example, her film *I Dish*.

The one exception was Ron Lane, who was working in Wolverhampton and London during the mid-70s, at a time of the first reactions against structural hegemony. Lane's films did not follow the general line of revolt (Brecht-Godard-Straub influenced), but proclaimed their toughness and provocation, with Warhol as their recognised predecessor. Insistently hand-printed, grainy close-ups and long-held shots were as potentially disturbing as the often overt sexual content. Like most work of the period, all action – or lack of it – was interior-shot. Starkly silent, the films had minimal narratives and slow, gestural acting. An edge of raw realism recalled the earliest, most troubling, Warhols.

Warhol's wider response lessened as his image

The Last of England, *1987 by Derek Jarman*

changed. As an international socialite, he had little to offer the British scene, and in general the earlier films were preferred to the later. The splintering of the structural movement also took place in a more urgent political climate, the Heath-Callaghan years. The turn to new narrative forms, sometimes used as an anti-structuralist slogan, was partly pre-empted by the older generation themselves. Le Grice made a neo-narrative 'domestic trilogy', the final film, *Finnegans Chin*, reaching a large TV audience (it also dealt less with process as such, than with the complex codes of sound and montage). William

Almost Out, 1984 by Jayne Parker

Raban and Marion Halford anticipated new work to come in their *Black and Silver* by reinventing symbolism within the framework of the narcissistic dance-film. Lis Rhodes mixed autobiography and structural cinema in *Light Reading*.

The real rebellion came in the later 70s, pioneered by a new generation of students, many of whom had been taught by Le Grice, Gidal, Dwoskin, Welsby and David Parsons. Perhaps the real link between the first and second avant-gardes is provided by less formal contacts, those between the new film-makers and David Larcher. Larcher began as a key figure in the underground cinema. Often abroad, he has made intermittent forays on the

British scene (as with his Channel 4 video-film *EETC*) and continues to work at the Co-op. His first films date from the Royal College of Art in 1967 (where Dwoskin and Gidal later taught, and which was a seedbed for many new tendencies, up to the 'New Romantics' of the 80s).

Larcher's hand-treated and scratch-painted films are perhaps closer to Brakhage than most British work, as is their epic scale and their blend of personal drama and landscape images. Their ambiguous eroticism, and Larcher's interest in games, play and fantasy, bring them closer to the 'Baudelairian Cinema' proclaimed by Jonas Mekas in a review of Jack Smith. Sharing some of the same concerns as the structural movement (process, manipulation, linguistic theory, location), Larcher's films have also integrated an aspect of outrage and extremism that was often excised from Warhol's work by British artists, but which was quickly seized and welcomed by neo-romantic film-makers.

This most recent phase can only be outlined. In contrast to the structural era, the film-makers of the 1980s were not drawn to theory or discussion; far less so, paradoxically, than a mentor from the older generation, Derek Jarman. Jarman's mixture of avant-garde and mainstream, his willingness to mix styles and media, his taste for outrage and his avoidance of academicism were among the near-Warholian qualities which made him a key figure for film-makers in a new period. The image was back, as were club-venues and Beat Film revivals. This generation also revived an avant-garde tradition by fringe-work in the commercial world, so that rock-video techniques filtered into their films and live-action events.

Warhol has a diffuse part in this later chain of developments. His laconic and ironic attitude, his sheer style of being an artist, is perhaps more important than any particular work. In some ways, his influence can be seen in ways that merge formerly distinct impulses. If earlier film-makers extracted the grain of pure modernism from

Warhol's films, the new generation insert him into a looser post-modernist context – less determinate, more open, but with an arguable loss of focus.

The earliest films of John Maybury and Cerith Wyn Evans, for example, recall the Brakhagian psychodrama, but also a performance-art sense of ritual flavoured by overtones of sex and sadism out of Kenneth Anger. Shaven-headed and internalised actors, intermittantly aware of the camera, enact symbolized events to soundtracks which reflect rock, high culture and synthesized sources. In both their contributions to *The Dream Machine* (1984) these elements jostle with Warholian echoes; quasi-voyeuristic camera, hypnotic rhythm and camp myth. They richly uncover a seam of threat and imminent disturbance which can be found in the best of surrealist and underground cinema, and which is intimately bound to the sense of a social crisis which ran through much work of the early 80s, from scratch video to the Miners' Tapes.

In such later films as *Big Love* Maybury explores myth in the stylised manner pioneered by Gregory Markopoulos, and in a performance-based 'rehearsal scene' plays on the mixture of improvisation and confrontation found in mature Warhol. His collage-video *Circus Logic* similarly explores duration and texture. The recent films of Cerith Wyn Evans, such as *Epiphany*, are openly indebted to Kenneth Anger (and – perhaps via Jarman – Sergei Eisenstein), but his contrast between tacky glamour and high technique, and his ability to weave contemporary icons (stars and skinheads) with classic myths, may have a distant Warholian aspect. Such conjunctions are also found in the links betwen these film-makers (and others such as Jarman, Steve Chivers and Sophie Muller), and pop-promo production has also reinvented the traditional link between advanced film/video and avant-garde rock. The Factory – which included 'Andy Warhol's Velvet Underground' – and its European variants from the Arts Lab to the Diorama had explored such connections outside the music industry.

The crucial difference between the early and the later periods of British film-making has been in the gradual move away from critical and self-critical analysis; the equally gradual diffusion of Warhol's image as a film-maker, and the resultant loss of definition, is almost a figure of this development. Interestingly enough, a recent film (*Neon Queen*) by Jean Mathee (who has studied at two key colleges for the British avant-garde movement, the Slade and the Royal College of Art) attempts to weld the two directions. Image-slippage and colour manipulation (both 'structural' hallmarks) are combined with extended duration, minimal change and repetition, but the central image contains vivid and glamorous overtones; tellingly, it is a portrait of Marilyn Monroe, whose reincarnation through Warhol's famous prints is now almost indistinguishable from her own image.

One way to summarise Warhol's impact on the British is by looking at how he was seen to mediate or transform the consumer culture of the USA. This aspect of his work links up his general impact in the 60s, because the repetition of objects (bottles, tins, banknotes, stars) was familiar from his prints and paintings. Their presence was perhaps akin to the slow variation of images in the continuous frames of a filmstrip. While Le Grice regarded Warhol's art as a Dada attack on his society, Dwoskin argued the opposite. He saw Warhol as the necessary artistic product of industrial America, which had long embedded repetition into its culture (such as the objects of Andy's attention – cans, money, stars). Here the artist matches the work of art in the age of mechanical reproduction.

Warhol, in Dwoskin's reading, copied the Hollywood system to become a mirror in which all its values are reversed. 'These children of the American multiplicity of tin cans and Hollywood romance made their "camp" mirror their own environment, using the manufactured cult names as their own.' Dwoskin wrote. 'They became their own product by the obsessive play upon the artefacts of the commercial propaganda of the Hollywood cult.' Films such as *Screen Test*, *Hedy* or *Harlot* show this aspect of Warhol, just as *Poor Little Rich Girl* reverses the rigid control of the studio system in Edie's random actions, the out-of-focus shooting, off-screen sound and the noise of the running camera motor.

These facets were taken up but shorn of their Hollywood traces by the more aggressive English avant-garde. A part of Warhol's attraction lay in the nature of the period, when the barriers between

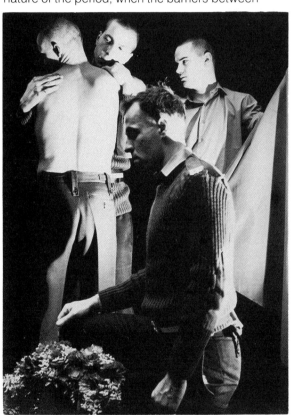

Imagining October, *1985 by Derek Jarman*

media appeared to crumble. Warhol was a key figure in this operation. Like him, the British avant-garde had begun with experimental work involving music, painting, sculpture and print: Le Grice showed his paintings as well as his films when he first exhibited, and also did live-action work and multi-screen projection. Like other British artists, he pared down the multi-media formula, stripping it of underground and baroque metaphor. Even so, there long remained in Le Grice's work a residue of the visual hypnographia and lurid colour of the epoch (two Warholian hallmarks which Warhol himself had blended into a mixture of avant-garde and kitsch condemned twenty years before by Clement Greenberg). They appear in the rough colour overprinting of *Berlin Horse* and as late as the ripe colour-negative conclusion in *Blackbird Descending*.

It was Warhol's stress on the physical nature of film, not his camp playfulness, which attracted the British. Twenty years later, when Warholian strategies appealed to a new wave of anti-structural romantic-revivalists, the reverse was true. They eschewed raw material in favour of an assertive style and perfectionist technique, focusing on precisely the camp and erotic play which most of Warhol's first admirers had rejected on ethico-political grounds.

It is easier to trace Warhol's influence on the first wave of film-makers, for they themselves attested to Warhol's importance and authority. Their theoretical writing on the question of film duration and content has become part of a speculative critique of cinema which begins with Walter Ruttmann's definition of the 'time-based medium' in 1919. The essays and books of the 60s period are still of intense interest, by-passing most film writing today in sheer intelligence. Warhol's influence is also present to a degree in the films which were made, although by way of ideas rather than style (aside from such early acolyte-pieces as Gidal's superstar portraits in *Heads*). Dwoskin's visual debt to Warhol is, however, clear in *Girl*, a long-take of a naked woman in which her increasing discomfort matches that experienced by the viewer. Other films originate in post-Warholian figuring out of the consequences of his work, as in Le Grice's 4-screen polyvision *Le Déjeuner sur l'herbe: After Manet*.

Nonetheless, it is still difficult and probably foolish to try to extract essence of Warhol from the formation of the British avant-garde. Its sources were diverse, and it did things that Warhol did not: films without lenses (John Du Cane), films resprocketed by being passed through a sewing machine (Annabel Nicolson), didactic lightplay (Le Grice), performances with self-duplicated image (Guy Sherwin), and the whole movement towards direct intervention through the printer. For the earlier period, the different views of Warhol do illuminate different pulls within the avant-garde. These can be seen by comparing, for instance, Dwoskin's broad-front defence of international avant-gardisme, Le Grice's assertion and enumeration of positive film virtues and values, and Gidal's stringent negative attack on all affirmative statements.

Warhol was a prime mover in the milieu of the experimental arts of the 60s. He had a special allure for the film-makers of the period because of his radical iconoclasm. This still underpins Warhol's appeal for youth culture. A decade after his first impact, the generation influenced by Warhol was under siege from younger artists for whom Warhol was also an exemplary figure, perhaps even more galactic. Warhol as influence acted as a bridge between the period of artistic minimalism and the era of aesthetic flamboyance. He emerged unscathed, and no one seemed troubled by the double-act, even though (unlike the perennial survival of the anarchic Velvet Underground, once 'Andy Warhol's') he was so variously interpreted. Warhol's immaculate style appeared to be impervious, solid as a star; white light, white heat ■

Notes

1 'Every strong poet caricatures tradition and every strong poet is then necessarily mis-read by the tradition that he fosters. The strongest of poets are so severely mis-read that the generally accepted, broad interpretations of their work actually tend to be the exact opposites of what their poems truly are ... "influence" clearly is a very troublesome trope, and one that we substitute with continually, whether we want to or not, because "influence" appears also to be another term for another apparent opposite, "Defence".' This formulation, from Bloom's *Kabbalah and Criticism* appeared in 1975, a year after the first edition of P. Adams Sitney's influential *Visionary Film*, indebted to Bloom's earlier books, and the final pages of which dealt with Warhol and the 'structural' film. For the British avant-garde (who generally have been among Sitney's more hostile, or anxious, readers) it can be suggested that Warhol's 'influence' was a 'Defence' against an equally strong artist, Stan Brakhage, whose work partly provoked Warhol's counter-Romantic film-making.

2 Apart from such rarities as *Sleep*, shown in 1964 along with Sitney's first European tour (too early an event to have a real impact), the big explosion in Warhol screenings took place – according to David Curtis's 'Chronology' – in 1969. The New Cinema Club showed *Hedy* (Curtis programmed it with Le Grice, Dwoskin, Keen and Barucello) and a year later *Lonesome Cowboys* and *Flesh* came to London, to be followed by NFT and RCA screenings of *Bike boy* and *My Hustler*.

During recent years, the films which have circulated here show an odd appropriateness to the British context and its fascination with interior space: *Couch*, *Kitchen*, fragments of longer films, *The Chelsea Girls*, and the later Morrisey features with which they were easily confused. The longer, rigorous works were not shown, nor those which forced the conceptual rather than the visual issues.

3 Dwoskin finds quotations in Aristotle (rather than Marx) to assert that meaning derives from the objective apprehension of an external world, which includes those Hollywood films that for many future film-makers provided 'the shape of thinking'. Hollis Frampton talking to Gidal in a 1972 interview: 'Aristotle talks somewhere of six kinds of intelligence. And we've whittled it down to one kind of intelligence, right, goodness, being able to talk, to write something which is like talk. Being articulate. That leaves five kinds of intelligence as recognised by Aristotle shivering in the cold. Well, one of the kinds he talked about was *techne*, which is the kind that lets people make things, presumably good things. We get *technical* from that ... But he didn't mean it as pertaining to a craft, he meant it as the whole faculty of mind that makes it possible for a Brancusi to march up to a billet of bronze and get the "Bird in Space".'

THE PRODUCER AS AUTHOR
DAVID JAMES

**From *Wide Angle*,
vol. 7 no. 3, 1985**

Andy Warhol's intervention in American film may be contrasted with that of Stan Brakhage; the latter's innovation of a theory and practice of film as categorically other than the industrial use of the medium is matched by Warhol's similarly remarkable but entirely contrary project, that of taking art film ever and ever closer to Hollywood. In his attempt to identify film with the psychological and even physiological processes of the individual psyche, Brakhage largely abjured the forms evolved in the commercial cinema. Warhol on the other hand was preoccupied with the industrial apparatus of mass fascination in which vision as an optical faculty is transcended and distributed through the pan-sensual play of memory and desire in the operations of the culture industries. If for Brakhage the issue was seeing, for Warhol it was being seen; in his work the construction of a personal discourse is inseparable from the process of securing prominence in the discourse of others. Warhol realised that if in the spectacular society the logic of *esse est percipi* makes being quantifiable as publicity, then the privileged ontological investigation is that into the mechanisms of the mass media, and art an enteprise that is fundamentally entrepreneurial. The progress of his film-making may best be understood then as the extension of various interests connected with filmic processes to parallel issues in the cinema industry as a whole, that is from the *medium* to the *media*.

Accordingly, the industrial function of the film producer, the agent who arranges and coordinate the various apparatuses of cinema, suggests a concept that articulates the aesthetic and the commercial components in his practice; it signifies his peculiar strategies of own-ing.

Warhol's career as a film-maker contains so many abrupt lurches into new directions and shifts to different scales of production that description of in terms of a single expressive urgency is as difficult as organizing it in terms of standard generic categories. But all the singular achievements as well as the desultory, incomplete projects that lie between the silent rising and falling of John Giorno's abdomen in *Sleep* in 1963 and th logo 'Presented by Andy Warhol' splashed across the ads for the Carlo Ponti Company's production *Frankenstein* in 1974 do refer to a trajectory of whi Warhol's own distinction between 'the period wher we made movies just to make them' and a subsequent decision to make 'feature length movi that regular theaters would want to show'[2] is as jus an anatomy as any. Though the caesural pivot that both joins and separates the autotelic art and the commercial enterprises is difficult to place – does lie after *Empire* (1964)? – or *The Chelsea Girls* (1966)? – or *Lonesome Cowboys* (1967)? – or *Tra:* (1970)? – certainly a distinction between an early Warhol and a late Warhol can be elaborated in bot formal and biographical terms. It corresponds to

Donovan in Fifty
Fantastics and Fifty
Personalities, *1964–66*

increasingly sophisticated technological investments, the shift from private Factory showings to public exhibition, and an engagement with the grammar of industrial cinema, with scripting, fiction and narrative as commonly understood. The products of the two periods have been differently evaluated: critics with allegiance to independent film tend to find, for example, that after *The Chelsea Girls* Warhol 'quickly faded as a significant film-maker'[3] or that 'something absolutely grotesque happened to Warhol's two finest gifts: his visual intelligence and his taste. It was simply this: Degradation'.[4] Those with investment in feature film see the opposite; that, for example, Warhol came 'of age as a film-maker ... around the time that his collaboration with Paul Morrissey began'.[5]

Such a categorical distinction between different Warhols is a pre-condition of the valorization of one over the other and to a biographical narrative by which either a good artist sold out to the media or an elitist, pretentious one became popularly accessible. The larger story of Warhol's whole career calls into question the thematics upon which these depend, and any use of essentialist concepts of pure and commercial art to produce a binary opposition that would distinguish parallel functions in Warhol's entire *oeuvre* is precluded by the subversion at all its stages of the grounds upon which such an anti-thesis could be based.

Throughout his career the same tensions – and the same interdependence – between art and business are present. In his film-making phase, Warhol both engaged the medium and, in a series of meta-filmic and meta-cinematic strategies, represented that engagement, formalistically laying bare its conditions. His investigation of the technological and social mechanisms of the recording apparatus, originally of the processes of photography and eventually extending from the camera *per se* to the media industry as a whole, runs parallel to the industrialization of his mode of film production; the thematic and iconographical

explorations of Hollywood accompany his replacement of artisanal production by a division of labor in which the different stages in the production process – writing, acting, shooting and editing – are distributed. Warhol delegated more and more responsibility until in some of the late films he was no more than a name attached to a product completed essentially without participation on his part other than the marshalling of production expenses and the publicity. In the expansion of his activity from being the operator of a camera to being the operator of an industry, his erasure of authorship – his most characteristic authorial gesture – was recontextualized according to the requirements of the different spheres. But in each his formal organization of the art object was inseparable from his organization of its social insertion. It is this continuity of his role as a *producer*, according to one definition 'a combination of shrewd businessman, tough taskmaster, prudent cost accountant, flexible diplomat, and creative visionary,'[6] that allows the homologies between style, content and social location of his work to be specified as thoroughly as in the case of Brakhage. Consequently it allows for the understanding of his intervention in both underground and industrial film in social terms as a social act.

Of the various Warhols produced by commentary – the anti-filmmaker, for example, or the formalist precursor of structural film – none has been more tenacious than Warhol-the-documentarist, and the supposition that he democratically documents people 'being themselves' provided the basis for the endemic supposition that his cinema was voyeuristic.[7] While initially useful in specifying the observation of deviant sexuality in the pro-filmic by the uninflected stare of the camera, the notion that Warhol's was such a form of direct cinema, without significant determination of the pro-filmic by the cinematic apparatus, is entirely misleading. It runs aground not only like other absolute realisms on its elision of the mediation of the apparatus and of generic and formal codes, but more crucially on the nature of the pro-filmic situation. For rather than unfolding in ignorance of the camera's presence or being unaffected by it, the spectacle is produced for and *by* the camera. Only if you are unconscious (*Sleep*) or a building (*Empire*) can you be unaware of media attention in Warhol's world. Otherwise the recording apparatus, by itself capable of transforming life into art, introduces itself as a presence that constitutes the space of its attention as the theater of self-construction. Since the task of the pro-filmic is to accommodate itself to the demands of the camera, conducting itself always in full recognition of the apparatus as both recording technology and as a social implication, the defining condition of voyeurism – 'repetitive looking at *unsuspecting* people'[8] – is denied. The metaphor has to be reversed, recontained in an antithetical coupling in which the self-conscious pro-filmic subject, narcissistically exhibiting himself or herself as a means of attracting attention, is complemented by a camera whose power lies in its threat to look away.

Though the elaboration of these issues frequently returned upon itself, it can be schematized as three main stages: investigation of the process of being photographed, of being made the subject of film; the construction and deconstruction of artificial selves by means of roles appropriated from film history or metaphorically related in some other way to Hollywood; and the internalization within the diegesis of the issues of exhibitionism and spectatorship in narrative features which themselves begin to approach Hollywood's formal and economic terrain. The photographic apparatus has throughout a double role; on the one hand it is the means of reproduction, and on the other it is the signifier of mass industrial reproduction, both metaphor and metonym for Hollywood, holding out the promise of mass consumption and thus the means of negotiating a private event into a public spectacle. It promises the transformation of the individual into the star.

The earliest films – *Eat* (1963), *Henry Geldzahler* (1964), *Blow Job* (1963), *The Thirteen Most Beautiful Women* (1964) through the sections of *The Thirteen Most Beautiful Boys* (1965) and *Fifty Fantastics and Fifty Personalities* (1965) and the 100-foot rolls of Factory visitors shot by Billy Name – simply isolate a single figure before the camera, but rather than documenting the ability of the subject to manifest an autonomous, unified self, these portraits narrate the sitter's response to the process of being photographed. The camera is a presence in whose regard and against whose silence the sitter must construct himself; it makes performance possible, constituting being as performance. The situation is that of psycho-analysis and the camera is the silent analyst who has abandoned the subject to the necessity of his fantastic self-projection. But unlike parallel situations later in video portraiture, where the immediate mirror-like feedback of the monitor allows the negotiation and renegotiation of the narcissistic image to the point of its stability, allowing the 'fragmented body-image' to assume a 'form of its totality,' even to assume 'the armour of an alienating identity,'[9] here film supplies only the implication of observance, displacing its documentation and proof of the future moment of projection. Alone in the anxiety caused by knowledge of being observed but denied access to the results of that observation, the subject must construct himself in the mental mirrors of his self-image or the recollection of previous experience of being photographed.

As Warhol elaborated on these issues he became interested not in the structuralist investigation of the means of reproduction but in the complication of the pro-filmic itself and specifically with various kinds of tensions between an implied, though never fully achieved, self outside the medium and various ways in which that self is

Joe Dallesandro and Viva in Lonesome Cowboys, *1967*

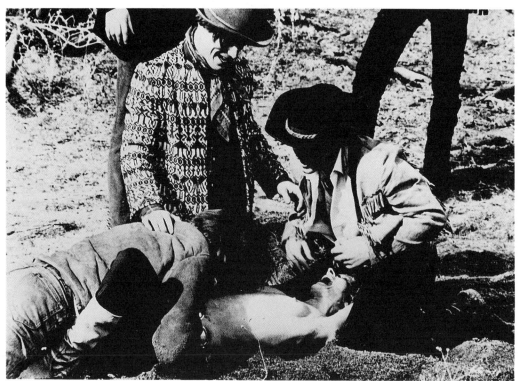

inflected in the experience of it.

Two main areas overlap: the creation of a self through the dynamics of social interaction and the fabrication of a self through the demands of more or less fictional situations, of narrative and hence of characterization. This latter eventually allowed confrontation with the conventions of role playing, that is with the vocabulary of acting, and so provided the vehicle upon which Hollywood as a historical and economic institution could be approached. The personae assumed in the fictional narratives as well as the more consistent if not more real personae the actor assumes in everyday life remain unstable, and the drama of the Warhol narratives, even through the most 'commercial' of the Morrissey collaborations, resides in the interplay between the different levels of artifice in any one actor/character as much as it does in the interaction between the separate characters, even though each is the means of production of the other. Up to *The Chelsea Girls* and *Four Stars* (1966), the primary interest lies in people assuming roles; after that point, as genre and narrative provide more stable fictional frames, in people falling out of them.

The more and more complex narratives that evolved from the one-shot, non-dramatic situations of the early films involved more fully articulate locations instead of the Factory, a greater degree of fictional pre-scription and incorporation of the conventions of role playing. As quasi-therapeutic acting-out gave way to acting proper, iconographical and histrionic reference to Hollywood came in focus. And as the imitation of industrial production methods and production values eliminated the grammatical crudeness that had insistently maintained filmic self-consciousness, that reflexivity was relocated as an intra-diegetic consideration of Hollywood, culminating in the complex intertextuality of the late films where Warhol's interest in the shifting ontologies of media reproduction lead to a revival of Thirties and Forties cinema as satire on the present state of the industry.

This analysis of the history of Hollywood may be schematized in three main phases: the first entails the fragmentary appropriation of names, roles and gestures from the golden age in narratives depicting the off-screen life of the stars (e.g., *Hedy* [1965], *Screen Test # 2* [1965], *Harlot* [1964], *More Milk, Yvette* [1965] and *Lupe* [1965]); the second consists of generic imitations (e.g., *Lonesome Cowboys* [1967] and *Blue Movie* [1968]); and the third of remakes of specific films (e.g., *Heat* and *Frankenstein*). Each of these phases manifests a thematic and formal doubleness in which affection and debunking are each other's precondition. This simultaneous satire upon the industry and homage to it is not simplified as the mediation on Hollywood more closely approaches the condition of its object, and all the films attack whatever industrial point of reference they originate from. In the second stage, for example, metageneric works like *Lonesome Cowboys* and *Blue Movie* foreground their refusal to reproduce key generic motifs, even while they insistently invoke their reference forms. Most obviously the sexual inversion of the cowboys ricochets back through all the Howard Hawks/John Wayne clichés of male camaraderie, eroding those conventions by caricaturing what is most central in them. This quotation of generic references can be pushed to the point where the production itself becomes entirely self-conscious. The tensions of the silent portraits are again activated and the camera engaged directly. Viva is often the means to this dialogue between the film and its actors; she often verbalizes the conditions of her role, the terms of her performance of it, even as she alternately fulfills them and rejects them. In *Blue Movie* for example, she comments on both the difficulties and pleasures of acting in a pornographic film, sometimes engrossing herself in its requirements and then discussing them with her co-star or the camera: she mockingly accuses Waldon of being disgusting for exposing his genitals 'right in front of this lens' and all through the sex play she winks and smiles at the camera/spectator.

The generic debasement instanced by the tawdry sexuality and low production values places these films as anti-art, deliberately vulgar gestures of negation towards the commercial cinema as *Sleep* was towards the underground. Even *Blue Movie* subverts its genre by taking its conventions to what were at the time unacceptable extremes of explicitness. Similarly *Flesh* (1969) or *Trash* (1970), essentially strings of sexual encounters spaced by desultory narrative interludes in the form of pornography accepted by Warhol as early as *Couch* (1964), shock commercial expectations, not least by their interest in the stars rather than the narrative. In these, Warhol's investigations of role playing opens up into a double critique of Hollywood in which a formal element – the revival of the star system of the Thirties – and a thematic element – the foregrounding of the process of visual consumption – make each other possible. The mixture of satire and affection in the invocation of 'the movies' is subsumed in what is at once a dramatization and a valorization of the use of the medium for extravagant self-presentation.

Given Warhol's interest in the politics of glamor, his and Morrissey's revival of the star system of the Thirties and Forties was entirely logical, even if it did take place when Hollywood was being re-written as a director's cinema. The range of histrionic modes produced by the transition from the mannered, gestured styles inherited from stage melodrama and the silents to the closer identification between actor and role had made acting highly self-conscious, allowed it to 'acknowledge its own abstraction' and 'enjoy its dissimilarity to existential modes of behaviour'[10] in a way exactly appropriate to the intricate ambiguities of the self-presentation of transvestites and prostitutes, the characteristic subjects of the late films. The split between actor and role in these films extends Warhol's previous interest in relaying already artificial constructs through further levels of artifice, especially through the intrinsic ambiguity of the transvestite and the hustler. As Stephen Koch has pointed out, both the denial of anatomical reality in the former and the distinction between sex and body employed by the latter to distinguish himself from his johns produce a confusion in sexual identity: 'Sexuality is the pivot of a conundrum about being and appearing.'[11] In the extra-diegetic Warhol world of surfaces, multiple reproduction and sexual disguise, let alone in the world of his films, any such polarization of reality and appearance cannot be maintained, but it does provide the basis for a more or less consistent and recognizable acting style in which the actor neither fully inhabits the role nor creates any constant distance from it, for example by quoting it as in Brechtian theory. The role is engaged fitfully and often tangentially in such a way that its authority is constantly on the point of disintegrating even as the actor that is thus revealed can never be fully independent of the persona.

Whereas for Dallesandro and the other hustlers the female role of being looked at entails their absence from their bodies and so produces a minimalist acting in which they are never fully present except as visual objects, the transvestites need to maximize rather than minimize their presence. Their acting consequently is a hyperbolic, highly gestural pastiche of fragments of different codes of femininity, with the interaction between the different degrees of it and the various vocabularies for it being the source of multiple narrative ironies. The hustler and transvestite roles are wittily juxtaposed in a single scene in *Flesh* in which on one side of a room Joe Dellasandro is being blown by Geri Miller and on the other Jackie Curtis and Candy Darling are reading old Hollywood fanzines, mentally recasting themselves in the image of Joan Crawford. Orally consumed by Miller, Dellasandro is visually consumed by Curtis and Darling. With his back to the camera he looks away from everyone, presenting his face in profile upon which may be read the effect of Miller's ministrations, themselves, as in *Blow Job*, out of sight. The camera pans from one to the other so that, as in the twin-screen projections, one scene is in competition with the other, the exchange of glances passing from screen to screen, from the image of the subject of visual consumption to the image of the object of visual consumption, a doubled relay which dramatizes the real and the fantasy roles within spectatorship.

Even as the late films moved, if not to Hollywood exactly at least to a place in the popular culture

Taylor Mead, Viva and Tom Hompertz in Lonesome Cowboys, 1967

parallel and adjacent to it, they still reserved for themselves a formal and an economic difference. At his most commercial and despite his scorn for the 'artiness' of Warhol's early films, Morrissey retained their key motifs: the largely uninflected gaze of the camera with its movement restricted to pans and zooms and the long take which together construct the coherent spatial and temporal extensions inside which the stars mobilize the interplay between the various levels of their roles. Cuts are not bridged by sound continuity nor are scenes broken down into shot/reverse-shot form and so orthodox editing, specifically the nesting of close-ups inside masters and the suturing of the spectator inside reconstituted diegetic space and time, is

impossible. In place of that optical and ideological incorporation, the spectator is stranded upon the self-consciousness of the performance. The cautious and reserved approach to Hollywood grammar and modes of audience involvement are then the form of appearance of an institutional migration whose controlling level is economic and social. In addition to the formal consequences – the different filmic strategies set in motion – several other material concomitants of this relocation from the art world through the underground film subculture and into the wider public realm of pure publicity and industrial cultural production are important, especially the constitution of the audience and the nature of authorship.

The move from amateur, domestic projection at the Factory to public commercial screenings, first at the Cinémathèque and then the Regency Theater where *The Chelsea Girls* provided Warhol's first popular and financial success, and eventually to suburban theaters produced, even as it was produced by, a quantitative and a qualitative transformation in the terms by which the audience was constituted. In the earliest films the audience was essentially nonexistent, a largely theoretical implication of the performing situation and the technology of reproduction. Many of the films were never shown, or only shown at the Factory when other things were going on, or shown as part of multiple sensoria like the Exploding Plastic Inevitable; or they were screened publicly and the audience walked out. Reflecting the primacy of shooting over exhibition in Warhol's early cinema, this audience, where it was not merely a fictional construct allowing the camera to signify spectatorship and so produce anxiety and exhibitionism in the pro-filmic, was the means by which the fact that the films were essentially unwatchable could be put into public circulation. As a *de facto* audience materialized, drawn at first by the scandal and then by the figuration of scandalousness in pornography, and as the films began to be exhibited in public theaters, its physical presence and optical engagement allowed the films to be certified as a pop phenomenon in the publicity apparatus of consumer society. For only a genuinely popular audience could open the full register of the star roles and fully mobilize the ambiguities within them. As the agent of perception became the general public, the actors entered the world of magazine stories, talk show appearances, conversational references and became part of the vocabulary of public intercourse and so achieved existence in the media at large. The disparity between fantasy and reality set into motion in the early appropriations of Hollywood iconography was bridged as stardom became a habition rather than a pretense, an actuality rather than an artifice. The audience for any specific film and in fact any specific spectating activity were both subordinate to audience-in-general, the subject of the communications industry as whole.

This redefinition of the audience across the development in Warhol's production from transactions in the medium of film to transactions in the social and economic systems of film production and consumption is the complement of parallel continuities and displacements in Warhol's own activity. Though his work, his professional status as an artist or film-maker is predicated on his ability to compose visual phenomena, these technical skills are only the point of origin for the manipulation of entrepreneurial possibilities in the material contexts of these visual phenomena.

The various stages of his work, considered as formal and iconographical constructions, run parallel to an evolution in his role in its production; while it apparently involves substantial ruptures, in fact it only extends the scope of a limited pattern of operations that can be summarized as his systematic withdrawal of authorial presence as the means of asserting authorship of the process of production and proprietorship of its fruits. Whereas other film-makers of the period when Warhol was in

the underground specified both their own particular achievements and the whole scope of their engagement as the inscription of self in the production of film whose generic characteristic was that they were personal, Warhol chose to forego both highly idiosyncratic work on the film material and the creation of a personal vision of the world and to proffer this very refusal as the mark of ownership and authorship. The assumption of the industrial division of labor, the delegation of responsibility to Paul Morrissey and others and the reservation of his own activity largely to the administration of this organization, and even the intra-diegetic attention to the history and forms of the public imagery of Hollywood thus do no more than extend the terms of his early interests. As his control of the pro-filmic space modulated into his control of the public space of mass cutural consumption, it allowed him the privilege of controlling access to the cinematic apparatus and the machinery of publicity, and so of making performers either famous or non-existent.

All his strategies may then be described as negations or systems of exclusion: the stationary camera excludes off-screen space; the moving camera allows him to reject different areas in the pro-filmic; later, twin and multiscreen projection forces different films to compete with each other and finally in the feature films he is able to deny stardom to all but the few he admits into the public arena of self-exhibition, the cinema. Finally, the films themselves will be made unavailable and all that will remain will be reputation, fame, publicity. Warhol's installation of himself as a device for securing public attention, a device for mediating between a product and the public, begins as a feature of style and ends as a marketing strategy. To this extent then all his investigations on film of the play between the pro-filmic and the apparatus are autobiographical allegories; they all dramatize his career in the media.

An episode in his life-long engagement with the

media industry, Warhol's films were both an investigation of the condition of being in the attention of film and a means of securing his own prominence in the media, of underwriting the move from quasi-artisanal production to control over productive and distributive resources parallel to those of the major studios. Like his previous move from the world of advertising to that of fine art, this social and economic migration was facilitated by social changes in the relation of the art and film worlds to the needs and possibilities of capitalism as much as by his own peculiar visual ability and historical sense, but his manipulation of the moment of consumer capitalism by art work was uniquely successful. Other painters and sculptors of the period affected changes in the formal concerns of social location of underground film, but even the most successful entrepreneurs among them like Michael Snow never attained any impact outside the art world. Warhol's medium was the media itself, his business was the production of art and the metaphor of the producer specifies his achievement in appropriate industrial terms.

While producers have only rarely been considered *auteurs* (Val Lewton is a conspicuous exception), Warhol demonstrated how that function controlled and determined all others in the communications industry and so called into question the rhetoric of romantic authorship, clarifying film as commodity production, writing itself as textual production. He thus brought into visibility what such romantic rhetoric has obscured, that making film is a social and material act taking place in history. His genius was to arrange it so that the 'creative visionary' and 'shrewd businessman' in their joint operations consistently ratified the other's activity. But even as he did so he reserved that space, a narrow one finally but a space nevertheless, from which the entire operation could be illuminated by its own self-consciousness. As the title of his very first film suggested, Hollywood was regained . . . but only 'sort of' ■

Notes

This article was prepared with assistance from the National Endowment for the Humanities.

1 Andy Warhol, *The Philosophy of Andy Warhol* (New York: Harcourt Brace Jovanovich, 1975), p. 92.
2 Andy Warhol, *Popism: The Warhol '60s* (New York: Harcourt Brace Jovanovich, 1980), pp. 251–52.
3 P. Adams Sitney, *Visionary Film: The American Avant-Garde*, 2nd ed. (New York: Oxford University Press, 1979), p. 371.
4 Stephen Koch, *Stargazer: Andy Warhol's World and his Films* (New York: Praeger, 1973), p. 100.
5 John Russell Taylor, *Directors and Directions: Cinema for the Seventies* (New York: Hill and Wang, 1975), p. 137.
6 Ephraim Katz, *The Film Encyclopedia* (New York: Thomas Crowell, 1979), p. 933.
7 The fullest elaboration of Warhol's voyeurism is in Koch. He writes, 'Even more than it does most movies, voyeurism dominates all Warhol's early films and defines their aesthetic' (p. 42). Despite his extensive use of the metaphor, Koch repeatedly recognizes that the reverse is true: 'That was Warhol's gift – he made everybody in his world watched. And what is being watched has a meaning, even if it's only the meaning of being watched' (p. 6).
8 *Diagnostic and Statistical Manual of Mental Disorders*, 3rd ed. (Washington, DC: American Psychiatry Association, 1980), p. 272. My emphasis.
9 Jacques Lacan, 'The Mirror Stage as Formative of the Function of the I as Revealed in the Psychoanalytic Experience,' *Ecrits: A Selection* (New York: Norton, 1977), p. 5. Lacking video's 'mirror,' Warhol's cinema approaches more closely the therapeutic situation which Lacan describes in 'The Function of Language in Psychoanalysis,' a text which Rosalind Krauss has used in 'Video: The Aesthetics of Narcissism' (*October*, no. 1 [Spring 1976], pp. 51–64.). Krauss' article is especially useful in its formulation of the distinction between the modernist reflexive foregrounding of attention to the medium and the (postmodernist) 'psychological condition of the self split and doubled by the mirror reflection of synchronous feedback' (p. 55). Though Warhol's cinema lacks synchronous feedback, it approximates the therapeutic situation even more closely than does video, which in the monitor allows for the closure of the mirror stage. In Warhol's shooting situation the role of the therapist, who is both silent (absent) and present, is recreated in the silence of the camera and the presence of people around the set, often including press invited precisely to intensify the self-consciousness of the performers.
10 Charles Affron, *Star Acting: Gish, Garbo, Davis* (New York: Dutton, 1977), pp. 5–6.
11 Koch, p. 122.

FLESH OF ABSENCE
RESIGHTING THE WARHOL CATECHISM

PAUL ARTHUR

A substantially different version of this piece appeared in *The Independent*, December 1988, and I would like to thank the editor for permission to cannibalise it here.

At the limit, thought would be the intense contemplation from close up – to the point of losing oneself in it – of stupidity; and its other side is formed by lassitude, immobility, excessive fatigue, obstinate muteness, and inertia. Michel Foucault[1]

Let's pretend for, say, the proverbial fifteen minutes that the films have nothing to do with the paintings, boxes, wallpaper, photographs, multiples, or collections of bric-à-brac. Let us further imagine they are immune from the pressures and rewards of wealthy patrons, art-market trends, publishing coups, gossip columns, auctions and other byplays of institutionalisation; separated in short from the rampant apotheosis variously called the 'Warhol Effect' or 'Warhol Phenomenon'. Such a characterisation is not entirely far-fetched. After nearly twenty years they are once again being shown, dragged to light in the wake of museum and gallery retrospectives and buoyed by a sea of critical and theoretical discourse. No longer literally consigned to the warehouse of history, they are ensconced in a more alien terrain, far from the motley array of Factory couches, Cinemathèque basements, disco walls, and art-and-schlock houses in which they flourished. Unlike the settings given to the chunks of real estate they are intended to 'supplement', the sepulchral screening rooms of the Whitney, MOMA, *et al.* deny interactions of a specifically social space wherein aspects of film production, publicity, and spectatorship were tumultuously collapsed. But paradoxically (and, given their source, perhaps predictably), the current unavoidable displacement offers as well a vantage from which old perspectives appear cloudy and new ones are suddenly brought into focus.

The issue of context is really twofold, that of space *and* time. Made under and through the promise of mutability, having to 'fit into' a variety of occasions and emplacements – as in a parody of their Taylorised (not Mead) ancestral movie machine, individual segments of the early work had to be labile enough to endure dis- and reassembly excision, etc.[2] – their radical reductions of movie language were nonetheless held to be of a 'timeless' nature, free from History's wallops, a perverse rereading of classical stability. This has not come to pass. Instead, stripped of the contingent sociality of their 'scene', the films' historical rootedness is all the more in evidence, amplifying Jonas Mekas's early sense of Warhol as cinéma vérité documentarist.[3] They have 'aged' and done so in determinable ways. Yet what has been retained is equally striking. Even the most conservative museum-goer now assimilates the paintings like the household goods they represent and have become – with a combination of recognition and exchange value. The films, shunted aside in the exhibition layout (at MoMA placed literally underground), are another story; after twenty years

va and Taylor Mead in
nesome Cowboys,
'67

147 PAUL ARTHUR

the audience still cannot sit still for them.

The fresh sparks of outrage and mass desertion are more than simply a sign of continued cultural resistance in the age of postmodernism. The films' newly visible invisibility contributes to a canted version of 'aura'. Hidden for so long, the power of their intervention was related to a scarcity which produced a fertile conceptual residue in the precinct of alternative film-making. They were, and are again, preciously authentic precisely because of their absence, or better, the complex manner in which they nurture an impossible presence.[4] Stephen Koch astutely claimed that Warhol was the first artist in the history of cinema for whom a viewer's 'disinterest' becomes an active term in the creation of meaning.[5] Through the material abnegations of Warhol himself ('misplacing' entire films, leaving cans of footage unmarked by date, title, whatever) and the sensibly tremulous exertions of museum film departments (whose tasks must mirror the preservation of pre-1900 cinema, a fitting irony), this disinterest is becoming institutionalised. Thus we have the spectacle of a hushed if meagre audience watching a forty-two minute excerpt of an six-hour movie that few, if any, would have watched for twenty minutes straight in its original form; or the serving up of what Amy Taubin has called a 'nap-sized' portion of *Sleep*.

Deracinating not only the spatio-social ambiance of the work but its impossible temporal scaffolding accomplishes two seemingly incompatible things. It elides the crucial confrontation of interminable image with the spectator's own quotidian desires and frustrations, a destabilising phenomenology of 'seeing' or 'not seeing' film under an attenuated logic of social constraint. And it sharpens the need to re-attribute Warhol's global and local dynamics on the basis of exactly what is available and its method of sequencing. The irreducible gestures of his formal approach, framing and the structuring of time – part of cinema's ontological bedrock – are in this way inadvertently shifted to yet another level of productivity. There is a 'body' of work; it will always be fragmentary, always exfoliate the blank surfaces of the fragment as against the unified whole; and it is incumbent on us to address this experience in the knowledge of, but without instant recourse to, what surrounds the immediate image. It must be met, therefore, with something of the 'stupidity' with which its shaping apparatus confronted the pro-filmic world, even if that stance finally elicits just a different set of categories.[6]

'There are two kinds of people in the world,' Warhol might have said in one of his favorite aphoristic gambits, 'those who regard my early films as ungainly epistemological jokes, capable of undermining (or sustaining) whole systems of belief, and those who just don't *get* them.' Like a lot of other things Warhol said (or didn't say), there is in fact little choice. Bald assertions turn in on themselves, caught in a web of frangible signification. The films issue forth an ambivalence in the form of questions normally taken for granted even in the domain of avant-garde practices. What is a shot, a sequence, a dramatic action? How are we to fix the boundaries between fiction and documentary effects, between narrative and nonnarrative, architectonics and randomness? What is the seat of authorship and the extent of its agency: does it reside in cinematography, direction, acting, writing, the social contexts of image consumption?

If such concerns have helped enhance Warhol's theoretical currency, that does not blunt the historical specificity of their presentation. The roughly four years in which his principal energies were devoted to movie-making – also a period of astonishing productivity in his painting – constitutes a moment overseen by the twin breakup of the Hollywood studio system into 'free-floating' affiliations and the surging of independent documentary and avant-garde movements. Without wishing to oversimplify his positioning within these two trajectories (or to disregard the reciprocity with themes in his plastic work), Warhol distilled and mediated a fundamental axiom from each camp: the primacy of narrative and the suffusion of a sexualised image of the body in and through the text. The meeting of these meta-processes in time, their intersections and divergences, animates the 'drama' of Warholian cinema. Unlike the more rarified enterprise of structural film-making, to which his films are often tied, Warhol never veers from the domain of sociality (no depopulated exterior or interior landscapes). His self-lubricating superstars with their given or projected stories precede the filmic apparatus into the space of the image, even if what occurs in that space is completely governed by the camera's running stare.

The playwright Ronald Tavel, the Factory's early 'scenarist', said that in a uniquely lucid directive Warhol asked him to compose 'not plot but incident'. True to this mandate, stories gather themselves around conjunctions of handy props (e.g. a mushroom, a cigar) and offhand situations (e.g. a roll-length kiss, an attempted seduction). A pre-text triggers the gradual unfolding of narrative which operates in an oscillating field of role-playing, its dramatised breakdown, and the disavowal of that which is not merely literal. Nothing replaces anything else. As in *Henry Geldzahler*, a cigar is just a cigar. For the director, this would be called simply 'letting people be themselves and talk about what they usually talked about', but an emphasis on the surface often masks what is not and cannot be accessible to vision or, strictly speaking, speech. Sleepers do not dream; meditative subjects do not think; buildings are not symbols of capitalist power. The duration of the shot insures this proscription as it provides a medium for stories devoid of fictional psychology and allegory. Or more precisely, if there is an effect of interiority it must come from elsewhere, from the spectator and his or her phantasmatic mapping of 'self' onto the image – the contents of gaps filled in, of visual cues

augmented by immediate circumstances.

In another register, the films as a progression in historical time, even or especially the truncated and fragmentary progression we are currently offered, limn a similar set of narrative exigencies. It is a commonplace that Warhol recapitulated the history of industrial film-making, moving from silence to sound, black-and-white to color, unscripted to scripted, artisanal to hierarchical labor, and from photographer to director to producer. Yet this larger narrative emerges in retrospect less as a natural or predetermined course than a matter of 'incident', the input of particular personnel and access to technology, the manifestation of a sustained notoriety as opposed to a series of calculated innovations. There are, however, at least a couple of provisos to this picture. Warhol's investment in film history extends past Hollywood's system of glamour and voyeuristic display to the actual codes of industrial film language, making for an intertextual dialogue more intricate than is usually allowed.

An example of what Warhol squeezes from commercial cinema is the infamous eight-hour, ostensibly minimal, *Empire*. Apart from its phallic joke, its play on postcards, and its hilarious revision of a tradition encompassing Monet's cathedrals and Cézanne's mountains, it delivers the longest 'establishing shot' in movie history. Freezing the opening moments of hundreds of standard Hollywood melodramas, 'New York' is signified as a monument around which the clichéd 'eight million stories' may or may not be taking place. Unwilling or unable to generate the 'next' shot, we are left with a backdrop whose minute variations in light and technical coding (flares, printing errors, etc.) acquires a morbid dramatic urgency. It looks by turns graphic, fluid, solid and a negative x-ray of itself; a piece of flickering wallpaper and a moment by moment contest between an image, an image twice-removed by cultural standing, and a material surface.

Kiss, another inside historical joke reprising

Edison's 1896 landmark, molds a series of fixed-camera two-shots into a dramatic *ronde* or miniseries through sheer accumulation. As with a number of other films, what was held originally to be vacuous and starkly formal has given way to the impression of a complex performative arena. Couples kiss in a surprising range of rhythms and phrases, their untranslatable actions gaining in three minutes the lineaments of characterisation. The movements of one man are inferred as annoyingly detached, another is labelled falsely eager. The desire to substitute affect for physical gesture is mobilized only to be rendered absurd, as when a figure from an earlier sequence later returns with a different 'style'. Some sequences take on a comedic structure while others seem to condense an entire romantic courtship. Hairstyle and clothing offer cues to an actor's social status, milieu, vocation. In delivering a radically-cropped sign of climactic movie passion, Warhol stimulates the viewer's capacity for differentiation, for providing a broader context deemed appropriate to the sign. But the functional schism between action and fictive attribution eventually results in a self-conscious realization of how notions of character screen out the perception of physical performance.

A viable encapsulation of a whole group of Warhol films might be: 'what people do with their mouths'. Orality is a constant theme of the silents and the talkies, albeit with different ramifications. *Kiss*, the first film to be publicly screened, sets in motion a more general problematic involving sight and tactility. Obviously, a sense of touch is conveyed in cinema only in the most indirect fashion. By simultaneously reducing, fragmenting, and attenuating the field of action – the body in space – Warhol enforces our active recognition of sensory absence as he relentlessly exploits its representation. Deprived of a comforting charade of fictional involvement, the appeal to certain bodily sensations becomes almost pornographically direct. Robert Indiana eating a mushroom or Henry

Geldzahler smoking a cigar bear a suggestiveness that is at once exclusively visual and extra-visual. Clearly neither one is 'acting'; extended exposure verifies the realism of performance and bends our normal abstractive response to images of bodily penetration of all sorts. And herein lies a paradox of Warhol's inscription of the detached 'stare', the 'gaze' of noninvolvement. It can work as a relay in the hyperawareness of our own corporeality, as if in compensation for what is withheld. One would have to return perhaps to Courbet and Flaubert to discover a more intensive staging of a textual sensorium.

The film that, as it were, comes to mind as the trickiest separation/bonding of looking and feeling is *Blow Job*. As a trope of film history, it is the longest 'reaction shot' on record, a thirty-five minute close-up that refuses as it continuously invokes an 'other' space of causal activity adjacent to the frame. There is as well a third space, that of the camera, and as usual it is the hub around which all else is organized. Like other portrait films in which a subject reveals himself through prolonged engagement with a single stimulus, the blow-job recipient carves a geometry of shifting sightlines, glancing at, away from, or past the camera, above or below the frameline. His largely inexpressive face tightens and unfurls, twists and dips, composes itself in a succession of planes and angles (in *Eat*, Indiana uses the action of a swivelling rocking chair to constantly alter perspective while in *Sleep* new camera setups reframe the body). Attempting once more to track the course of a rising action through deflection, we begin to calibrate small affective gradations linking boredom, pleasure, and pain. The frame is a confinement that doubles, as it is responsible for, the encircling manipulation that remains offscreen.

The tension established between camera and subject, subject and offscreen presence, recalls the formal dynamics of Dreyer's *The Passion of Joan of Arc* and it is not hard to see *Blow Job* as a judicial transmutation. Aside from the actor's striking resemblance to Falconetti, there is a section in which his focus narrows and he seems to shake his head slightly in response to verbal questions or directions, inverting the ratio in *Joan* of verbal to physical interrogation. But instead of burning at the stake, the hero of *Blow Job* merely strikes a match and enjoys a final cigarette, his head wreathed in smoke.

Virtually alone in owing a discernible debt to a work of the American avant-garde – Anger's *Scorpio Rising* – *Vinyl* internalises within the frame and plot

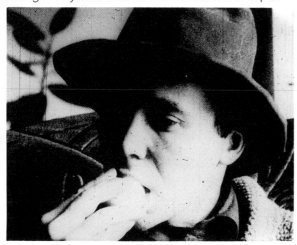

the complex exchange of looking and feeling while maintaining a play of on- and offscreen space. Verbal speech, with its attached ambiguity of reading (from cue cards) versus improvising, is factored into the process of adapting the novel *A Clockwork Orange*. Alongside a succession of poses and sightlines deployed around the camera's stare, a collection of as many as seven figures are arranged within the shallow playing area, interacting at four distinct planes with each other and the ubiquitous machine. Simple props such as a candle, a leather mask, cigarettes, cans of beer, serve as markers for the intersection of fictional roles and, for lack of a better term, spontaneous

behavior. What is determined as 'fake' – for instance, an inquisitor tearing off the pants of a seated victim in the background or Gerard Malanga yelling 'No more, no more, I can't take it' – suddenly caves in and we infer outbursts of 'real' anger, pain, sexual desire.

The stunning density of composition (having distinct echoes in Fassbinder and Jarman, among others) creates a visual excess which is thematically connected to the story's device of psychic reprogramming via overload, with the camera here doubling the symbolic mechanics of movie-introjection. But this oddly reflexive construction buries what is most potent in other films, the camera's vacancy, its *faux* indifference. A smarmy complicity infects relations between visual presence and absence and it is capped by the layering of pop songs (à la Anger) as ironic foils to the action: 'Shout', 'This Could be the Last Time', and 'Tired of Waiting' only schematise the performances they were intended to puncture. Threatening to degenerate into a conventionally literary spectacle, *Vinyl* at last grabs hold of itself, exhausting its fictional purchase and degenerating into a desultory (post-production) party.

Located somewhere between the centred isolation of the one-man portraits and the fullblown *mise en scène* of *Vinyl*, *Beauty #2* convokes the limit-point of Warhol's fascination with bodily equivalence in/as the cinematic apparatus, with the push-pull of material function and the constitution of the subject. The brilliance of execution is due in part to the gender switch; reigning superstar Edie Sedgwick, for whom *Beauty* is an ostensible screen test, is a woman engulfed by male pressure (even the dog 'Horse', 'found like everything else', is male). In this film particularly the camera is felt as a gendered eye, and the disparate terms by which sexual power is exercised and defeated are split into separate trajectories on a grid of visible-invisible space. Sedgwick, in underwear, lolls on a brightly-lit bed drinking and smoking and talking almost continuously to an offscreen Chuck Wein and perhaps to Malanga. She is joined by minor 'beauty' Gino Piserchio whose role is that of blank seducer. There is a bit of kissing and fondling but the real action takes place elsewhere.

Under the pretence of trying to draw from Edie heightened emotional responses, 'finding something real to talk about', Wein conducts a sort of interview laced with taunts and existential conundrums. They discuss earrings, haircuts, hustlers, beauty, feelings, the price of things. Wein disparages her tepid lovemaking and reads a passage from John Lennon's *A Spaniard in the Works*. He is stationed off to her left, Piserchio is slightly behind her on the bed, and the camera and Malanga loom to her right. Encircled but never victimised, she engages the tangled lines of (mis)communication with the shifting parries of words, looks, and movements. One male position stares silently but cannot touch. Another issues a torrent of jealous insults but remains off-frame and at times does not even seem to be looking. Her on-screen partner hardly speaks, is able to rub perfume over her body, but elicits the least effective claim on her attention. The focus of multiple intrusions, Edie's performance essays the borders of psychological dispersal without relinquishing the privileges of a controlling passivity. Not just a center of consumption, she is the locus of a powerfully divisive, almost comical, impotence.

Countering the Warholian assertion of 'I am a machine', the subject of *Beauty #2* anchors a minimal representation in a surprising fullness of person. Her radiance is gathered from the palpable limitations of her entourage, and it is not less touching for its dark symbiosis. Edie emerges as a warped paradigm of the types of characters 'laid bare' in cinéma vérité documentary or Italian neo-realism. Pared away to a single proposition, the narrative is *precisely* the process through which a belief that she is knowable and known – sharing our assumed humanity – is instated. Why on earth, one might ask, do we need a humanist Warhol, a tender purveyor of individual autonomy (minus interiority) and social significance? Without begging the issue, a possible answer would be to re-place him in the history of 60s culture as the illegitimate son of Bazin and the various filmic realisms he championed; to save him from 'himself', from being paraded as the father of postmodernism (a mantle tirelessly promoted by Peter Wollen, Barbara Kruger, and others) rather than the deeply ambivalent figure newly apparent in his films.

Role-playing in Warhol's world takes time. Even the most straightforward showing and/or telling does not occur instantaneously. The reason for this is grounded in a reciprocity between the building and demolition of formal parts, layering and evacuation, the sutured and unsutured. The fixed camera long-take, therefore, is not a mere device, a provocation for its own sake, but the container or body out of which conditions of narrative flow. Although they hardly seem like it, his films are races against the clock: time is always running out, something dramatic should and must happen in order to redeem the heavily coded confrontation of viewer and image. And of course something can scarcely *not* happen. Depending on what we make of the image, we may leave the theatre, doze off, fantasise, yell at the screen, treat it like a 'normal' movie experience. The list is not endless but it is distinctly Warholian. Duration is not a monolith in this work, it is textured and variable in its structure. Broadly speaking, there are three categories of internal duration corresponding roughly to historical stages in Warhol's production. In the first, something with the elements of narrative accumulates out of the nothing of a flat 'incident'. Protocols for what can or might happen next – sequence and cadence – are derived gradually, the case in *Eat*, *Haircut*, *Blow Job*, etc.

At a second stage, there is less waiting and finally less transformation in time. Characters have their roles 'ready-made' and offer them to the camera not without contradiction but without the threat that no role, and hence no action, is available. This more or less comfortable inhabiting of the arc of representation could be deemed 'fiction', were we not speaking of films such as *Vinyl* and *The Chelsea Girls*. The third mode of duration is the rarest and most transgressive. It is not mutually exclusive of the others but requires a certain exhaustion that is felt only in Warhol's later work. As being before the camera became naturalised within the Factory troupe, it was harder to find situations in which characterisation in Warhol's terms could be built up or peeled away. It was exasperatingly there. Only the endless running of the camera offered a chance of outlasting star-bought schticks of campiness and burlesque (e.g. *Lonesome Cowboys* and after). The 'Sunset Beach on Long Island' section of the twenty-five hour **** allows a brutish *nothing* to evolve out of a coyly-calculated *something*, a sort of revenge of the apparatus. Surfside horseplay dissolves into boredom, then irritation, then action more charged as, for instance, Ondine displays an inventory of hostile responses at least the equal of his *The Chelsea Girls* incarnation of the Pope.

By any standard, Warhol knew how to add and subtract. He was a master accountant long before he absented himself from the frontlines of film production to take the role of silent partner. Among the things he knew for a fact was that time was money, that the unwinding of roll after roll of film was a wantonly profligate gesture (even in a different economic climate) and the only one capable of altering the epistemological balance of classical Hollywood construction. He knew that time was narrative, that given enough time the chemistry of passive camera and human subject would coalesce into a story. Time carries the seeds of diegetic procreation. In the end, the lifelong fan of the industrial film product knew that narrative was money, that it constituted an economy at once

material and formal, social and psychological, and he cannily exploited what he could of this with a minimum of labour. That the glorious enterprise was likely less profitable than a single soup can manufactured between the edges of stretched canvas does not, except perhaps by his own lights, make Warhol a less successful film-maker ■

Notes

1 Michel Foucault, 'Theatrum Philosophicum', in *Language, Counter-Memory, Practice*, trans. Donald F. Bouchard and Sherry Simon (Ithaca: Cornell University Press, 1977), p. 190.
2 The best assessment of Warhol's relation to industrial cinema is David James's brilliant 'The Producer as Author', *Wide Angle* 7, no. 3, 1985, a cornerstone of his ground-breaking materialist study of 60s film culture, *Allegories of Cinema* (forthcoming from Princeton University Press), and reprinted in the present volume.
3 See Jonas Mekas, *Movie Journal* (New York: Collier, 1972), *passim*. What this view ultimately punctures is the sort of high-modernist attribution found in Sitney's *Visionary Film*.
4 Carter Ratcliff, although limiting himself to traditional 'pop' manifestations, takes a recent and well-deserved potshot at the art-historical marshalling of a 'Benjaminian' refutation of aura in: 'The Work of Roy Lichtenstein in the Age of Walter Benjamin's and Jean Baudrillard's Popularity', *Art In America*, February 1989, pp. 112–19. I have previously written on this aspect of Warhol's film in 'Structural Film: Revisions, New Versions, and the Artifact', *Millennium Film Journal* 1, no. 2 (Spring-Summer 1978), pp. 5–13.
5 Koch's celebrated study, *Stargazer* (New York: Praeger Publishers, 1973), remains a vital account of formal and psychological constructs, although subsequent developments in film theory have opened up certain culs-de-sac and bare spots.
6 In his essay on Deleuze cited above, Foucault enlists Warhol, along with Bouvard and Pecuchet among others, as 'acategorical beings', p. 189. Although I do not think I intend the relation between fragment and presence as the same order as Foucault's decentering 'stupidity', they are adjacent in their impact upon cohesive thought.

WARHOL: WON'T WRINKLE EVER
A FILM-MAKER'S VIEW

VIVIENNE DICK

Found photo of Andy Warhol

All quotes from Jonas Mekas taken from his essay (reprinted in the present volume) and filmography in John Coplans, *Andy Warhol* (1970).

The closest I ever came to Andy Warhol was a photo I found of him once in a garbage can not far from Max's. He's jumping in the air with his arms and legs outstretched and he's wearing a 'bad' T-shirt. I think he's even smiling.

People used to mention seeing him at art openings or at Studio 54 – this was in the late 70s. *Interview* magazine was around – I used to read the half page Glenn O'Brien wrote about the new music scene in downtown Manhattan. As far as I was concerned that's where it was all happening. Some of the Warhol stars were still around – Taylor Mead and John Giorno usually performed at those all-night poetry/performance sessions at St Marks church; Nico played a few times with John Cale at CBGB's; Lucinda Childs was working with Robert Wilson. I would occasionally see Jackie Curtis at Slugger Ann's – his grandmother's bar on Second Ave and Tenth St. Renee Ricard had a part in Eric Mitchell's *Underground USA* – a parody of a Warhol film. I would sometimes see Jack Smith lurking around 1st Avenue. He would put on performances with titles like *How Can Uncle Fishhook Have A Free Bicentennial Zombie Underground?* – he made a lot of films – most of which are stashed in his apartment.

Jack Smith
Andy Warhol bought himself a Bolex in 1963. He had been regularly attending Jonas Mekas's film screenings at the Filmmakers Co-op on Park Avenue South. These were informal film screenings where independent film-makers could screen finished and unfinished work – people like Ron Rice, Ken Jacobs, Marie Menken and Jack Smith. When Warhol started filming he used many of the actors who had been working with these film-makers. The second film Warhol shot was a 'newsreel' of Jack Smith shooting *Normal Love*. Jack Smith usually used a lot of drag queens as actors. The film was never as important to him as the making of it – the elaborate preparations with the sets, the make-up, the glitter and the coloured gels. His inspiration was the Hollywood movies of his childhood – Maria Montez in lurid technicolour, and his own surreal imagination. Warhol admits being influenced by him – the way he didn't bother with rehearsals or conventional plots, the way he would use anybody who happened to be around – and carry on shooting after the actors got bored. Some early Smith-inspired films Warhol made were *Mario Banana* and *Camp* (with Mario Montez and Jack Smith acting).

The Early Films
The first film Warhol made is called *Sleep*. Eight hours of John Giorno asleep on a couch. He says he was shy in the beginning with a camera and that it was easier to shoot someone asleep with no one else around. After each roll, the camera changes

Kiss, 1963

angle and focuses on a different part of the body. Some of the rolls are repeated twice. Like all Warhol's films this is a film about time and our perception of it – the process of looking – and our personal capacity to transform what we see.

We are watching someone asleep in real time – real film time, that is – which runs parallel to our time as it's not happening simultaneously. And the film is projected at 16 fps, which slows the film down a little – gives it a sort of hallucinatory effect (this is the case for all Warhol's silent films). And the person we are watching is sleeping – existing 'out of time'. The person is twice removed from us. Warhol has always been interested in what's real and what's fake. He says, 'all my films are artificial. But then everything is sort of artificial. I don't know where the art stops and the real begins.' This can be applied to people, emotions, television . . . He says, 'I think once you see emotions from a certain angle you can never think of them as real again. That's what more or less has happened to me.'

Jonas Mekas has described how during screenings of *Sleep* people would get up, go out for coffee or a chat (or leave) and come back in again to continue watching. In one instant Warhol makes us aware that our time and the time on the screen is different, that we have control over how we are seeing – we can let ourselves be absorbed into a meditative state or we can withdraw. The film will go on nevertheless in its own sweet time.

After *Sleep* he made *Kiss* – 100 ft rolls of close-ups of people kissing. Other films around that time are *Eat* – 40 minutes of eating a mushroom; *Haircut* – Billy Linich getting his hair cut. *Drunk* – 70 minutes of Emile De Antonio getting drunk on a bottle of whiskey, and *Blow Job* – showing the face of the person on the receiving end only. Warhol was as fascinated with the moving image as the very first film-makers were. He made hundreds of 'portraits'. Everyone who came into the 'Factory' (the loft he worked in) would be sat on a chair and a roll of film was run off – 3½ minutes per person. *13 Most*

Beautiful Women and *13 Most Beautiful Boys* came out of these sessions: static close-ups that are just like photographs. A lot of drag queens, speed freaks and male hustlers had started to hang out at the factory – many of whom were friends of Billy Linich, who along with Gerard Malanga was Warhol's assistant.

The last silent film Warhol shot was *Empire*, eight hours of the Empire State building shot from the 44th floor of the Time Life building. This was in 1964, when he bought an Auricon camera. He had Jonas Mekas help him with it as he was unfamiliar with the camera. He subsequently used this camera for many of his sound films. The thing about it was it was a sync-sound camera – like a Super–8 camera – a camera developed during the war for news-gathering. It made the production of sound films very straightforward – especially as he didn't bother editing.

Edie
In 1965 he met Edie Sedgwick – a rich girl who had just left college and now wanted to be a model in New York. He says, 'after one look at Taxi (Edie) I could see that she had more problems than anyone I'd ever met. So beautiful but so sick. I was really intrigued.' She looks like someone who has stepped out of the late 70s or early 80s. Androgynous with short blonde hair and heavy eyebrows. There's a picture of her wearing bondage arm bracelets in Stephen Koch's book *Stargazer*. For about six months she and Andy were inseparable – constant partying and going to openings. She invented a look – Fruit of the Loom T-shirts over ballet tights, long earrings and a short white mink coat over that. She had her picture in *Vogue*, *Life* and *Time*. She was a kind of Lulu of the 60s. A cool Lulu. In 1965 she appeared in twelve Warhol films. Warhol was in love with the way she moved and looked. He wanted to film her for a whole day. The films he did with her are largely documentary with a little fiction thrown in via Tavel's scripts. In *Poor Little Rich Girl* 'Edie

moves about her bed and telephone, tells about her spent inheritance and shows her beautiful coat' (Jonas Mekas' description). The film is unavailable. *Restaurant* is 'Edie and her guests at the table as they drink, argue and wait for their meal' (J.M.). *Afternoon* – 105 mins – Edie is at home with her friends. *Kitchen* (40 minutes) was written by Ronald Tavel. Warhol describes it in the film-makers' Cinemathèque programme notes; '*Kitchen* is illogical, without motivation or character – completely ridiculous. It is very much like real life.'

The cast is as follows: Edie as *Jo*. Roger Trudeau

Edie Sedgwick in Poor Little Rich Girl, *1965*

as *Mickey*. Donald Lyons as *Joe*. Electrah as *Nicki* and Renee Ricard as the *Busboy*, David MacCabe as *Photographer*. A static camera in an ordinary-looking kitchen with a table in the middle foreground. Edie's voice informs us (between sneezes) that the scenario is hidden in a calendar on the wall and under a book on the table. She enters. She is wearing a pair of sheer tights and a striped T-shirt. She opens her bag and takes out a mirror and starts putting on eye make-up. Someone is messing with dishes at the sink. Mickey (Trudeau) comes in. He's wearing a pair of trousers and no shirt. His kisses her on the neck. She continues applying make-up. Then they have a conversation about litterbaskets. Edie (in a hoarse drawl): 'I do rummage around in litterbaskets – that's how I found you.' Mickey: 'They're always throwing away worthwhile things into the litterbasket.' Edie seems quite at home here with her friends. She sits on the edge of the table exercising her Barbie doll legs. He kisses her on the ankle. Every so often a photographer comes in to take a flash photo. Mickey tells Edie about how he had sex with Jo(e) in the shower. He massages Edie's neck and suggests going to the beach. She doesn't want to go. She puts him over her knee and slaps him, telling him to go and do his lessons. Mickey then accuses her of throwing his underwear into the litterbasket. He goes on about second-hand clothes. Something about if you wear second-hand clothes you will adopt the personality of the previous owner. 'If you can't understand yourself you might as well get to understand someone else'. He keeps repeating himself but it's hard to hear him anyway because the blender is on now, the busboy is clattering the dishes, the photographer is running in and out and Edie is sneezing and paying no attention to him.

The film runs to white emulsion and into reel two; more clattering at the sink. We can hear Edie muttering: 'Ah know I'm going to forget when to come in.' There's an announcement off-screen listing the cast and describing the props (a layercake, silverware, marshmallows, stove, instant coffee) and there is a special direction: 'The part of Jo is to be played for high camp at all times.' Edie doesn't come across as a good actor. She doesn't play for high camp either, she plays herself.

Joe enters now with Nicki. 'I might add business is not too fabulous these days up and down Greenwich Avenue.' Edie asks him how he wants his coffee; 'I like my coffee hot, sweet and black, just like my men'. She spills the coffee and offers him layercake. Throughout the film whispered prompting is heard off-screen. Edie gets mad at him over something and jumps on him. Nicki fixes her hair, pokes in a bag and chews gum. An airplane passes overhead. Then she starts off 'in high camp'. It's hard to make out what she is saying. Sound was not a high priority with Warhol and they never had a proper sound recordist working on the crew. She says something to do with 'between your legs' and 'getting raped in the subway' and generally seems to be annoyed with Jo (Edie) for 'going round with a bunch like this'. Edie calls her a 'raving maniac', 'and besides, I never listen to other women'. Mickey meanwhile jumps on top of Joe. Nicki does her nails and brushes her hair. Edie gets a fork and toasts a marshmallow on the stove. Then she's put (unresisting) on the kitchen table and 'strangled'. She sits up. Her finger hurts. She's burnt it with the fork. The script is forgotten. For the next five minutes everyone fusses around her. Someone gets the ice out. Someone else looks for some Band-Aid. Renee offers her a paper towel to dry her hand with. The crew join in, definitely a slice of 'real life'. Warhol directed these films in his own remote way. He would just let the actor carry on talking about what they would usually talk about. Sometimes he would give them a theme to work with. Sometimes he got Ronald Tavel to write the script. But the scripts were peripheral to the movie. They were something for the actors to hang on to if they dried up. And the most interesting parts of the film were usually when the actors forgot about the script. Warhol is not so much interested in the action as in what happens in between – the incidental – the throwaway part. He had nothing to do with some of the best moments in the films. He just set up a 'readymade' situation. He watches and records. He said, 'What I liked was chunks of time all together – every real moment.'

Although he is probably the most passive of film-makers ever, he did interfere in the content of the films by taunting and humiliating the actors, indirectly of course. He would get Tavel to interview any potential superstars to find out their personal secrets. This information would then be inserted into the script in order to provoke a response in front of the camera. This happens in *Beauty #2*, apparently; Edie is taunted by someone off camera to the point of anger. And the big scene in *The Chelsea Girls* is where Ondine loses his temper with the woman who calls him a phoney.

Warhol disrupted any attempts to rehearse for *Vinyl* (an adaptation of *A Clockwork Orange*). Just as Tavel would be trying to put Gerard Malanga through his lines, he would send him off on a long errand. Then he invited a lot of people – the press, etc. – to come and watch the filming, making it difficult for the actors to concentrate.

Several of Edie's last films are unavailable – though they may turn out to have been stored at Warhol's house. There's one called *Outer and Inner Space*. In it Edie 'talks with her image on a TV set. The dialogue is about space, mysticism and herself' (J.M.). The last film Edie was in with Warhol is called *Lupe*. He describes the background: 'We'd all heard the stories about Lupe Velez, the Mexican Spitfire who lived in a Mexican-style palazzo in Hollywood and decided to commit the most beautiful Bird of Paradise suicide ever . . . She then took the poison and lay down to wait for this beautiful death to overtake her, but then at the last moment she started to vomit and died with her head wrapped around the toilet bowl. We thought it was wonderful.'

Edie didn't want to be in any more films after this

She became paranoid about her ability to act and she didn't know if she was being made fun of or not. She was also taking a lot of drugs. Warhol wanted to do a retrospective of her films around this time. She refused.

Nico and Viva

By 1966 Nico had arrived and Warhol was paying more attention to her and trying to set her up as a singer with the Velvet Underground. In 1971 Edie died of 'acute barbital intoxication'.

Warhol's women are usually in competition with

Viva in Midnight Cowboy
by John Schlesinger

each other and with the drag queens. They spend a lot of time putting on make-up and brushing their hair. There's a lot of exaggerated anxiety. Edie in *Kitchen* says: 'My life is just like that layercake – year after year one meaningless layer after another.' Some of them are funny. Viva and Mary Woronov are more the dominatrix type. There's a lot of spite between the sexes – none of the tenderness we see between the men. Viva is making out with someone in *Lonesome Cowboys*:
Viva: 'Put your tongue back in and stop digging me with your fingernails!'
Man: 'I'd rather go and feed the chickens!'

Lonesome Cowboys is essentially a bunch of gay men horsing around among the cactus. Viva wears riding boots and carries a whip. She gets raped and spends a lot of time singing Latin hymns. It was ironic Warhol would end up getting shot by someone like Valerie Solanis, a feminist fanatic who had founded an organisation called SCUM (The Society for Cutting Up Men). She had been hanging around the Factory and had even been in one of his films. She had given Andy a script (presumably to make a film with) called *Up Your Ass* which he said was 'so dirty he thought she might be working for the police department'.

He never made any films after *Lonesome Cowboys*. Around this time he seemed keen on doing a big-budget Hollywood-type film. He was very conscious of Hollywood moving into, as it were, his territory. While he was recovering in hospital from the gunshot wounds John Schlesinger was shooting *Midnight Cowboy* and a lot of the Factory people had small parts in it. Anyway, he left the film-making to Paul Morrissey after this. He had never really been interested in technical perfection.

He was fascinated with people, the vulnerable, narcissistic, witty, beautiful people he collected around him, who were the subject of his films, who sustained his creativity. He had withdrawn from emotional connectedness to people a long time ago and replaced it with an obsession to record the people around him – thousands of tape recordings, polaroids, reels of films.

A child of the media age, he succeeded in becoming what he had always wanted – a famous presence, a mysterious transparency. He said: 'It's not what you are that counts – it's what they think you are' ■

DEATH AT WORK
EVOLUTION AND ENTROPY IN FACTORY FILMS

TONY RAYNS

'Actually, the audience has grown bigger and bigger, and I think we're hitting a popular audience. Degenerates are not such a great audience, but they're a step up from the art crowd; we would always rather play a sexploitation theatre than an art theatre.' Paul Morrissey, interviewed in *Cinema*, nos. 6–7, August 1970

'I have had many interesting and exciting conversations with Warhol and Morrissey, but, in retrospect, I cannot think of a single statement either of them ever made to me – and precious few ever made to anyone I know of – that, upon examination, turned out to be true.' Stephen Koch, *Stargazer*, 1973

The big unanswered question about Warhol the film-maker is: *Why did he team up with Paul Morrissey?* It's a question not even broached in the 500-odd pages of Victor Bockris' recent biography – which sees every tree but misses both the wood and the forest – where Morrissey's arrival in the Factory is noted as a 'fortuitous accident'. Morrissey joined Warhol's amorphous entourage in August 1965, just before the filming of *My Hustler*, and was a solid fixture until January 1975, when he left to make films elsewhere. The longstanding relationship reportedly began to break down during the wrangles over the financial debacle of *Flesh for Frankenstein* and *Blood for Dracula*, and ended soon after, when Morrissey tried to involve himself in the production of a Broadway musical (to which Warhol had flippantly lent his name) that closed overnight. For a decade, though, Morrissey worked on the production, distribution, exhibition and promotion of Factory films, and he began making 'Warhol films' on his own initiative in 1968, while his employer was convalescing after Valerie Solanas' assassination attempt. The first commercially exhibited Factory films with credit titles carried the credit 'Directed by Paul Morrissey'.

It's clear that Morrissey became one of the kingpins of Andy Warhol Enterprises Inc., alongside Fred Hughes, Bob Colacello and Vincent Fremont; he was the business manager who took care of Warhol's film affairs, dealing with all the mundane practicalities that Warhol himself had no interest in. But it's harder to get a fix on Morrissey's role in the first three years of the association. Insofar as any of the people who thronged the original East 47th Street Factory could be considered anomalous, Morrissey was an anomaly. Introduced to Warhol by Gerard Malanga, he fitted none of the Factory stereotypes: he was neither a sex object nor a speed-freak, he had neither the intellectual background nor the social connections that might have appealed to Warhol's snobbery, he was (or soon became) aggressively reactionary in all his opinions, and he was openly contemptuous of the art world. By his own account (Bockris, page 232),

Sylvia Miles and Joe Dallesandro in Heat, *1972*

Morrissey was attracted less by Warhol himself than by the *louche* personalities and behaviour of Factory regulars like Ondine and Brigid Polk, and by the prospect of working in film. What did Warhol see in him?

The question matters, because there was a fundamental difference between Morrissey and the many other men who contributed ideas, scripts and technical assistance to Factory films over the years. (The long list includes John Palmer, who conceived and helped to execute *Empire*, Billy Linich, Ronald Tavel, Jerry Benjamin and Chuck Wein – leaving aside all the many 'actors' who contributed on-screen improvisations to the films.) Unlike the others, Morrissey's stance was interventionist from the very start; he was not content to let Warhol *assimilate* his input into the films, but instead insisted on *imposing* his own ideas, which were generally diametrically opposed to Warhol's. The two men clashed the first time Morrissey joined a Warhol crew, for the shooting of *My Hustler*; Warhol shot the first reel as an uninterrupted, fixed-camera stare at the muscle queen on the beach, and Morrissey reshot it with languorous pans between the beach and the verandah of the beach-house. *My Hustler* was not exhibited commercially in New York until 1967, after the success of *The Chelsea Girls*, at which time Morrissey naturally supplied the cinema with his own version of the first reel. Warhol's version has never been exhibited anywhere.

Although it constantly threatens to erupt in films like *The Loves of Ondine* and *Lonesome Cowboys*, the underlying schism between Warhol cinema and Morrissey cinema was more or less contained until 1968, when Morrissey profited from Warhol's absence in hospital by making *Flesh*: a film that borrows some of Warhol's actors and methods but categorically rejects the arbitrariness and detachment that were the foundation stones of Warhol's cinema. Morrissey went further down this road in *Trash* (1970) and *Heat* (1972), progressively abandoning the visible in-camera edits and the improvisations that had survived in *Flesh* as vestigial Warholisms. Morrissey reportedly walked out on the filming when Warhol reasserted his own film aesthetic in *Blue Movie*, which he shot one afternoon and evening in David Bourdon's apartment only a month after leaving the hospital. After that, though, Warhol seemed content (resigned?) to let Morrissey follow his own direction – except perhaps in the case of *Women in Revolt*, filmed intermittently between 1970 and 1972, which looks and plays very much like the work of two 'authors' in conflict. In essence, this means that Warhol finally let Morrissey hijack Factory film-making for his own ends. Morrissey was the only collaborator ever allowed to get away with this; others were dropped, excluded or vilified in much the same way that communist parties tend to purge their ranks.

Warhol made films for 14 years, from *Kiss* (1963) to *Andy Warhol's Bad* (1976). That is, from a series of silent shorts to a brand-named commercial feature; from a studied 'anonymity' to a loudly advertised authorship. (In some markets the horror movies made in Rome also co-opted Warhol's name for their release titles; perhaps the intended signification was really closer to *ownership* than authorship in the usual sense. But Warhol learned to his financial cost that 'ownership' is a much more fluid concept in film industry circles than in the art world.)

There are many possible takes on this extraordinary trajectory from the minimal and private to the lurid and public. It could be seen as a gradual sell-out to business pressures, or as a neatly symmetrical reversal of the shift (from commercial drawing to gallery art) in Warhol's painting. It could be seen as an index to changing attitudes to sex in the USA, most particularly the rise of Gay Lib after the Stonewall Riot and the rise of porno theatres in the wake of the First Amendment battles against censorship. It could be seen as Morrissey saw it: as a weary rejection of avant-garde values and an attempt to meet mass-audience needs and tastes at least half-way. More interestingly, if dispiritingly, it could be seen as a highly idiosyncratic reinvention of cinema in somewhat deviant terms: Warhol's reprise of cinema's evolution from primitive beginnings to absent-minded old age.

It's known that Warhol was inspired to take up film-making by seeing numerous 'underground' films at the New York Film-makers' Co-op in 1962. Aside from discovering 'personalities' like Jack Smith and Taylor Mead, who found their way into his

own early films, Warhol undoubtedly responded to the realisation that films could be made at an independent, personal level, without need of the money and technical mystiques associated with Hollywood. He must also have warmed to a milieu that was decidedly relaxed about homosexuality, unlike the predominantly homophobic art establishment. Warhol's starting point, exactly like Jack Smith's, was a characteristically gay nostalgia for the tawdry glamour of Hollywood movies of his childhood and adolescence – less the impossibly remote production values of 'A' movies than the

Bad, 1976

visibly makeshift exoticism of 'B' movies – and traces of this impulse ran right through his film-making career, from the creation of low-life 'superstars' to the final wallows in bad-taste genres. In Warhol's case, though, the impulse led him to the false start of *Tarzan and Jane Regained . . . Sort of*, a little seen and long suppressed vehicle for Taylor Mead and Naomi Levine, presumably made on orthodox home-movie lines. The 'real' Warhol emerged immediately afterwards in the *Kiss* shorts (run by Jonas Mekas at the Film-makers' Co-op as a kind of serial) and the feature *Sleep*.

Sylvia Miles, Joe Dallesandro and Pat Ast in Heat, 1972

One of Edison's first exhibited Vitascope films was the scandalous *Kiss of May Irvin and John C Rice* (filmed from a stage performance in April 1896, although some film historians dispute Edison's authorship), and the myth goes that Warhol took both the idea of filming osculating couples and the method of filming – a silent, fixed-angle, monochrome stare – from an archive viewing of the Edison short. Whatever basis this myth may have in fact, there is no doubt that Warhol's earliest films were materially governed by the technical limitations of the equipment in use, much as Edison's pioneering experiments in cinematography had been. Warhol started out with a hand-wound 16 mm Bolex camera, which takes 100-foot rolls of film (approximately 2¾ minutes when projected at 24 frames-per-second), but needs rewinding every twenty seconds or so. He then added a motor, which enabled him to run 100 feet of film continuously, without pausing to rewind. He shot with this equipment throughout 1963, and then in 1964 switched to an Auricon camera with a larger magazine (it took 400-foot rolls); the first film shot on the Auricon was the eight-hour 'portrait' of the Empire State Building. Within a year he switched again to a camera that took 1200-foot rolls and permitted synchronous sound recording. The steady technological upgrade was completed by the purchase of a tripod with a swivel-head and a zoom lens. Only the last four Factory films – *Heat*, the Frankenstein and Dracula movies and *Andy Warhol's Bad* – were shot on 35 mm.

Of course, nothing *forced* Warhol to make technical limitations govern the form of his films. He might equally have shot hand-held films or bought himself editing equipment. But his instinctive withdrawal from 'art', guided by his idolisation of Duchamp and fuelled by his recent successes with serial silkscreens in New York's galleries, led him back to a 'degree zero' of film-making, emphasising the primacy of the cine-camera as a recording instrument and embracing the technical processes of shooting and editing (from whited-out reel-ends and wrong aperture or focus settings to the laboratory marks that tend to appear on negatives) as integral parts of the work. The resulting films drastically reduced the roles of director and viewer alike. The director's function was limited to choosing the subject, setting up the shot, turning the camera on and off and deciding whether or not to exhibit the result. And the viewer, for the first time in the history of the commercial exploitation of persistence-of-vision, was relieved of the obligation – perhaps even a large part of the desire – to *pay attention* to the screen. The standard 'film-as-wallpaper' definition of the early Warhol films doesn't stand up, since their entire meaning and effect spring from the fact of their projection on a screen in a darkened room. The interest of films like *Kiss*, *Blow Job*, *Eat* and *Empire* is precisely that they *command* attention without *demanding* attention.

It's worth noting that it took Warhol some little time to discover the minimum necessary directorial role to achieve this balance. In the exceptional case of *Sleep*, he worked on his film material as intensively as he had lately worked on the silkscreens: six 100-foot rolls (each of them an uninterrupted take of John Giorno asleep, each taken from a different angle) are repeated and permutated at very great length, projected at a slower speed than the original speed of photography and finally reduced to freeze-frames. But Warhol quickly realised that he didn't need to devote such energy or run up such large laboratory bills to produce the desired anaesthetic effect. It was initially enough to point the camera at a more or less passive subject; in the case of *Empire*, it wasn't even necessary to screen the finished film, since the concept carried virtually all the meaning and public awareness that the film actually existed (thanks to Jonas Mekas' 'Movie Journal' column in *The Village Voice*, 30 July 1964) produced virtually all the effect.

In 1964, as Warhol added sound recording to his technical repertoire and turned increasingly to human subjects, he remained entirely faithful to the non-interventionist principles of his silent films. The camera remained static, vagaries of photography and sound recording were accepted as integral elements, and no serious attempt was made to impose direction or narrative on the 'actors'. The first sound film was *Harlot*, shot in December 1964, which immediately established Warhol's preference for off-screen sound: four 'actors' pose on-screen in a huddled group, registering minimal interest in or indifference to each other, while three men (Ronald Tavel, Harry Fainlight and Billy Linich) improvise a desultory off-screen conversation, comprised of scatology, gossip and bad puns. This, too, could be seen as a phase in the reinvention of cinema history: an echo of the period (most marked in Chinese and Japanese cinemas) when late-silent movies were accompanied by live commentaries. (A transcript of the *Harlot* soundtrack and a surprisingly lucid account of the making and showing of the film by Ronald Tavel can be found in *Film Culture* no. 40, reprinted in the present volume). Just as Chaplin or Ozu fought shy of making talkies until the last possible moment in the mid-1930s, so Warhol clung to the concept of off-screen commentary on on-screen performance for most of 1965. The turning point was *My Hustler*. It's clear that Warhol's version of that film's first 1200-foot reel would have closely resembled *Harlot*: a static shot of Paul America doing next to nothing on the beach, accompanied by the drooling improvisations of three off-screen lechers. When Morrissey insisted on panning the camera from the sex object to the speakers, he not only ruptured the formal integrity of Warhol's methods but also, at a stroke, turned Factory films into vehicles for 'actors'. From there, it was a small step to *The Chelsea Girls*.

There had been on-screen dialogue in many of the earlier Factory films made in 1965, but it had either taken the form of response to aggressive or hostile off-screen prompting (as in *Screen Test #2* and *Beauty #2*) or been limited to the actors' attempts to cope with visibly unrehearsed scripts (as in *Kitchen*). Such films had already marked a shift in Warhol's attitude to the cine-camera. He had begun by using the camera as a more-or-less neutral recording instrument, whose technical

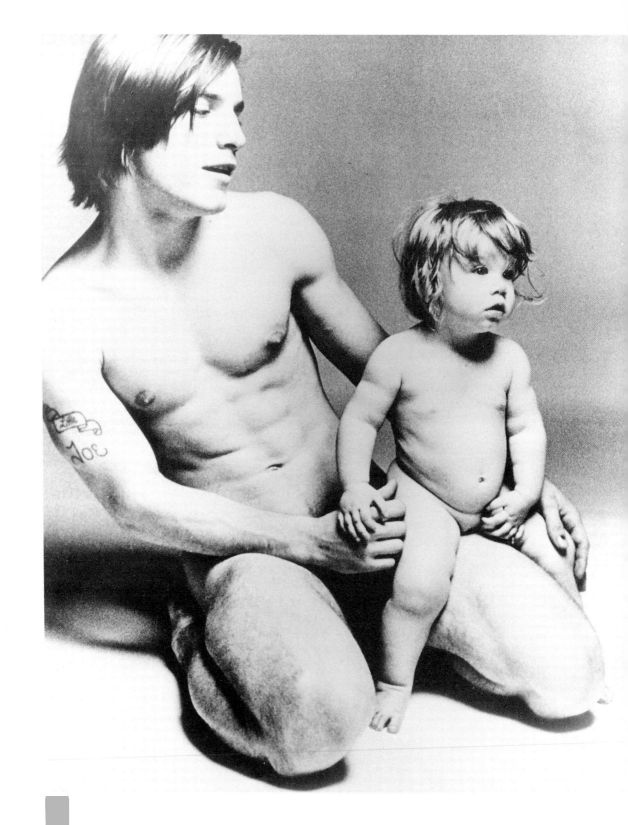

Joe Dallesandro in
Flesh, *1968*

specifications were allowed to determine the material form of the films; when he grew more interested in film portraiture, picking his subjects from the flotsam of speed-freaks, poseurs, meat-marketers and hangers-on at the Factory, he evidently came to see the camera as a combined weapon and shield. On the one hand, the camera became an instrument of aggression, goading the 'actors' into performances by its very presence even as it implacably recorded their resilience, their inadequacies and their humiliations. On the other, it served to detach the film-maker from both his subjects and, by extension, their world of narcissism, egotism and sexual display. In short, the cine-camera was co-opted into Warhol's armoury of defences against an amoral and potentially frightening society – alongside the dark glasses, the wigs, the tape recorders and the Polaroid camera. The sado-masochistic gestalt in play here (investigated by Stephen Koch in *Stargazer*) is less important for the present discussion than the evolution of the camera's function. By accident or design Warhol hit upon a means of rhyming his own abdication from the traditional role of the artist with the manufacture of objects that would stand as very precise and very material 'statements' of social, sexual and psychological import. It was the cine-camera in all its mechanical autonomy that made the rhyme perfect.

As soon as Morrissey began panning the camera, the rhyme became false. The pan from the beach to the verandah of the beach-house in *My Hustler* was the first directorial intervention in the *process* of Factory film-making since Warhol's own abandoned experiments with repetition and permutation in *Sleep*. Moreover, it was an intervention explicitly at the service of the actors, designed to show them off, to assert the value of seeing them as well as hearing them. In Hollywood terms, it put the names of the 'stars' above the title. There are two distinct (but not mutually exclusive)

ways of looking at this. They might be thought of as 'Warhol's perspective' and 'Morrissey's perspective'. The latter would see the change as the next 'logical' step in the evolution of Factory cinema: the introduction of 'stars', a relaxation of formal constraints, a move towards film-making with definable, human-interest subjects. The former would see the change as a retreat from the randomness and detachment of earlier Factory films, and a risky step into the arena of conventionally directed film-making. Morrissey's perspective was the one that ultimately prevailed – right up to the production of *Andy Warhol's Bad*, which was a Morrissey film made without Morrissey, just as *Flesh* and *Trash* had been Warhol films made without Warhol.

This brings us back to the question we started with: *Why did Warhol surrender to Morrissey?* We can only speculate on the answers, although there are several objective factors to take into account. Warhol and Morrissey both came from Catholic backgrounds, and shared a detached fascination with the blatantly immoral behaviour of the Factory crowd. They may well also have shared certain sexual proclivities, although Morrissey has never, to my knowledge, publicly declared his sexuality. Morrissey's assertive self-confidence was *yang* to the *yin* of Warhol's insecurities and paranoid withdrawal from responsibilities and relationships. Morrissey was introduced to Warhol as a person with film-craft skills at just the moment that Warhol was giving up painting and turning his full attention to film. And Morrissey had hucksterish ideas about marketing films, earning money with them, at a time when (as Bockris' tireless ear for minutiae reminds us) Factory overheads were rising and the values of Warhol's paintings were not.

Did Warhol then simply sell out to Morrissey? Did he let Morrissey take over Factory film-making simply because Morrissey seemed ready and able to guide it into profit? Or were there deeper reasons for the surrender? Perhaps Warhol felt some unexpressed need to assert a directorial personality or a moral point of view, but shrank back from asserting it himself. Did he use Morrissey to assert it for him? To look at it a slightly different way, did Warhol feel the need to move his cinema into another new phase and choose Morrissey as his executive assistant for this express purpose? Or perhaps Warhol's instincts told him that he had taken his idiosyncratic reinvention of cinema in deviant terms as far as it could go without lapsing into endless repetition. Did he sense this impasse and embrace Morrissey's Hollywooden skills as a way out? How did Warhol see Morrissey's input: as a further evolution of Factory cinema? Or as a way of adulterating his own film aesthetic and pushing it towards entropy and ultimate oblivion?

Coincidentally or not, earlier Warhol collaborators like Ronald Tavel and Chuck Wein found themselves edged out as Morrissey settled into the Factory; there was less and less need for the kind of 'scripts' and 'situations' they had supplied. Around the end of 1965, Warhol/Morrissey began concentrating on shooting 1200-foot rolls featuring improvisations by one or more 'superstars'. These were always shot as uninterrupted takes and projected (if at all) exactly as they ran through the camera. Following the precedent set in *My Hustler*, many of them featured minimal directorial touches, like panning shots to follow action and use of the zoom lens. The twelve reels eventually selected for twin-screen projection as *The Chelsea Girls* came from this prolific output, and so did the countless reels used for the one-off screening of **** (*Four Stars*) in December 1967. During 1967, though, Morrissey tired of these obviously impractical and 'uncommercial' experiments. Heartened by the modest commercial success of *My Hustler* in New York, he suppressed most of the experimental 'portrait' reels and produced instead a number of conventional-length features, all of them containing plentiful male (and occasional female) nudity.

There's no reason to doubt that Warhol was fully complicit in the making of films like *The Loves of Ondine*, *Bike Boy*, *I, a Man* and *Nude Restaurant*, which were not only conceptually geared to the sexploitation market but were also the first Factory films since *Sleep* to feature any kind of editing. At its 'purest', this editing was engineered simply by stopping and restarting the camera and projecting the resulting reel exactly as it stood; Warhol retained enough of his old commitment to the *process* of film-making to leave in the soundtrack blip and image-track flash-frame that mark the start of each new shot, thereby emphasising the fact of each 'cut'. These rough, in-camera edits became a kind of trademark of Warhol's cinema up to *Blue Movie*; Morrissey retained them for *Flesh*, but abandoned them from *Trash* onwards. Of course, the appearance of in-camera edits is not in itself a guarantee that the projected film is identical with the film that passed through the camera; in films like *Lonesome Cowboys* and *Flesh* it is very obvious that further, more conventional editing has also been carried out. But *Blue Movie*, which comprises four 1200-foot reels, one of them a continuous take and the other three containing in-camera edits, is clearly faithful to the Warhol ethos that defined a finished film as whatever passed through the camera.

Blue Movie is by far the best of the 1967/68 Warhol films, and the only one that suggests that Warhol's approach to cinema reached a sophisticated maturity. By documenting its own time-frame (one afternoon and evening) and limiting its subject to conversation and sexual relations between two people (Viva and Louis Waldon), the film succeeds in upholding the principles of concentration, arbitrariness and serendipity that were cornerstones of Warhol's cinema from the sta The domestic intimacy of the content and the obvious absence of directorial control (both Viva and Louis make it clear that they themselves determine what happens) turn the film into a flow o random thought associations, gestures, mannerisms, whims, speech-slips, in fact a glossary of unconscious self-expression, all brought into focus by the fact that the two people on screen are adults who have agreed to be filmed chatting and making love. Some of the 1967 sexploitation features also contain scenes or sequences that play like vaudeville variations on Freud's *Psychopathology of Everyday Life*, but they are too scrappily conceived and constructed to achieve the 'authentic' Warhol blankness. The crucial factor, as in Warhol's earliest films, is the material emphasis on *process*, which provides a defined common ground between the (non-) director, the performers and the viewer and thereby delineates the space in which things may or may not happen, may or may not be discovered. Take away that factor and you're left with a film like any other – a film like *Flesh*.

In abandoning the formal integrity of Warhol's cinema and deliberately setting out to make films which would catch and hold an audience's interest, Morrissey also introduced a transparent vein of moralism: *Flesh*, *Trash*, *Heat* and the horror diptych are chronicles of all the ills that flesh is heir to. These are not only conventionally authored films, but films whose scripting and casting more or less explicitly express an authorial point of view – a mixture, as it happens, of prurience, condescension and supercilious contempt. Are these hardline attitudes a legitimate extension of whatever lay beneath Warhol's studiously detached voyeurism? Or did Morrissey simply take the blank sheet of Warhol's moral silence and fill it with Republican bigotry? Maybe these questions find their oblique answer in Warhol's seemingly lapsed Catholicism. Compare Richard Avedon's celebrated 1969 photograph of Warhol – showing only his torso, pitted, scarred and sutured after the assassination attempt – with Morrissey's jokes about spare-part surgery and necrophilia in *Flesh for Frankenstein*, where the line about 'fucking death in the gall bladder' directly anticipates the cause of Warhol's own death. The Warhol who professed dispassion when one Factory denizen after another burned out, who produced the serial silkscreens of disasters, car crashes and suicides, whose diaries and writings are obsessed with ageing and death and who bared his own stigmata for Avedon's camera, was also the Warhol who put his name to Morrissey's gleeful graveyard humour. A death wish is a death wish is a death wish, and public piety is nothing more than an optional extra.

Warhol maintained the same serene detachment from Morrissey's crassness and B-movie ambitions that he did from the behavioural excesses of his Factory 'superstars' in the 1960s. His own art, on canvas, on paper and on film, is quite different from Morrissey's cinema. Warhol's films, up to *Blue Movie* and parts of *Women in Revolt*, share with many of his paintings a tendency towards absolute stillness. Inexorably chronicling the passage of time, they correspond with Cocteau's definition of cinema as 'death at work'. That's fine, but the overall trajectory from *Kiss* to *Andy Warhol's Bad* insists that neither life nor death is usually that simple – and reminds us that there's more than one way to skin a cat ∎

Notes

Victor Bockris, *Warhol* (London: Frederick Muller, 1989).
Stephen Koch, *Stargazer* (London: Marion Boyars, 1973, 1985).
Jonas Mekas, *Movie Journal: The Rise of the New American Cinema 1959–1971* (New York: Collier Books, 1972), especially the columns dated 30 July 1964 and 9 January 1969.
Viva, *Superstar* (London: Sphere Books, 1970).
Andy Warhol, *The Philosophy of Andy Warhol (From A to B and Back Again)* (London: Picador, 1975).
Issues no. 40 (1966) and no. 45 (1967) of the magazine *Film Culture*.

Also, see my earlier writings on the cinema of Warhol and Morrissey in *Cinema* (nos. 6–7 1970) and *Monthly Film Bulletin* (December 1970, June 1971, July 1972, February 1973, August 1973).

WARHOL'S EARLY FILMS
REALISM AND PSYCHOANALYSIS

MICHAEL O'PRAY

'The only piece of action in the dream was the opening of the window; for the wolves sat quite still and without any movement on the branches of the tree, to the right and left of the trunk, and looked at me. It seemed as though they had riveted their whole attention upon me, – I think this was my first anxiety dream.' The Wolf Man – Sigmund Freud

Freud's 'From the History of an Infantile Neurosis' of 1918, better known as the Wolf Man case, contains the most elaborate account of the content and mechanisms of unconscious phantasy to be found in his writings. More importantly, for the purposes of this essay, it has at its core a dream which is strangely reminiscent of the early Warhol films, say, *Empire*, *The Thirteen Most Beautiful Women*, *Sleep*, *Eat* and *Henry Geldzahler*. That is to say, it shares qualities with the films which use not only the fixed camera but also a relatively still subject-matter. Freud, in his analysis of the Wolf Man's dream, identifies a characteristic which signals its most powerful latent content. In a footnote on the dream wolves he remarks:

> *They sat there motionless*. This contradicts the most striking feature of the observed scene, namely, its agitated movement, which, in virtue of the attitudes to which it led, constitutes the

connection between the primal scene and the wolf story.

The 'observed scene' was, of course, the Wolf Man parents performing 'coitus a tergo, three times repeated' during a siesta on a hot summer's afternoon, which the Wolf Man allegedly perceived when a very small child. One piece of theory behind Freud's analysis here concerns a familiar psychoanalytic idea, namely that an extreme feeling or affect, if denied, will disguise itself by adopting the characteristics of its opposite. In the Wolf Man's dream the violent movement of the observed copulation becomes the passive, still image of the dream-wolves. Warhol's obsession with stillness and duration in his films similarily point to unconscious ideas of the kind found in Freud's analysis of the wolf-dream. It also seems remarkable that these early films can be divided between the silent still-life films and ones which depict frank and real scenes of sexual activity. In the case of the mass of material which formed the largely unseen film *Couch*, rumoured to be twenty-four hours long,[1] Warhol displays a polysexuality closely associated in Freud with the pre-oedipal infant's unconscious mental life. The two meanings of the Wolf Man's dream – one manifest, the other latent – reflect the two aspects of Warhol's films; the asexual still *Empire* and *Eat* are to be replaced by *Couch* with its endless sexual couplings.

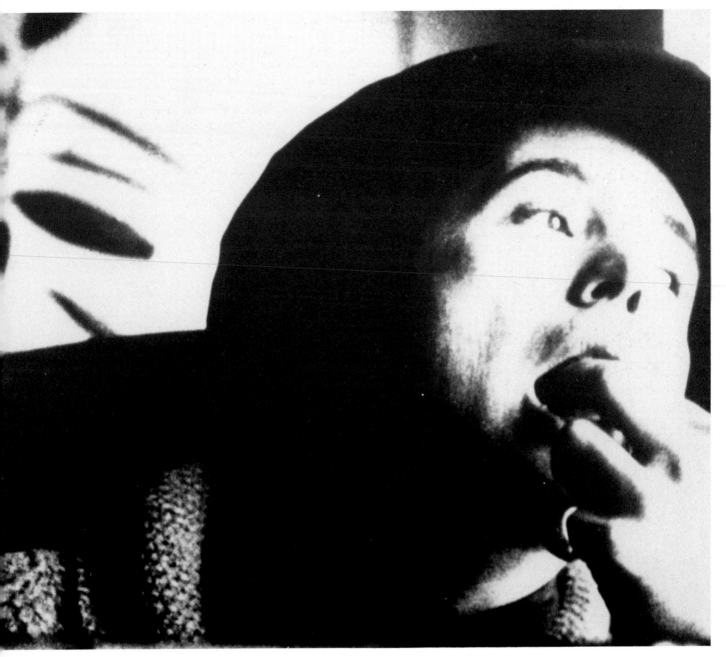

Robert Indiana in Eat,
1963

It was precisely the motionless, long-held stare of the camera that eroticised so much of the early material, even *Empire* as Warhol himself was quick to realise. The issues here are complex[2] but in this essay, I want to address Warhol's early silent films (*Sleep, Empire, Eat, Henry Geldzahler, Thirteen Most Beautiful Women* and *Blow Job*) in terms of other aspects of psychoanalytic theory, emphasizing the ideas of Melanie Klein as filtered through the art-critical work of the neglected English aesthetician, Adrian Stokes. The essay also represents an attempt to apply Stokes' ideas in painting, sculpture and architecture to film.[3]

The mundane subject-matter of Warhol's early minimal films is, of course, a legacy of the first onslaught on content in art carried through by the Impressionists and crystallised in Duchamp's ready-mades. The retrieval of the urban environment of Western capitalist society and the concomitant rise of the subjective, the private and the domestic and, inevitably with Freud, the psychical during the same period, has been one of the underlying if unconscious aims of art during this century. But equally, there has been a willingness to blur and even eradicate the traditional difference between form and content. More often than not this has meant treating form as content, whereas it is also possible to treat content as form. There is no strict demarcation between the two, only a matter of adopting a particular attitude toward the object. In the Warhol films in question, the form is treated as one with the subject matter and in this respect Warhol can be conceived momentarily as falling under the aesthetic rubric of André Bazin. For at least in one version, the cruder one, of Bazin's realist theory of cinema, Warhol is a perfect example of a cinematic project which holds the object at a distance in its wholeness and integrity *qua* object, which treats of reality as intrinsic to the filmic process and where montage-like construction seems to have no hold. The exclusion of editing, the use of the fixed camera, duration, and the 'mundanity' of the events filmed, all would lead us to identify Warhol as a realist. Therefore it seems apt that we find in Bazin's 'The Evolution of the Language of Cinema'[4] written between 1950 and 1955, a description of a Warholian film in the context of some remarks on Stroheim: 'One could easily imagine as a matter of fact a film by Stroheim composed of a single shot as long-lasting and as close-up as you like.' Bazin also states that Stroheim has 'one simple rule for direction. Take a close look at the world, keep on doing so, and in the end it will lay bare for you all its cruelty and its ugliness.' The technique and aesthetic of realism (in this version at least) adumbrated by Bazin would embrace, it seems, many of Warhol's earlier films. But it is in Stokes's writings that we find the link being forged between a realism of sorts and certain psychological concepts.

Adrian Stokes has remarked upon the anti-art project endemic to twentieth century art in terms of a stress on the real. He states:

> There has been a great broadening of the possible objects for aesthetic contemplation at the sacrifice of precise imagery, delineated symbolic content, in favour of a presentation of the pre-existent, the actual.[5]

Whilst Stokes may have had ready-mades and collage in mind here with his notion of the 'actual', the quotation seems apt in discussing a concept with a family-resemblance to 'actuality' – realism. In cinema, the commonly-held division between montage film-makers and realist ones (the Eisenstein/Bazin distinction) is not simply to be taken as a technical one but, as Bazin believed, marking something more profound, something running deeper than method. At this point, it would seem opportune to turn aside from Bazin and discuss Adrian Stokes' views in order to explore a parallel between montage and filmic realism and a fine art distinction more applicable to painting, sculpture and architecture.

It was Stokes who grasped a distinction in art, traditionally made, between carving and modelling and then, quite originally, deepened it so that the categories became ones of psychical import. Briefly, in carving Stokes conceived a relationship to the stone which involved ideas of how phantasies were projected by the artist onto the materials. In sculpture, for example, the stone when carved is treated traditionally as if the finished object was already *in* the stone block. This ideology of the carving mode implied a respect for the integrity of the stone's expressive properties – the carver released the image in form (Stokes' phrase) from the material, that is, stone. Such sculpture, exemplified most satisfyingly for Stokes in his book *Stones of Rimini* by Agostino di Duccio's low-relief carvings, was characterised by a self-sufficiency of the object dependent on an attention to texture, inner light (exemplified in the use of marble) and the even progression of surfaces. In contrast with the modelling mode of work, the art object *qua* object was somehow intact; it was an otherness.

Modelling, on the other hand, in Stokes's earlier

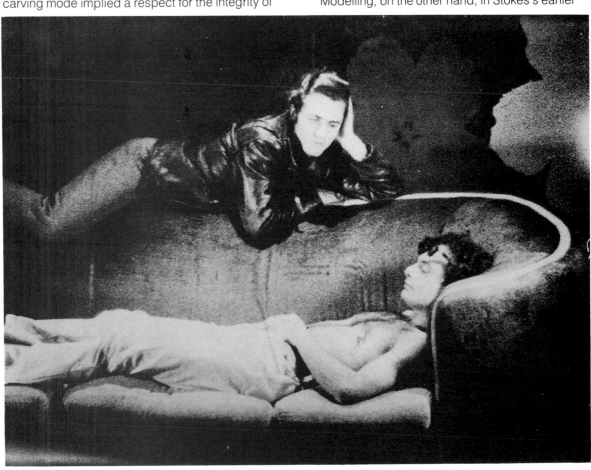

Gerard Malanga and Piero Heliczer in Couch, 1964

writings, suffered by being associated with the idea of art springing, so to speak, from nothing. Through the use of molds and traditional materials like brass and bronze, the modelling mode was marked by sharp transitions, a profusion of internal differentiation and an attack on the materials, often running counter to their natural properties. So much of this description seems reminiscent of the realist/montage distinction with carving associated with realism and modelling with montage. The use of expressionistic chiaroscuro lighting or extensive editing techniques runs counter to the otherness established in carving or broad realist modes; rather an envelopment takes place, a drawing in of the spectator which denies the self-sufficiency and externality of the film.

The ontological and epistemological foundations of the two positions are quite distinct. For the realist, the Bazinian, the pro-filmic event is paramount, whereas for the Eisensteinian, the construction of relationships between parts of given footage into an entirely 'new' object is central to the act of 'true' film-making. It needs hardly stressing how much the montage method has been associated with fragmenting violence in the work of Eisenstein, Hitchcock, Brakhage and Anger, whereas the realism of Dreyer, Rossellini and Renoir elicits descriptions of calmness, a subdued sensibility lacking the violation of surfaces found in the montage film-makers. Moreover, in, for example, *Eat* and *Henry Geldzahler*, there is not only the fixed camera, unedited reels and the non-staged events but also a love of the subject matter so often associated with that aesthetic. This idea flows out of Bazin's notion that 'there is ontological identity between the object and its photographic image', and is central to his defence of Italian neo-realist cinema. But in Warhol's early films, this fixed loving gaze of the camera is always dangerously poised on the edge of a sadism, a cruel murderous gaze. This is reminiscent of the Wolf Man's dream where the extreme properties of the image – the

motionlessness, the fixed stare denote a latent content of quick movement and aggression. The Warhol films we have isolated from the body of his work, it is argued, fall into the realist aesthetic.

Notably in his later post-war writings, Stokes shifted away from this prejudice against modelling, a prejudice obviously in sway during his own analysis with Melanie Klein in the 1930s after the two books in which this position was articulated were written. He stressed eventually the importance of both modes or attitudes being present in art. This was to respect the Kleinian theory of the two positions – the depressive and the paranoid-schizoid, associated respectively with carving and modelling. In this way, and through intense struggle, Stokes rendered a technical distinction into a psychological one and ultimately, an aesthetic one. In modelling we are dealing with the part-objects, severe splitting and fragmentation of Klein's paranoid-schizoid position, whereas the carving mode is associated with the whole objects of the depressive position.

In such films as *Empire*, *Henry Geldzahler*, *Eat* or *Sleep* carving qualities seem dominant. The film-as-representation is self-sufficient and independent. It stands apart from us with no enveloping tendencies except those associated essentially with cinema's viewing conditions – the darkened auditorium, the screen's scale, the intimate sharing of spectatorial space with others and the intrinsically dramatic qualities of white light projected onto the screen. The fixed camera and still-life pro-filmic event are mesmeric but suffused with boredom. Refusing the drama, the narrative and the semantic constructions of editing, Warhol stresses the photographic aspect of film, its 'mechanical reproduction' and what can be achieved by simply flipping the switch and walking away. Michael Snow's *La Région Centrale* has the same Romantic anti-art gesture but the machine of that film insinuates the montage of the modelling position, providing the drama of movement. Warhol eschews this for a more manic

Robert Indiana in Eat, *1963*

form of omnipotence in which stasis, withdrawal and denial are encompassed by an unflinching acceptance of the subject as image, any subject as image. But only to a point, for John Giorno (the sleeper in *Sleep*) Henry Geldzahler, Robert Indiana (the eater of mushrooms in *Eat*) are portraits of friends. There is no equivalence in the history of the avant-garde cinema, for whilst the film-maker's friends have peopled the narratives of many avant-gardists from Buñuel to Maya Deren to Jack Smith, rarely have their films been simply portraits in the same way as Warhol's.

Gerard Malanga in The Thirteen Most Beautiful Boys, *1964–65*

Importantly, Annette Michelson[6] has felt the need to link Brakhage with the montage work and theories of Eisenstein, and Warhol's films have often been seen as direct responses and in opposition to Brakhage. Brakhage would seem to fit into a modelling mode of work – the constant movement, use of close-up, strong dramatic colour and lighting effects and the use of editing and subjective hand-held camera. The object is not held at a distance, but envelopes the spectator through these dramatic devices. There is a strong attack on the film and a sense of construction by which the pro-filmic event is only one stage towards the piecing together of a filmic reality that provides notably a metaphor for

consciousness and nature itself. All of these qualities oppose the aesthetics of Warhol.

As a final support for this argument (in its present stage, an argument of association rather than of logic), it would seem appropriate to look at some remarks made by Walter Benjamin which relate to the idea of realism in Warhol's early films. 'The camera introduces us to unconscious optics as does psychoanalysis to unconscious impulses,' writes Benjamin.[7] In section XIII of his essay 'The Work of Art in the Age of Mechanical Reproduction', he speaks of the visual possibilities of the movie camera in terms of its mechanical properties:

By close-ups of the things around us, by focusing on hidden details of familiar objects, by exploring commonplace milieus under the ingenious guidance of the camera, the film, on the one hand extends our comprehension of the necessities which rule our lives; on the other hand, it manages to assure us of an immense and unexpected field of action.

He goes on to expand this idea in a more aesthetic mode:

With the close-up, space expands; with slow motion, movement is extended. The enlargement of a snapshot does not simply render more precise what in any case was visible, though unclear: it reveals entirely new structural formations of the subject.

Benjamin perhaps had in mind here the idea of the documentary, the kind of work now produced in films on the natural world – the flower's growth speeded up, the insect magnified, the lion's kill slowed down, etc. In other words, the film equivalent to Muybridge's and Marey's photographic studies. Jonas Mekas made the connection between Warhol's cinema and cinéma vérité when discussing *Empire*, *Eat* and *Sleep*. But it seems no accident that in Benjamin's famous essay on the concept of the aura, so widely applied to Warhol's art, this conception of cinema should also be articulated, a conception superficially close to Warhol's. His use of the slowed down images, the mundane acts of sleeping, eating and kissing and later, in *Couch* for example, fucking and messing around on a sofa, are all reminiscent of Benjamin's concern for a cinema of 'unconscious optics'. This revelatory aspect is central to Warhol's cinema.

But slowed-down film is only one method among many. The most innovative in many ways was duration itself, the immense length of the film in relation to its minimal subject-matter. This introduces different ideas to those found in Benjamin, ideas concerning spectatorship, voyeurism and self-reflexivity. To this extent, and unlike aspects of Benjamin's, the Warholian aesthetic is modernist, in the widest sense of that word. For like the Dada artists Warhol delights in laying bare the materials – the fogged ends as the reel runs out, the fixed camera and the partially improvised theatre organised in front of the camera as in *Vinyl*, *Kitchen* or *Couch* are all intimate with the ideas circulating in New York at the time. Nevertheless Warhol's modernism is one deeply penetrated by a realism not conspicuous in Brakhage or for that matter, Jack Smith. There is no editing or camera effect conspiring towards either an illusionism or a heightened poetics. Duration confronts the spectator with film itself as material and as a process of representation. *My Hustler* stands out for the very fact that it does use devices like editing, fast pans and narrative pacing (of sorts), seemingly under Morrissey's influence. The minimal films are very much the poetics, if we wish to use that word, of the real and in so much, are at one with Benjamin's remarks.

In summary, these remarks are offered as hypotheses, as suggestions for possible connections to be made between different conceptions of cinema and aesthetics in relation to Warhol and perhaps avant-garde film in general. In the past, film theory, too often owing to Lacanian semiotics, has stumbled before avant-garde cinema. The latter's rejection of linear narrative has meant that good analysis, when it occurred, found its critical and theoretical impetus often in literary sources (Sitney and Koch). In Adrian Stokes' work, the psychoanalysis of Melanie Klein and aesthetics itself were brought together, and it is Stokes who is most suggestive in terms of an art that is saturated with the desire for formal innovation, for he understood that the formal is as imbued in phantasy as is so-called content. In Warhol's early films we find some kind of instantiation of this idea ∎

Notes

1 Ronald Tavel in interview with Patrick S. Smith in the latter's *Andy Warhol's Art and Films* (p. 489) states that *Couch* is twenty-four hours long, although the version usually seen is about forty minutes long.
2 For example, Warhol's sadistic voyeurism is well documented and often on screen for us to see. Koch has said much about this in his book *Stargazer*; however a full-scale psychoanalytical reading of Warhol has yet to be done.
3 See *Tonight the Ballet*, Adrian Stokes (London: Faber, 1942) for Stokes' only serious discussion of film. The vast quantity of Stokes's work is gathered in *The Critical Writings of Adrian Stokes*, (ed.) Lawrence Gowing (Thames and Hudson: 1978). For other writing on Stokes and cinema see my articles: 'On Adrian Stokes and Film Aesthetics', *Screen* vol. 21 no. 4, 1980/1 and 'Primitive Phantasy in David Cronenberg's Films' in *David Cronenberg*, (ed.) Wayne Drew (London: BFI Dossier 21, 1984).
4 In *What Is Cinema?*, André Bazin (Berkeley: University of California Press, 1967).
5 Adrian Stokes, 'The Future and Art' in *A Game That Must be Lost* (Cheadle, Cheshire: Carcanet, 1973).
6 See Annette Michelson, 'Camera Lucida/Camera Obscura', *Artforum*, January 1973.
7 Walter Benjamin, 'The Work of Art in the Age of Mechanical Reproduction' in *Illuminations* (London: Fontana, 1973) p. 239.

THE WARHOL FILE
MARGIA KRAMER

From *The Village Voice*, 17 May 1988

Margia Kramer's book *Andy Warhol et al. The FBI File on Andy Warhol* was published by UnSub Press in 1988

In 1968, the FBI began to gather information toward an obscenity case against Andy Warhol and his friends, and film, *Lonesome Cowboys*. A file entitled 'Andy Warhol; (deleted line) Andy Warhol Films, Inc.' was created under the category 'ITOM: Interstate Transportation of Obscene Matter.' After his death, I obtained from FBI Headquarters in Washington, D.C., the FBI file on Warhol – 71 pages – through a Freedom of Information Act request.

In November 1967, Warhol, Paul Morrissey, and Viva went to Tucson, Arizona to scout locations for a new film. Audiences heckled them during local appearances and screenings of Warhol's film **** (1967). According to newspaper accounts, however, the director, undaunted, said they would return within a few week's time. (Morrissey claimed that they planned to make a movie called *The Unwanted Cowboy*, a western spoof starring Viva as a bareback rider.) At the end of January, 1968, the cast and crew went to Oracle, Arizona, and began shooting on the Old Tucson set, where John Wayne movies had once been made.

Warhol shot the film – now called *Lonesome Cowboys* – in just four days. It was the first 'location' movie of his career. Photographed in Eastman Color and 16 mm, it was edited down to 110 minutes and released for national distribution in 35 mm. More mainstream than his previous films, *Lonesome Cowboys* was distributed in the US by Sherpix, Inc., a subsidiary of Art Theatre Guild, Inc., a pioneer in art film exhibition, which, according to the film's press release, 'owns and operates 40 Art Theatres throughout the United States, and was responsible for the successful introduction of art films in the mid-west.' According to *Variety* (7 May 1969), Warhol and Morrissey began to aim for major money with *Lonesome Cowboys* and *Flesh* (1968); *Flesh*, made for $4000, grossed an average of $2000 per week during its New York run; *Lonesome Cowboys*, an average of $3000 to $4000. This film – now shot on location, feature-length, and distributed nationally – generated interest outside the art world in Warhol's work. (His next project, a $100,000 feature to be filmed on location in Los Angeles, was never made; he was shot on 3 June 1968.) But it also captured the attention of the FBI.

At the 1968 San Francisco Film Festival, FBI agents monitored *Lonesome Cowboys*. The following quotations from their three-page description are found in a document from the Warhol file dated 4 November 1968:

> All of the males in the cast displayed homosexual tendencies and conducted themselves toward one another in an effeminate manner.
>
> One of the cowboys practiced his ballet and a conversation ensued regarding the misuse of mascara by one of the other cowboys.
>
> There was no plot to the film and no

a in Bike Boy, *1967*

Flesh, *1968*

development of character throughout. It was rather a remotely-connected series of scenes which depicted situations of sexual relationships of homosexual and heterosexual nature.

The history of the Warhol file is instructive. The first entry is dated 2 February 1968. In a document dated 23 February, the name of the initial informant in Tucson is deleted. His or her single complaint had been sufficient cause for the FBI to begin the file and monitor Warhol and his friends around the country, in connection with the production,

rash, *1970*

distribution, and exhibition of *Lonesome Cowboys*. The file contains large areas of encoded deletions; 33 pages, including the last 9 (before the final summary), are totally withheld.

Documents from the file are revealing. By 8 March 1968, the New York field office of the FBI had taken over the investigation from the Phoenix office, and a criminal investigation was requested. (The file remained active until 3 September, when it was retitled 'Andy Warhol, ET AL,' and its status changed to 'Pending Inactive.') On 5 August 1969, the film was seized and audience members photographed during a police raid at a commercial screening in Atlanta. According to *Variety* (31 December 1969), '. . . last week . . . the film was given the green light by Fulton County district attorney Lewis R. Slaton and solicitor general Hinson McAuliffe only after six cuts were made. . . .' In states where the film was shown, the FBI did in fact suggest to local law enforcement authorities that they press an obscenity case against *Lonesome Cowboys*. Finally, in June 1977, the Warhol file on *Lonesome Cowboys* was summarized in two pages, which were sent (along with the description from the 1968 San Francisco Film Festival) to the Carter White House, for reasons unknown.

At a time when Warhol was attempting to reach a broad commercial audience, the monitoring of activities surrounding *Lonesome Cowboys* exacted a high price from both the artist and Sherpix, Inc. – cuts in the original film, costly legal fees, court delays, and prior-restraint, all helping to prevent its unhindered distribution. The government would use prior-restraint again: *Blue Movie* (1969) was seized by New York City police. Between 1969 and 1971, city and state courts declared the film hardcore pornography. The case went to the US Supreme Court, which upheld the use of prior-restraint, deciding against Warhol. But this was 1973: Cuts would be required if the film were to be distributed again. Four years of profits had been lost ∎

I'LL BE YOUR MIRROR
GARY INDIANA

From *The Village Voice*,
5 May 1987

A thorny, twisty subject: Andy Warhol. The Andy Warhol Phenomenon. The vacant but obdurate public presence – relentless, in fact – famed from the outset for its entourage. At first the entourage consisted of amiable lunatics, charmingly damaged heiresses, beautiful street boys, miraculously loquacious speed freaks, fallen Catholics, people with a flair for 'suggesting ideas'. Later the shimmering mask surrounded itself with buttoned-down professionals, social climbers, dewy millionettes. Since the new people risked nothing, and felt nothing much about anything, they provided few ideas. The product lost its quality of selective inanity. It became an example of surplus vacuity. The Presence no longer wondered at his inability to feel.

Then the death. The private duty nurse, who sounds like someone who might have changed her name from Valerie Solanis. And the incredible obsequies. Years ago, Taylor Mead told me that Andy's problem was that he wasn't content with being a genius, he wanted to be a saint, too. And so, the speakers at his memorial service stressed his unflagging Christian spirit, his charity. How he multiplied the loaves and fishes. One speaker made the curious argument for sainthood: it wasn't for Andy to be his brother's keeper. The understatement of the century, surely. As further proof of Andy's intense spirituality, his eulogist quoted the line about wanting to be reincarnated as the ring on Liz Taylor's finger. Clearly, Catholicism is exactly what it used to be.

One former superstar put it quite succinctly: 'I'm going to Andy's funeral, but I doubt if he would go to mine.' Outliving Andy must be, for some, a surprise. As usual, excellent timing. The culture was becoming weary of Andy Warhol. The inanities had ceased to charm, having reached a brutal apotheosis with the picture-book *America*. Lately, Andy had resorted to flirtation.

Although his influence is pervasive in the best contemporary art, the best contemporary artists were having none of him. The inspired, breathtakingly easy Duchampian gesture can only come off against a background of resistance, of entrenched tradition. When it works today, the background it works against is precisely the seduction of the glamorous surface. Richard Prince had already inverted Andy's best-known, most-misquoted maxim. In the future, no one will want to be famous. A nice twist on Dorothy Parker's line: 'If you want to know what God thinks about money, just look at the people he gives it to.'

'Either wear a work of art or be a work of art,' said Oscar Wilde, an aesthete with an attractively messy private life. Andy Warhol became a much less convincing work of art after the demimonde clasped him to its jeweled bosom. His eerie gift, until then, had been the ability to confer celebrity – on a soup can, a Port Authority rent-boy, or a wacked-out

Joe Spencer and Viva in
Bike Boy, 1967

socialite. The Factory was a church. The Church of the Unimaginable Penis, or something. Andy was the father confessor, the kids were the sinners. Which is why he didn't need to be involved with them when they finished confessing. The sanctity of the institution and its rituals is what's important, not personal salvation. Maintaining the eternal surface.

After turning his back on the zanies who'd been his inspiration, Warhol no longer bestowed celebrity, but instead sustained his own through increasingly ludicrous associations, chiefly through his magazine, *Interview*. The upscale *Interview*

Bike Boy, *1967*

chewed its way through acres of glossy trash at Studio 54 before arriving among such 'interesting' people as George Will, Nancy Reagan, Jerry Zipkin, and the Shah of Iran. Whatever Warhol was trying to do, it didn't 'read' as anything except venality.

For example, the I'll-paint-anybody-for-$20,000 approach. Art critics committed to the myth of Warhol-as-bellwether suggest that Warhol has simply done the same thing Goya did, or other court painters in the past. But an artist of Warhol's affluence isn't faced with starvation if he turns down a commission; say, from Idi Amin, or the Sultan of Brunei. Contrary to the Warhol philosophy, modern life still does require choices. Quite a few people

with money wouldn't piss on Nancy Reagan if her guts were on fire, and many of them commission portraits. At any rate, the 'court paintings' are Andy's weakest work – unless you look at them a certain way, and think their very lack of depth tells you something about their subjects.

They're bad as paintings. This is of less concern than the fact that they're bad as images. One of the usual objections to Warhol's paintings is that he's not a 'painterly painter' in the traditional sense. People who miss the point that Warhol, long ago, brilliantly made about mass culture. Robert Hughes for example. Hughes's essay, 'The Rise and Fall of Andy Warhol,' is one of those luminously nasty pieces of writing that clears the air of accumulated piety. But to ignore the importance of Warhol's art, especially in the 60s, simply because it isn't *arduous* the way a Francis Bacon is, negates almost every worthwhile development in art in the past 20 years. Painting and image-making are sometimes the same thing, and sometimes are quite distinct. The emphasis can be here, or there. They don't have to have a hierarchical relationship. Hughes seems to believe that some aesthetic utopia existed in the past, a utopia that art will return to after the current, doleful period. Many people think this way. Warhol understood something hateful but true: we aren't going to lose the past in quite the same way as before. And we're not going to find it again, either.

Nothing Andy ever said was true, but that is beside the point. There are less cogent objections to Warhol than Hughes's, less respectable ones. Sometimes they're mixed up with valid ones. Homophobia was one of the first reactions to Warhol, especially from the Cedar Tavern set, the Abstract Expressionists. You could be a fag back then, like Frank O'Hara, as long as you could pass, and understood you were supposed to suffer over it lusting after those *real* guys painting their heroic, tortured canvases. Andy was a swish.

A swish was somebody who couldn't hide it. It was just the way you were. Something from the 40s and 50s and before, when gays were either butch or femme. You find less and less of this when sexual role models disintegrate, as they did in the 60s and early 70s. Andy wrote somewhere that he exaggerated his swishiness because it wasn't something he thought he should change.

One of the most liberating experiences of my life was seeing *Bike Boy* at a theater in Cambridge. I was with some ultrastraight but *sensitive*, tolerant Harvard boys who froze in horror after the first two minutes. Viva was in a bathtub with a man, telling him if he wanted to make plastic sculptures he

Edie Sedgwick in Poor Little Rich Girl, *1965*

should just do it and shut up about it. 'We're into other things, now,' she whined. As I watched this film I thought: 'That's for me.'

It's bizarre that Warhol's films have been out of circulation for so long. Or perhaps not so bizarre. When Warhol said, in his last interview, that the films 'are better talked about than seen,' it occurred to me that a certain crust of the haute monde might have been less welcoming to Andy if it had been exposed to his movies. Which, I believe, compose his richest body of work. Who will ever forget Ondine, with his face buried in Joe D'Allesandro's underpants, in *Loves of Ondine*? Or Ingrid Superstar's recipe recitation in *Bike Boy*? The draft-

dodger's soliloquy, or Viva's epic monologue, in *Nude Restaurant*? Taylor Mead scampering about in *Lonesome Cowboys*: 'Oh you jingle, and you jangle, but you seldom wrangle . . .' I haven't seen these films in 20 years, and I remember every frame. I've already forgotten *E.T.*

Warhol's films are gloriously erotic, as sculpture is erotic. They're honest. Pornography – which every American should enjoy at least as much as having Edwin Meese for an attorney general – is dishonest. Perfect faces on perfect bodies do not blissfully couple without any problems, in real life; they only do that in California. When Ondine's about to get into Little Joe's BVDs, the bathroom door flies open and in walks Brigid Polk, demanding to know what that cheap little hustler is doing with her husband. Sexual pleasure is immanent in the Warhol movies, a possibility; but pornographic fulfillment is always shown as a deluded ambition. Real people are too complicated.

We should be wary about praise and damnation of Andy. He helped open thousands of closet doors. If the things he lent himself to in recent years fill me with distaste, I still admire the frosty slap he gave America before he became America's favorite vanity mirror. One should especially mistrust portraits like the concoction in *Edie*, a book compiled by George Plimpton and Jean Stein – surely two of the most privileged individuals in America, born with silver spoons, and zealous defenders of their class. Andy was a working boy. He worked hard, he made his money, they buried him with the blessings of his church. A saint for all the wrong reasons. And isn't that what America is all about? ∎

FILMOGRAPHY

The best filmography of Warhol remains Jonas Mekas's uniquely annotated one in John Coplans' *Andy Warhol*. Stephen Koch reworked it with his own annotations and revisions in his book *Stargazer*. As the Warhol films are being catalogued by the Whitney Museum of American Art at this very moment, we will have to wait for some years for the definitive filmography, although the notion of 'definitive' would seem hardly appropriate to the nature of Warhol's films and the spirit in which they were originally made and shown. No doubt, since Mekas's viewing of the films, certain films will have ceased to exist, and yet others will have other 'versions', and perhaps new ones will be discovered. The Whitney's own filmography in its catalogue *The Films of Andy Warhol* (1988) complies utterly with Koch's with the exception of *The Closet* (1965 #B1966), which leads one to believe that the real research had not begun at that point. Bockris's biography *Warhol* has a filmography which includes other films: *Whips* (1966), *The Closet* (1966), *Withering Sighs* (1967), *Construction-Destruction* (1967), *San Diego Surf* (1968). Dates have also changed in Bockris and are marked in this filmography by (B. . . .). Bokris has included *Imitation of Christ* from **** (aka *Four Stars*) as a separate film for 1967. A film not included in any of the filmographies and which was advertised by the Factory Films is *Tub Girl* (colour, 90 mins) with Viva, Taylor Mead, Bridget Polk, Ultra Violet and Tom Baker.

The filmography which follows owes everything to the work of both Mekas and Koch. Unfortunately, it has been impossible to see much of the work since Warhol's death. None of the following films are in distribution in Britain with the exceptions of *The Chelsea Girls*, *Lonesome Cowboys*, *Heat*, *Trash*, and *Flesh*.

All films are black and white with sound, unless stated otherwise.

1963

Tarzan and Jane Regained . . . Sort of 16 mm, 16 fps. 2 hours, sound on tape by Taylor Mead. Naomi Levine, Dennis Hopper, Claes Oldenburg, Pat Oldenburg, Wally Berman.
Kiss 16 mm, 16 fps, 50 mins, silent. Naomi Levine, Ed Sanders, Rufus Collins, Gerard Malanga, Baby Jane Holzer, John Palmer, Andrew Meyer, Freddy Herko, Johnny Dodd, Charlotte Gilbertson, Phillip van Renselet, Pierre Restaney, Marisol.
Sleep 16 mm, 16 fps, 6 hours, silent. John Giorno is the sleeper.
Andy Warhol Films Jack Smith Filming 'Normal Love' 16 mm, 16 fps, 3 mins, colour, silent. Seized by police March 1964 and no print exists.
Dance Movie (aka *Roller Skates*) 16 mm, 16 fps, 45 mins, silent. Freddy Herko.
Haircut 16 mm, 16 fps, 33 mins, silent. Billy Linich. Numerous versions existed.
Eat 16 mm, 16 fps, 45 mins, silent. Robert Indiana.
Blow Job (B1964) 16 mm, 16 fps, 45 mins, silent. Sound version existed.
Salome and Delilah 16 mm, 16 fps, 30 mins, silent. Freddy Herko and Debby Lee.

1964

Batman Dracula 16 mm, 16 fps, 2 hours, silent. Jack Smith as Dracula, Baby Jane Holzer, Beverly Grant, Ivy Nicholson.
Empire 16 mm, 16 fps, 8 hours, silent. Co-director: John Palmer, cameraman: Jonas Mekas. First film made with Auricon camera.
Henry Geldzahler 16 mm, 16 fps, 100 mins, silent.
Couch 16 mm, 16 fps, 40 mins, silent. Gerard Malanga, Piero Helzicer, Naomi Levine, Gregory Corso, Allen Ginsberg, John Palmer, Baby Jane Holzer, Ivy Nicholson, Amy Taubin, Ondine, Peter Orlovski, Jack Kerouac, Taylor Mead, Kate Helzicer, Rufus Collins, Joseph LeSeuer, Bingingham Birdie,

Mark Lancaster, Gloria Wood, Billy Linich. Koch gives the above running time, which is about right, but according to Ronald Tavel there is a longer, 24-hour version (see *Stargazer*).

Shoulder 16 mm, 16 fps, 4 mins, silent. Lucinda Child.
Mario Banana (aka *Mario Eats a Banana*) 16 mm, 16 fps, 4 mins, silent. Mario Montez.
Harlot 16 mm, 70 mins. Gerald Malanga, Philip Fagan, Carol Koshinskie, Mario Montez. Off-shot dialogue: Ronald Tavel, Harry Fainlight, Billy Linich.
The Thirteen Most Beautiful Women 16 mm, 16 fps, 40 mins, silent. Baby Jane Holzer, Anne Buchanan, Sally Kirkland, Barbara Rose, Beverly Grant, Nancy Worthington Fish, Ivy Nicholson, Ethel Scull, Isabel Eberstadt, Jane Wilson, Imu, Marisol, Lucinda Childs, Olga Kluver.
Soap Opera (aka *The Lester Persky Story*) 16 mm, 16 fps, 70 mins, silent. Co-director: Jerry Benjamin. Baby Jane Holzer.
Taylor Mead's Ass 16 mm, 16 fps, 70 mins, silent.

1965

The Thirteen Most Beautiful Boys (B1964) 16 mm, 16 fps, 40 mins, silent. Freddy Herko, Gerard Malanga, Dennis Deegan, Kelly Eddy, Bruce Rudo.
Fifty Fantastics and Fifty Personalities (B1964) 16 mm, 16 fps, (no running time available), silent. Allen Ginsberg, Ed Sanders, Jim Rosenquist, Zachary Scott, Peter Orlovski, Daniel Cassidy, Harry Fainlight, and others.
Ivy and John 16 mm, 35 mins.
Suicide 16 mm, 70 mins, colour. Scenario: Ronald Tavel.
Screen Test #1 16 mm, 70 mins. Scenario: Ronald Tavel.
Screen Test #2 16 mm, 70 mins. Scenario: Ronald Tavel. With Mario Montez.
The Life of Juanita Castro 16 mm, 70 mins. Scenario: Ronald Tavel. Marie Menken, Elecktrah, Waldo Diaz Balart, Mercedes Ospina, Marina Ospina. Ronald Tavel.
Drunk 16 mm, 70 mins. Scenario: Ronald Tavel. Larry Latrae, Gregory Battcock, Daniel Cassidy Jr, Tosh Carillo.
Horse (B1964) 16 mm, 105 mins. Scenario: Ronald Tavel. Larry Latrae, Gregory Battcock, Daniel Cassidy Jr.
Poor Little Rich Girl 16 mm, 70 mins. Directorial assistance: Chuck Wein. Edie Sedgwick.
Vinyl 16 mm, 70 mins. Scenario: Ronald Tavel. With Gerard Malanga, Edie Sedgwick, Ondine, Tosh Carillo, Larry Latrae, Jacque Potin, John MacDermott and others. Cameraman: Bud Wirtschafter.
Bitch 16 mm, 70 mins. Marie Menken, Willard Maas, Edie Sedgwick, Gerard Malanga.
Restaurant 16 mm, 35 mins. Assistance with shooting and scripting: Chuck Wein. Edie Sedgwick, Ondine.

Kitchen 16 mm, 70 mins. Scenario: Ronald Tavel. Edie Sedgwick, Roger Trudeau, Donald Lyons, Elecktrah, David MacCabe, Rene Ricard.
Prison 16 mm, 70 mins, 24 fps, sound (on tape). Edie Sedgwick, Bibie Hansen, Marie Menken.
Face 16 mm, 70 mins. Edie Sedgwick.
Afternoon 16 mm, 105 mins. Edie Sedgwick, Ondine, Arthur Loeb, Donald Lyons, Dorothy Dean. Reel One originally shown as part of *The Chelsea Girls* at Film-Makers' Cinematheque screenings and later taken out (J.M.)
Beauty #2 16 mm, 70 mins. Writer and assistant director: Chuck Wein. Edie Sedgwick, Gino Peschio. Off-shot: Gerard Malanga and Chuck Wein.
Space 16 mm, 70 mins. Edie Sedgwick, Eric Anderson.
Outer and Inner Space 16 mm, 70 mins. Edie Sedgwick talks with her image on a television set. Two reels projected side by side at Cinematheque screenings.
My Hustler 16 mm, 70 mins. Paul America, Ed Hood, John MacDermott, Genevieve Charbon, Joseph Campbell, Dorothy Dean.
Camp 16 mm, 70 mins. Paul Swan, Baby Jane Holzer, Mar-Mar Donyle, Jodie Babs, Tally Brown, Jack Smith, Fu-Fu Smith, Tosh Carillo, Mario Montez, Gerard Malanga.
Paul Swan 16 mm, 70 mins, colour.
Hedy (aka *The Most Beautiful Woman in the World*, *The Shoplifter*, or *The Fourteen Year Old Girl*) (B1966) 16 mm, 70 mins. Scenario: Ronald Tavel. Music: John Cale and Lou Reed. With Mario Montez, Mary Woronov, Harvey Tavel, Ingrid Superstar, Ronald Tavel, Gerard Malanga, Rick Lockwood, James Claire, Randy Borscheidt, David Meyers, Jack Smith, Arnold Rockwood.
More Milk Yvette (aka *Lana Turner*) (B1966) 16 mm, 70 mins. Scenario: Ronald Tavel. Mario Montez, Paul Caruso and Richard Schmidt.
Lupe 16 mm, 70 mins. Edie Sedgwick and Billy Linich.

1966

The Velvet Underground and Nico 16 mm, 70 mins.
Bufferin (aka *Gerard Malanga Reads Poetry*) 16 mm, 35 mins. Gerard Malanga.
Eating Too Fast (aka *Blow Job #2*) 16 mm, 70 mins. Gregory Battcock.
The Chelsea Girls 16 mm, 3 hours 15 mins, two-screen, colour and b/w. Hanoi Hannah reel scenario: Ronald Tavel. With Marie Menken, Mary Woronov, Gerard Malanga, International Velvet, Ingrid Superstar, Angelina 'Pepper' Davis, Ondine, Alberte Rene Ricard, Ronna, Ed Hood, Patrick Flemming, Eric Emerson.

1966–7
**** (aka *Four Stars*) 16 mm, 25 hours, colour. Shown once in full version (New Cinema Playhouse, New York, December 15 and 16 1967). For full details see Koch and Mekas, *op. cit.*

1967
The Loves of Ondine 16 mm, 86 mins, colour. Ondine, Viva, Joe Dallesandro, Angelina Davis, Brigid Polk, Ivy Nicholson and numerous unidentified men.
I, A Man 16 mm, 100 mins. Tom Baker, Ivy Nicholson, Ingrid Superstar, Valerie Solanis, Cynthia May, Betina Coffin, Ultra Violet, Nico.
Bike Boy 16 mm, 96 mins, colour. Joe Spencer, Viva, Ed Weiner, Brigid Polk, Ingrid Superstar.
Nude Restaurant 16 mm, 96 mins, colour. Viva, Taylor Mead, Louis Waldron, Alan Midgette, Ingrid Superstar, Julian Burroughs, and others.
Lonesome Cowboys (B1968) 16 mm, 110 mins, colour. Taylor Mead, Viva, Louis Waldron, Eric Emerson, Joe Dallesandro, Julian Burroughs, Alan Midgette, Tom Hompertz, Frances Francine.

1968
Blue Movie (aka *Fuck*) 16 mm, 90 mins, colour. Viva and Louis Waldron.
Flesh, 105 mins, colour. Joe Dallesandro, Geraldine Smith, Candy Darling, Jackie Curtis, Louis Waldron, Patti d'Arbanville.

1970
Trash 103 mins, colour. Joe Dallesandro, Holly Woodlawn, Jane Forth.

1972
Women in Revolt 98 mins, colour. Candy Darling, Holly Woodlawn, Jackie Curtis.
Heat 115 mins, colour. Joe Dallesandro, Sylvia Miles, Andrea Feldman, Pat Ast, Ray Vestal, Lester Persky, Eric Emerson.

1973
L'Amour 90 mins, colour. Max De Lys, Donna Jordan, Jane Forth, Michael Sklar.

1976
Bad 109 mins, colour. Carroll Baker, Brigid Polk, Perry King.

BIBLIOGRAPHY

The following is a very selective list emphasising Warhol's films and the avant-garde cinema in general. For a comprehensive list on writing relating to the paintings see *Andy Warhol: A Retrospective* (New York: Museum of Modern Art, 1989). On the films see the bibliography in *The Essential Cinema*, vol. 1, (ed.) P. Adams Sitney (New York: Anthology Film Archives, 1975).

Arthur, Paul, 'Beauty, Flesh, and the Empire of Absence: Resighting Warhol', *The Independent*, December 1988.

Battcock, Gregory, 'Superstar=Superset', *Film Culture* no. 46, Summer 1967.

Battcock, Gregory (ed.), *The New American Cinema: A Critical Anthology* (New York: Dutton, 1967).

Berlin, Gloria & Bruce, Bryan, 'the superstar story' *CineAction!*, December 1986.

Bockris, Victor, *Warhol* (London: Frederick Muller, 1989).

Brecht, Stefan, *Queer Theatre: The Original Theatre of the City of New York from the mid-60s to the mid-70s* (London: Methuen, 1986).

Coplans, John (ed.), *Andy Warhol* (New York: New York Graphic Society, 1970).

Cornwell, Regina, 'Ciao, Manhattan, Again', *New Art Examiner*, September 1988.

Crone, Rainer, *Andy Warhol* (London: Thames and Hudson, 1970).

Dwoskin, Stephen, *Film Is: The International Free Cinema* (London: Peter Owen, 1975).

Ehrenstein, David, 'An Interview with Warhol', *Film Culture* no. 40, 1966.

Gavronsky, Serge, 'Warhol's Underground', *Cahiers du Cinéma in English* no. 10, May 1967.

Geldzahler, Henry, 'Some Notes on *Sleep*', *Film Culture: An Anthology*, (ed.) P. Adams Sitney (London: Secker & Warburg, 1971).

Gidal, Peter, *Andy Warhol: Films and Paintings* (London: Studio Vista/Dutton, 1971).

Gidal, Peter, *Materialist Film* (London: Routledge and Kegan Paul, 1989).

Groot, Paul, 'Warhol Films', *Mediamatic* vol. 3 no. 3, April 1989.

Hanhardt, John & Gartenberg, Jon, *The Films of Andy Warhol: An Introduction* (New York: Whitney Museum of American Art, 1988).

Hill, Derek, 'Andy Warhol as a film-maker: a discussion between Paul Morrissey and Derek Hill', *Studio International*, February 1971.

Hoberman, J., 'Bon Voyeur: Andy Warhol's Silver Screen', *The Village Voice*, 17 May 1988.

Hood, Edward, 'Edie Sedgwick', *Film Culture* no. 46, Summer 1967.

Koch, Stephen, *Stargazer: Andy Warhol's World and His Films* (London: Marion Boyars, 1973, 1985).

Kramer, Margia, *Andy Warhol Et Al. The FBI File on Andy Warhol* (New York: UnSub Press, 1988).

Le Grice, Malcolm, *Abstract Film and Beyond* (London: Studio Vista, 1977).

Mekas, Jonas, *Movie Journal: The Rise of a New American Cinema 1959–1971* (New York: Collier Books, 1972).

Mussman, Toby, 'The Chelsea Girls', *Film Culture* no. 46, Summer 1967.

Ostrow, Stephen E., *Raid the Icebox 1 with Andy Warhol* (Providence, Rhode Island: Museum of Art, Rhode Island School of Design, 1969).

Pike, Susan, 'The Chelsea Girls', *Film Culture* no. 46, Summer 1967.

Rainer, Yvonne, 'Don't Give the Game Away', *Arts Magazine*, April 1967.

Ratcliffe, Carter, *Warhol* (New York: Abbeville Press, 1983).

Renan, Sheldon, *The Underground Film: An Introduction to Its Development in America* (London: Studio Vista, 1967).

Rowe, Carel, *The Baudelarian Cinema: A Trend within the American Avant-Garde* (Ann Arbor: UMI Research Press, 1982).

Sarris, Andrew, 'The Sub-New York Sensibility' *Cahiers du Cinéma in English* no. 10, May 1967.

Sitney, P. Adams, *Visionary Film: The American Avant-Garde 1943–1978* (New York: Oxford University Press, 1974; 2nd ed. 1979).

Smith, Patrick S., *Andy Warhol's Art and Films* (Ann Arbor: UMI Research Press, 1988).

Smith, Patrick S., *Warhol: Conversations about the Artist* (Ann Arbor: UMI Research Press, 1988).

Stein, Jean, *Edie: An American Biography* (London: Cape, 1982).

Tavel, Ronald, 'The Theatre of the Ridiculous', *Tri-Quarterly* no. 6, 1966.

Tyler, Parker, *Underground Film: A Critical History* (Harmondsworth: Penguin Books, 1974).

Violet, Ultra, *Famous for Fifteen Minutes: My Life with Andy Warhol* (London: Methuen, 1989).

Viva, *Superstar* (London: Sphere Books, 1972).

Warhol, Andy & Hackett, Pat, *POPism: The Warhol '60s* (New York: Harper & Row, 1983).

Warhol, Andy, *The Philosophy of Andy Warhol* (New York: Harcourt Brace Jovanovich, 1975).

Warhol, Andy, *From A to B and Back Again: The Philosophy of Andy Warhol* (London: Picador, 1976).

Wilcock, John, *The Autobiography & Sex Life of Andy Warhol* (New York: Other Scenes Inc., 1971).

INDEX

WITHDRAWN